love your library

Buckinghamshire Libraries

Search, renew or reserve online 24/7
www.buckscc.gov.uk/libraries

24 hour renewal line
0303 123 0035

Enquiries
0845 230 3232

follow us twitter

@Bucks_Libraries

PRE-CONTRACT – 'a pre-existing contract of marriage ... which precludes the making of another similar contract'.

Oxford English Dictionary.

'The queen [Elizabeth Woodville] then remembered ... the calumnies with which she was reproached, namely that according to established usage she was not the legitimate wife of the king'.

Domenico Mancini, 1483.

'King Edward was and stoode marryed and trouth plight to oone Dame Elianor Butteler, doughter of the old Earl of Shrewesbury'.

Act of Parliament, 1484.

'The bishop [of Bath and Wells] said that he had married them when only he and they were present'.

Philippe de Commynes, c. 1490.

'Edward [IV] had espoused another wife before the mother of Elizabeth of York'.

Eustace Chapuys to Emperor Charles V, 1533.

'There are no sufficient grounds for regarding [the marriage between Edward IV and Eleanor Talbot] as a mere political invention ... Perhaps rather an evidence of the truth of the story is the care afterwards taken to suppress and to pervert it'.

James Gairdner, 1898.

ELEANOR
THE SECRET QUEEN

*The Woman
who put Richard III
on the Throne*

JOHN ASHDOWN-HILL

The
History
Press

In memory of my cousin, Sheila Llewellyn.

First published 2009
This edition published 2010

The History Press
The Mill, Brimscombe Port
Stroud, Gloucestershire, GL5 2QG
www.thehistorypress.co.uk

© John Ashdown-Hill, 2009, 2010

British Library Cataloguing in Publication Data.
A catalogue record for this book is available from the British Library.

ISBN 978 0 7524 5669 0

Typesetting and origination by The History Press
Printed in Great Britain
Manufacturing managed by Jellyfish Print Solutions Ltd

Contents

List of Illustrations

Unless otherwise acknowledged, photographs are by the author.

1. Goodrich Castle, Herefordshire, where Eleanor spent part of her childhood. Photograph by Bill Benstead, courtesy of the Richard III Society – Worcestershire Branch.
2. The site of the Talbots' manor house at Blakemere, where Eleanor may have been born.
3. Sudeley Castle, Gloucestershire, home of Lord Sudeley. Eleanor lived here in the early years of her first marriage. Photograph courtesy of Sudeley Castle Estate Office.
4. Framlingham Castle, Suffolk, from the site of the Duchess of Norfolk's private garden. Elizabeth Talbot and her ladies would cross the moat by means of a vanished wooden bridge supported on the stone piers in the foreground.
5. Eleanor Talbot's descent from Edward I and Eleanor of Castile.
6. The two Talbot families.
7. Eleanor's mother, Margaret Beauchamp, Countess of Shrewsbury: a determined lady, but her children were devoted to her.
8. Eleanor's aunt, Anne Beauchamp, Countess of Warwick: wife of the 'Kingmaker', and mother of Richard III's queen.
9. Eleanor's aunt, Eleanor Beauchamp, Duchess of Somerset, who was perhaps also her godmother.

10. Eleanor's uncle, Edmund Beaufort, Duke of Somerset. The Beaufort connection was dangerous in Yorkist England, but was always acknowledged.

11.   The Mortimer descent of Edward IV and Eleanor Talbot.

12. Eleanor's relationship to the wives of Edward IV's brothers.

13. Eleanor's father, John Talbot, first Earl of Shrewsbury, was a great national hero – the 'Sir Winston Churchill' of his day.

14. Eleanor's sister, Elizabeth Talbot, Duchess of Norfolk, was also her greatest friend and protector.

15.   Eleanor's niece, Elizabeth Talbot, Viscountess Lisle. This portrait, probably painted in Flanders during Margaret of York's marriage celebrations, may suggest the possible appearance of Eleanor herself at the age of about 16. © Staatliche Museen Preussischer Kulturbesitz, Gemäldegalerie, Berlin (no. 532).

16. Hair of Eleanor's niece, Lady Anne Mowbray. The colour is genuine, but was probably darker in life. Eleanor's mother had fair hair, but Eleanor herself, like most of her family, was probably a brunette. © The Museum of London.

17. The descent of the lordship of Sudeley.

18. The family of Elizabeth Norbury, Lady Sudeley.

19. Sir Thomas Butler's cousins.

20. The tower of Burton Dassett Church. Eleanor and her first husband, Thomas, lived in the nearby manor house.

21. The Old Court, Corpus Christi College, Cambridge. Building in this courtyard was financed by Eleanor and her sister. Lithograph of a pencil drawing by W.G. Blackhall for S. C Roberts, *The Charm of Cambridge* (London 1927).

22. The great west doorway of the Carmelite Priory Church, Norwich, now re-erected in the Norwich Magistrates' Court. Eleanor's coffin must have passed beneath this archway.

23. Eleanor's hearse, displaying her arms as Lady Butler, at the office of Lauds for the Dead, celebrated for her at Norwich Cathedral, 1999.

24. The conjoined arms of Eleanor's parents, from the tomb of her grandfather, Beauchamp Chapel, Warwick.

25. The seal of Eleanor's father-in-law, Ralph Butler, Lord Sudeley. Warwickshire County Record Office, L1/82, reproduced by kind permission of the depositor.

26. Impression of the signet ring used as a seal by Eleanor when married to Thomas Butler. The ring bore her mother's emblem: the daisy, or marguerite. Warwickshire County Record Office, L1/81, reproduced by kind permission of the depositor.

27. Eleanor's memorial plaque at the Norwich Whitefriars site, bearing her arms as Lady Butler.

28. The young Edward IV in about 1461. Redrawn by Geoffrey Wheeler, from BL, Royal MS 18 D II, f. 6.

29. Eleanor in about 1462? A reconstruction based on the skull of CFII, and portraits of Eleanor's close relatives. © Mark Satchwill, 2008.

30. The site of East Hall, Kenninghall, Norfolk. Originally published in C.R. Manning, 'Kenninghall', *Original Papers of the Norfolk and Norwich Archaeological Society*, Norwich 1870.

31. Eleanor's heirs (simplified).

32. Eleanor? The skull of CF II, Castle Museum, Norwich. (Remains of a medieval noblewoman, found at the Whitefriars site in Norwich in 1958.)

33. Ruins of the Norwich Carmel *in situ*. This arch led to an anchorite's cell attached to the priory.

34. The Guild Hall, Henley-in-Arden. Eleanor's inquisition post mortem was probably held here.

35. The tomb of Eleanor's niece, Elizabeth Talbot, Viscountess Lisle (died 1487). Eleanor's tomb in Norwich may have borne a similar effigy. Astley, Warwickshire; photograph by Geoffrey Wheeler.

36. The ancient icon of Our Lady of Mount Carmel at the fourteenth-century church of *San Niccolò al Carmine*, Siena. According to tradition, the early Carmelites brought it with them from the Holy Land when they fled to Europe. Photograph courtesy of the Carmelite Monastery, Quiddenham, Norfolk.

37. Eleanor's signet, depicting the icon of Our Lady of Mount Carmel. Her ring became stuck in the hot wax. Detaching it blurred the image of the Christ child. Warwickshire County Record Office, L1/86, reproduced by kind permission of the depositor.

38. Evidence of congenitally missing Talbot teeth? Dental X-ray of the skull of CFII (Eleanor?). Photograph by Norwich Community Dental Services (now Norfolk PCT Dental Service).

39. The skull of Eleanor's father, John Talbot, Earl of Shrewsbury, showing the wound which killed him. Photograph by J.R. Crosse, 1874.

Introduction

Whichever way one looks at it, Eleanor Talbot was the rock upon which the royal house of York foundered. Unwittingly, and for her part, surely, unintentionally, she brought about the downfall of a dynasty. Through her relationship with Edward IV she ultimately shook the crown of England so severely that it dropped into the lap of the improbable Henry Tudor (Henry VII), remotely and illegitimately descended from Edward III. What the lovely Eleanor would have thought of that outcome is anybody's guess (though her younger sister, Elizabeth, who lived into Henry VII's reign, seems not to have been one of his fans).

Eleanor unintentionally brought about this dramatic outcome because the Yorkist claim to the throne was founded on the concept of legitimacy. In 1399 Richard II had been deposed by his cousin, Henry IV. The Lancastrian branch of the royal family thus usurped the throne, breaking the direct line of the royal succession. As the senior living descendants of Edward III the Yorkist princes subsequently argued that their right to the crown was superior to that of their Lancastrian cousins. Legitimacy constituted the foundation of their claim. But that legitimacy was inevitably compromised when questions arose as to whom Edward IV had married; as to whether his son and supposed heir was a bastard. It was Edward IV's relationship with Eleanor which gave rise to such questions.

In an attempt to save the Yorkist day, the crown was passed to Edward's undoubtedly legitimate surviving younger brother, Richard III. But Richard, too, found himself entangled in the web of uncertainty, since those who believed in the legitimacy of Edward IV's children viewed Richard's accession as usurpation. From the day when Edward IV married Eleanor, or pretended to do so, or allowed it to be whispered that he might have done so, the house of York (hitherto so secure in the purity of its bloodline) confronted a contentious and uncertain future. The dynasty was rent by internal divisions. Edward IV found himself obliged to execute his own brother, the Duke of Clarence. Later, following the death of Richard III, we confront the extraordinary phenomenon of a former royal family apparently in such total disarray that it preferred to promote the candidacy of false pretenders (Lambert Simnel and perhaps Perkin Warbeck) rather than advance the claims of its own legitimate heirs.

Ten years ago this book could not have been written. Little was then generally known about Eleanor Talbot. Even her parentage was a matter of dispute. Yet Eleanor's Talbot surname and her paternity are absolutely key issues. In a fifteenth-century context, the fact that she was the daughter of the first Earl of Shrewsbury was enormously significant. Lord Shrewsbury was regarded as a towering figure and a national hero. When the Act of Parliament of 1484 explicitly characterised Eleanor as his daughter, the effect of this was akin to that of a late twentieth-century writer describing someone as a daughter of Sir Winston Churchill. Eleanor's rank – and her plausibility as a potential royal consort – were immediately established beyond any question.

The only possible way to tell Eleanor's story is to seek to do what has not been done previously – to bring all the facts into the light of day. As a distinguished archaeologist has written, 'to start to understand what happened in a particular place long ago ... we must first list exactly what we find ... if I misinterpret the evidence, at some point I shall discover something that will prove my lines of research are wrong – the 'facts' will not fit'.[1] A great deal of evidence is there to be found, if one looks for it.

Why then has Eleanor been so completely neglected? She is, in her own way, a key figure of English history, a veritable 'Cleopatra's nose'.[2] If her marriage to Edward IV had been acknowledged in her lifetime, if she had actually been enthroned and crowned as England's queen-consort, all subsequent history must have been different. The house of York might still have been reigning today, in a separate kingdom, never united to Scotland. The despotic, paranoid Tudors would have remained unheard of outside their native Wales. Enormous consequences would flow from all this. The English

Reformation, which sprang from Henry VIII's dynastic and financial crises, and was neither generally desired nor supported by the English populace,[3] might never have taken place. England's monasteries, still undissolved, could have preserved to the present day their unrivalled cultural heritage. No Tudors would mean no Stuarts; no Civil War; no Oliver Cromwell. The story goes on and on. It all turns on Eleanor.

Some readers may be surprised that the title of this book assigns Eleanor a royal title. It is true that during her lifetime she was never acknowledged as queen. However, by explicitly recognising the legitimacy of Eleanor's marriage to Edward IV, while at the same time specifically denying the rank of queen to Elizabeth Woodville, the act of *titulus regius* of 1484 did implicitly accord posthumous queenship to Eleanor. Henry VII's subsequent repeal of this act and his reinstatement of Elizabeth Woodville's royal rank may seem to leave Eleanor in a kind of royal limbo. But let us remember that the subsequent marital shenanigans of Henry VIII – who of course cannot really have had six wives, since some of his 'marriages' were annulled, and at least two of them overlapped – apparently does not preclude all six of *his* putative spouses from rejoicing in queenship.

Even today Eleanor as a person remains largely mysterious. Much of her character is still inaccessible. This may yet change. Ten years ago much of the information presented here was either undiscovered or unrecognised. In the future we may know more. In the meanwhile, this is the first attempt to tell the story of Eleanor Talbot, the secret queen.

In the main body of the text, quotations from fifteenth-century documents in English have generally been modernised in respect of spelling and punctuation. In the presentation of documentary evidence in Appendix 1, original spellings are retained, though contractions are expanded without comment and there is some modernisation of punctuation. In keeping with good genealogical practice the women who figure in this study are consistently identified principally by their maiden surnames rather than their married surnames.

I

John Talbot

When the 55-year-old John, Lord Talbot, returned to England in February 1442, he had not set foot in his native land since 1435 – the year in which his daughter, Eleanor, had been conceived. He had therefore never yet set eyes on this latest addition to his family, the first daughter born to his current wife.[1]

For the past seven years Talbot had been continuously in France, serving the cause of Henry VI. In 1431 this half-French king of England had also been crowned king of France at the cathedral of Notre Dame in Paris. It was Henry VI's own cousin and representative in France, Richard, Duke of York, who had now dispatched Lord Talbot on a mission back to England. Talbot's task was to plead with the king for more troops and more money to aid the faltering war effort. However, he may also have been glad to have occasion to visit his homeland on his own account, since he had private business in England; business which concerned his children.

It was the first Sunday of Lent, 18 February 1442, when John Talbot set sail from the Norman port of Harfleur, a town recaptured from the French eighteen months previously. He was accompanied by a deputation comprising Norman councillors, the faithful Richard Bannes, and five other men-at-arms from the Harfleur garrison, all of whom wore the Talbot livery.[2] Lord Talbot had his own merchant fleet,[3] and the vessel which now bore him across the Channel from Normandy may well have been one of his own ships. There was, as yet, no standing royal navy, and it was normal for private ships to be used in the king's service.

Much of John Talbot's life had been spent out of England, often in France, sometimes in Ireland.[4] His family had served the house of Lancaster long before it attained the English throne. This allegiance even predated the creation of the Talbot baronial title, going back to at least the 1320s. John's Talbot's grandfather had fought in Spain for John of Gaunt, Duke of Lancaster, and it was in the service of the house of Lancaster that John Talbot himself had first gone to France.

He had been born in the reign of Richard II, before the Lancastrian accession to the throne.[5] In the same year that he was born his grandfather, the third Lord Talbot, had died in Spain.[6] Then in 1396, when John was still only about 9 years old, his own father, the fourth Lord Talbot, had also died. As a result, a significant influence in John's early life had been his stepfather, Thomas Neville, Lord Furnival – the second husband of his mother, Ankaret Lestrange.

John Talbot was one of Ankaret's nine children by her first husband, Richard, fourth Baron Talbot. As the couple's second son, he had not been the heir to the Talbot title, which had passed, when their father died, to John's elder brother, Gilbert. However, Ankaret's decision to take a second husband after Richard's death gave her an opportunity to promote the interests of her second son. Her new husband, Lord Furnival, had no son of his own, and Ankaret suggested that his daughter and heiress, Maud Neville, should be betrothed to John, who was thus placed in line to acquire the Furnival title when his stepfather should die.[7]

John Talbot is first known to have held a military command in the reign of Henry IV. That was in 1404, when he represented his stepfather, patrolling the Welsh border after the battle of Shrewsbury. It was at about this time that John's marriage to Maud Neville took place. This convenient arrangement paid dividends three years later, when his stepfather died and John Talbot inherited the Furnival title. In 1414 the new Lord Furnival was sent by the new king, Henry V, to Ireland as royal lieutenant. There Talbot quickly established a rather unattractive reputation for rapid response and for the calculated use of terror as a weapon.

It was also in Ireland, at Finglas, near Dublin, that, on 19 June 1416, Maud Neville gave birth to John's first known child, a son, baptised Thomas (presumably after Maud's father). Thomas seems to have been a sickly child, and died some six weeks later.[8] However, by 1419, when the family left Ireland, John Talbot's second son, and eventual heir, John Talbot II, had probably been born, and perhaps also his third son, Christopher.[9] It was also in 1419 that John's brother, Gilbert, head of the Talbot family, died at Rouen, leaving only a daughter, Ankaret, to succeed him.

In 1420 Lord Furnival served briefly in France. However, he returned to England at the end of the year, having been appointed to organise the English festivities celebrating the coronation of Henry V's bride, Catherine of France. John was one of the Lords who served the new queen at the banquet in Westminster Hall following her coronation, while his sister-in-law, Beatrice, Lady Talbot (the Portuguese widow of his brother, Gilbert) was among the ladies honoured by being invited to sit at the table to the left of the queen. As organiser of the festivities, Lord Furnival may have been responsible for the menu served on that occasion, which comprised:

First Course
Brawn with mustard, eels in burneus,[10] furmenty with bacon, pike, lamprey powdered[11] with eels, powdered trout, coddeling, plaice with merling[12] fried, great crabs, lesche lumbarde,[13] a baked meat[14] in pastry, tarts, and a subtlety[15] called pellican, &c.

Second Course
Jelly, blandesoure,[16] bream, conger, soles with myllott, chevyn, barbylle, roach, salmon fresh, halibut, gurnarde roasted, roget[17] boiled, smelte fried, lobster, cranys,[18] lesche damaske,[19] lamprey in pastry, flampayne.[20] A subtlety, a panther and a maid before him, &c.

Third Course
Dates in compost,[21] cream motley, and powdered whelks, porpoise roasted, minnows fried, crevys of douce,[22] dates, prawns, red shrimps, great eels and lampreys roasted, a lesche called white leysche,[23] a baked meat in pastry with four angels. A subtlety, a tiger and Saint George leading it.[24]

When he returned to France, in May 1421, Lord Furnival probably left his wife pregnant (a pattern often repeated later, in his second marriage). The birth of a daughter, Joan, probably in 1422, may have been indirectly responsible for Maud Neville's death, in May of that year, at the young age of about 30.[25] Maud's was one of two deaths in the Talbot family about that time. The other was that of little Ankaret, the Talbot heiress. As a result of Ankaret's death, John now succeeded to his family title of Lord Talbot.

To deal with the family business attendant upon the death of his wife, and his own inheritance of the Talbot title, John returned to England in the summer of 1422. There, news reached him that Henry V had also died. This probably came as something of a shock, for the 35-year-old king had been about the same age as John Talbot himself. Henry had died at the Castle of Vincennes, just outside Paris, on 31 August 1422.

The king had been 'fighting a losing battle against a disease which his doctors could not identify – probably either a form of dysentery or a gangrenous fistula. The king's sufferings were atrocious; his blood was poisoned and he had assumed a most terrible appearance, with lice crawling from his eyes and ears ... Instead of embalming the body after the king's death, it was taken down to the ground-floor kitchens where it was cut up and the various parts put into an enormous cauldron over a fire ... It was so well boiled that the flesh fell off the bones and these were then placed in a lead-lined casket with spices' to be shipped home to England.[26]

The sojourn in England of Lord Talbot and Furnival may not have been greatly welcomed by the royal council, governing on behalf of the new king, the infant Henry VI. John Talbot had already proved a somewhat turbulent subject, engaging in prolonged and violent disputes over precedence and over the inheritance of the honour of Wexford, with his cousins, the Earl of Ormond and Lord Grey of Ruthin. At all events, he was soon sent back to France, where, fighting at Verneuil in 1424, he earned himself the Order of the Garter.

It was probably towards the end of that year, perhaps on 6 September, that, in the chapel of Warwick Castle, he married his second wife, the woman who was to be the mother of his daughter, Eleanor. She was Lady Margaret Beauchamp, eldest daughter of the Earl of Warwick, and a lady some years his junior. Their first child, confusingly yet another John, was born in 1426.

Lord Talbot now returned briefly to Ireland, where, for the second time, he became the royal lieutenant. The following year, however, he was again back in France with the regent, the Duke of Bedford, fighting at the side of his new father-in-law, Richard Beauchamp. There, he encountered Joan of Arc. With the exception of the regent himself, the dynamic and forceful Lord Talbot was apparently the only English leader in France whom Joan of Arc knew by name. At all events, she addressed a letter to him and to Bedford, telling them that they must withdraw and return to their own land. Lord Talbot was subsequently captured by Joan's army at Patay in 1429, remaining a prisoner in France for several years. Prior to his capture, news must have reached him from England that, in this absence, Margaret had given birth to their second son, Louis.

The custody of Lord Talbot was claimed by King Charles VII, who perhaps hoped to exchange him for Joan of Arc (captured by the Burgundians in May 1430, and sold by them to the English). If this was Charles' plan, however, it was never realised. Eventually John Talbot was released as part of a mutual exchange of prisoners. He returned to England in May 1433, and was in the country long enough to leave Margaret pregnant once again. In July, Henry VI's government sent him back to France, to serve with the king's cousin, the Earl of Somerset.

Somerset's younger brother, Edmund Beaufort, was also serving in France, and at about this time became Lord Talbot's brother-in-law by marrying Margaret's younger sister, Lady Eleanor Beauchamp. Eventually, Talbot was appointed governor and lieutenant general in France and Normandy. In 1434, at about the time that Humphrey Talbot (his third son by Margaret) was born, the king's uncle, the Duke of Bedford, raised him to the rank of Count of Clermont. Subsequently John Talbot had made only one brief visit to his native island, in the summer of 1435. It was probably this visit that resulted in Eleanor's birth.

Although he had been born in England, Normandy was John Talbot's ancestral home. Several centuries previously his ancestor, Richard Talbot, had first crossed the Channel from Normandy to England in the invading army of Duke William the Bastard. When the latter became 'William the Conqueror', Talbot – not in the first rank of the new king's supporters – had been rewarded with a single manor in Essex. By the accession of Henry II, the then head of the family, Sir Richard Talbot, held the manor of Eccleswall in Herefordshire. Thereafter the family seems to have based itself on the Welsh border. In 1331, Gilbert Talbot was created first baron Talbot by the young King Edward III. [27]

Richard, the son and heir of this first Lord Talbot, married an heiress, Elizabeth Comyn. [28] As a result, the Talbot family inherited a fine new home: Goodrich Castle in Herefordshire. The castle's grey keep dates from soon after the Norman Conquest, but the red sandstone outer walls and buildings were added in the reign of Henry III. By the time the Talbots acquired the castle, the Norman keep was little used, and the main residential quarters were the more modern great hall and its associated buildings. [29] John Talbot's father, Richard, renovated and improved the castle in about 1380, and in the fifteenth century, sturdy, moated Goodrich remained one of the principal dwellings of the Talbot family. In addition, however, the family had acquired other, more up-to-date houses.

Perhaps as he travelled to England, John Talbot looked forward to revisiting his acknowledged favourite amongst the Talbot homes: Blakemere in Shropshire. He himself had been born at Blakemere, an estate which had come to the Talbots through his mother, the heiress, Ankaret Lestrange.[30] Blakemere was not, strictly speaking, a castle, but a manor house, set in a fine deer park, in which were three lakes. The largest of these was the Black Mere from which the estate derived its name. Licence to crenellate the house had been granted on 14 July 1322[31] and thereafter it was sometimes referred to as a castle (*castellum*) although other texts continue to call it a *mansum*. The house lay to the eastern end of the southern side of the Black Mere, only yards from the lake, which (together with a little stream which still runs down to the lake on the western side of the site of the house) once fed the moat. Blakemere stood about a mile to the east of the town of Whitchurch, whose church tower is still visible today from the site of the house.

Nothing now remains of this favourite Talbot manor house. Still discernible, however, are the ditches which once formed its moat, and within the rough rectangle formed by these ditches, the raised mound where the house itself once stood. Fragments of dressed stone from the building still scatter the site. In the fifteenth century Blakemere was a rich and productive property. Tenants maintained arable farming as well as both sheep and cattle. A dovecote supplied more than 1,200 pigeons a year for Lady Talbot and her household, and the forty-six beehives contributed more than eight gallons of honey and sixteen gallons of mead annually.[32]

John Talbot's own private business back in England, in the spring of 1442, concerned his children and the inheritance claims of his second wife. Through her heiress mother, Elizabeth Berkeley, Lady Margaret claimed a share in the Berkeley inheritance. This claim was dear to the hearts of Margaret and John, both of whom were well aware that Margaret's children – of whom there were now four – were extremely unlikely to inherit any part of the Talbot estates and titles. These latter were entailed, and would go to John's eldest surviving son, John Talbot II, the child of his first wife, Maud Neville.[33]

Already some seventeen years had elapsed since John Talbot had married Margaret Beauchamp.[34] The eldest son of this second marriage, young John Talbot III, was now 16 years of age, and starting to make his own way in the world. This young man's future was probably one of the things in John Talbot's mind as he made his Channel crossing. Moreover, the Talbot family was still expanding, as John's irregular visits to England continued to produce children. Little Eleanor, born about the end of February 1436,[35] was the couple's fourth child, and their first daughter. Perhaps as John Talbot made his journey back to England across the Channel, he also gave some thought to Eleanor, the child he had never yet seen. She would soon be 6 years old. He would be home in time for her birthday.

2

Margaret Beauchamp

At 38 years of age, Eleanor's mother, Lady Margaret Beauchamp, was a good deal younger than her husband. Unable to travel the world as he did, making war, Margaret was also, in her own way, a great fighter. Her character and determination were a match for John's. Yet their partnership, which has been described, possibly with justification, as a love-match, [1] had proved harmonious and conspicuously successful. This may have been due in no small part to John's prolonged absences abroad, and to the fact that Margaret had, in consequence, enjoyed considerable freedom to order her own household for the greater part of her married life. Her husband evidently trusted her completely.

Margaret was clearly able and highly intelligent. She was also unmistakably a woman of action, and capable of remarkable ruthlessness when she felt the occasion demanded. Despite being a woman, Margaret did travel a good deal. It is possible that she visited her husband in Normandy in April of 1441 – when a papal indult, allowing them to have mass celebrated at a portable altar in an area which lay under interdict, was addressed to them jointly there. [2] The mention of Margaret's name in this indult may, however, have been contingency planning, or papal politeness. It does not necessarily prove that Margaret had crossed the Channel at that time, although she certainly did so on one later occasion.

Ironic fortune, having apparently dealt Margaret an excellent opening hand of cards, had, nevertheless, negated many of her potential advantages by secretly distributing trumps to her rivals. As his eldest child, Margaret had long expected to be the heiress of her father, Richard Beauchamp, Earl of Warwick, but finally his second wife, Isabel Despenser, gave him a son. Then, through her mother, Margaret had a clear claim to the honours of Berkeley and Lisle. However, her mother's cousin, James, had laid claim to this inheritance and secured the greater part of it. Finally, Margaret had been favoured with a flourishing family of healthy children, whom she would naturally have wished to see as their father's heirs. Maud Neville, however, had pre-empted her, producing a senior brood who would keep Margaret's offspring from the Talbot inheritance. Undeterred by these shabby tricks of Fortune's wheel, Margaret fought to make the best of things for her children.

Like most of the English aristocracy, Lord and Lady Talbot were distantly related to one another, sharing a common descent from King Edward I. They were also both descendants of the houses of Clare and Despenser. Their relationship, however, was sufficiently remote that in their case no papal dispensation was necessary before they could marry. Their patently successful union had been crowned with a brood of promising and healthy children, born at irregular intervals as a result of John's periodic home leave. So far they had three sons and one daughter. This second Talbot family closely paralleled that produced for John by his first wife. Maud Neville had given her husband three sons (Thomas, John and Christopher) and probably two daughters (one whose name is unknown to us and Joan). However, Maud's brood had dwindled. Thomas, born in Dublin in 1416, had died at the age of six weeks, and the nameless daughter had died not long after the death of her mother, in 1424.[3] On the other hand all Margaret's children had so far survived.

Her eldest son, John Talbot III, had been born in 1426. The influence of his father's campaigning in France could be seen in the naming of their second son, Louis, born two years later. There had then followed a gap of several childless years, because Lord Talbot had been a prisoner of the French. Not until 1433 had he been available to father another child. Humphrey had duly made his appearance in the following year. He was named, probably, after the king's uncle, the Duke of Gloucester, who may have been his godfather. At about the time of Humphrey's birth, Margaret found herself for the first time raised to the rank of countess. On the vigil of the feast of St Louis (24 August) the Duke of Bedford, regent of France, had created her husband Count of Clermont.

A brief visit to England by the new count, in the summer of 1435, had resulted in the birth of Eleanor, Margaret's only daughter so far. The relationship between female members of aristocratic families in the fifteenth century was often particularly close, so that for Margaret, the birth of this first daughter may have been quite a special event.[4] Margaret herself enjoyed a close relationship with her own sisters, and it is evident that she also maintained very close ties with all her children. Later the children – and especially Margaret's two daughters – were to keep up close links with one another. The name selected for the little girl in itself marks the closeness of the family ties, for it was almost certainly chosen in honour of her aunt, the elder of Margaret's two sisters.[5] In fact, this aunt (who was herself pregnant at the time of Eleanor's birth) may well have been little Eleanor's godmother. About three months later, Aunt Eleanor gave birth to her own second child (the first by her second husband), little Eleanor's cousin, Henry Beaufort.[6]

Herself the first child of her parents' marriage, Margaret had been born in 1404, when her mother, Elizabeth Berkeley, was 18 years old, and her father, Richard Beauchamp (who had succeeded to the earldom of Warwick three years previously) was 22. Her parents had been married when her mother was not yet 10 years old, and for about six years the marriage had therefore remained unconsummated.[7]

Despite the fact that King Richard II was her father's godfather, Margaret's family, like that of John Talbot, had been drawn into the orbit of the house of Lancaster. Her paternal grandfather, Thomas Beauchamp, Earl of Warwick, fought for John of Gaunt in Spain. Subsequently imprisoned by Richard II in that part of the Tower of London which now bears his name,[8] Thomas only narrowly escaped execution. But he survived, to be pardoned and triumphantly set free by Henry IV. However, he had died before Margaret was born, so she had never known him.

Margaret could possibly just remember her father's mother, after whom she had been named. Margaret Ferrers, dowager Countess of Warwick, had been some years younger than her husband. Even so, she had not long survived him. Little Margaret had been barely 3 years old when her paternal grandmother had died.

Her maternal grandmother had been yet another Margaret — Margaret de Lisle. This grandmother had died twelve years before her grandaughter was born, and was therefore unknown to her except by name. The fact that she had been the heiress to the de Lisle title was not forgotten, however, and Margaret Beauchamp made use of this information in her ambitions for her own children.

As for her mother's father, Thomas, Lord Berkeley must have been very well known to Margaret. When he had died, in 1417, Margaret was already 13 years old. Old enough, certainly, to be well aware of the unseemly wrangles over land and titles which immediately followed grandfather Thomas' death.

The Berkeleys were of an ancient family line. They could trace their English ancestry back before the Norman Conquest. Elizabeth Berkeley thought she should have been her father's heiress; an opinion in which her father had concurred. Despite this, the Berkeley title was claimed by a male cousin. From this sprang the acrimonious and long-running Berkeley inheritance dispute, in which Margaret Beauchamp, as her mother's co-heiress, soon became a chief player.

Margaret's grandparents, Lord and Lady Berkeley, had been buried together in a single tomb at Wotton-under-Edge parish church in Gloucestershire. If their tomb inscription is to be believed, they had been a happy couple:

> *Nos quos certus amor primis conjunxit ab annis*
> *iunxit idem tumulus, junxit idemque polus.*
> In youth our parents joyn'd our hands, ourselves our harts,
> This Tombe our bodyes hath; th'heavens our better parts.[9]

As for Margaret's father, Richard Beauchamp, he had been knighted at the coronation of Henry IV, and had succeeded to the earldom of Warwick in 1401. He had served Henry IV in Wales, and, after fighting bravely at the Battle of Shrewsbury, on 21 July 1403, he had on the day following the battle, been made a knight of the Garter by the grateful king. This had been in the year preceding Margaret's birth. Not long afterwards, the king had licensed Richard Beauchamp to travel abroad. He had been away for two years, making pilgrimage to both Rome and the Holy Land, as well as travelling elsewhere in Europe. He had returned to England by 1406, and in 1407 Margaret's younger sister, Eleanor, had made her appearance.

On 9 May 1410 her father was appointed a member of the royal council, and he had emerged as a major figure in the reign of Henry V, at whose coronation he had served as Lord High Steward, deputising the same role for the Duke of Clarence seven years later when Catherine of France was crowned as Henry's queen. On this latter occasion he had presumably sampled the banquet served to her by John Talbot (then Lord Furnival).

The year after Henry V's coronation, Warwick had been appointed deputy of Calais, and shortly thereafter he had been sent to represent England at the Council of Constance. He had probably not returned to England until 1415.[10] Her father's absences abroad as pilgrim, tourist, soldier and diplomat, had caused a hiatus in the birth of his children, but in 1417 another daughter – Margaret's youngest full sister, Elizabeth – had been born. Elizabeth is the last known child of the Earl of Warwick by his first wife. After her birth he was abroad a great deal, in France, serving Henry V in asserting his claim to the throne of France. Thus the couple had no surviving son when Elizabeth Berkeley, Countess of Warwick, died in 1422, at the age of 36.[11]

At this time Warwick's co-heiresses were apparently Margaret and her two sisters. However, their father was only 40 when their mother died, so it can have come as no surprise to his daughters when, within a year or two of Elizabeth's death, he married again. Perhaps it seemed a little bizarre to Margaret that her new stepmother, Isabel Despenser (who was also her third cousin) should be only four years older than she was herself. Naturally, however, her father's second wife had to be young if his hopes for a son were to be fulfilled.

In fact, Isabel Despenser can never have seemed much like a stepmother to Margaret. Not only were they too close in age, but also Margaret left her father's house within a year or so of his second marriage, to marry John Talbot. She was already Lady Talbot when the news reached her that the new Countess of Warwick had succeeded where her own mother had failed. The birth of her half-brother, Henry, in March 1425, robbed her of the hope of her father's inheritance.[12] Henry remained the Earl of Warwick's only son, although the Countess Isabel bore the earl another daughter, Anne, in September 1426.[13]

Margaret's own mother, Elizabeth, the late Countess of Warwick, had been laid to rest beneath a fair marble tomb in Kingswood Abbey, Gloucestershire, a house of which she had been hereditary foundress and patroness. Nothing now remains of Kingswood Abbey except the gatehouse, and even the site of the former Abbey church is disputed, so Elizabeth's tomb is lost. Even by the early seventeenth century no trace of it remained. However, a record of the inscription which it had once borne was preserved at Berkeley Castle:

> Here lies the lady Elizabeth, late Countess and first wife of Richard de
> Beauchamp, late Earl of Warwick, and daughter and heiress of Thomas, late

Lord of Berkeley and of Lisle (the which lordship of Lisle was held by this same Thomas according to the law of England after the death of Margaret, his late wife, mother of the aforesaid Elizabeth), the which Richard and Elizabeth had issue Margaret, Eleanor and Elizabeth. Which Countess Elizabeth died in truth on the 28th day of December in the year of the Lord 1422, on whose soul may God have mercy, Amen. [14]

This was less a memorial inscription than a declaration of war by the countess' family on her cousin, James, the male claimant to the honour of Berkeley. The fight for the rights enshrined in this manifesto would occupy most of Margaret Beauchamp's life. It was a struggle which would blight her family down to the third generation, and which was destined ultimately to extinguish her male posterity.[15]

3

Lord Shrewsbury

John, Lord Talbot, and his retinue landed safely, probably in Portsmouth, soon after 20 February 1442. From the port he must have made his way rapidly to London, to impress upon the king the urgent need for reinforcements in Normandy. Evidently his requests fell upon receptive ears. Permission was given to raise a new army to reinforce with all possible speed the existing English forces in France.

Talbot himself seems to have remained in London. In March, commissioners were appointed by the king to requisition ships to convey the reinforcements to Normandy, and some were dispatched to the East Anglian ports, but on Tuesday 27 March, the Tuesday of Holy Week, Lord Talbot himself was commissioned to assemble ships from the Port of London and from Sandwich, which suggests that he was at that time living in or near the capital.[1]

It is probable that the Talbot family had a house in London at this period. There is an area known as Talbot Court off Gracechurch Street, not far from the site of St Benet's Church, just opposite the east end of Cheap Street, and north of London Bridge. This may mark the site of a former Talbot residence.[2] There is still a building there called Talbot House, though the present structure is of much more recent date. Later sources, however, have claimed Talbot Inn in Whitechapel as John Talbot's London home.[3]

Evidence certainly exists of Talbot connections with London. In 1467 John's second wife, Margaret, Countess of Shrewsbury, probably died (and was certainly buried) in London. Their youngest son, Humphrey, also seems to have lived in London for at least part of his adult life. He founded a chantry for himself and his deceased relatives at the Church of St Andrew-by-the-Wardrobe.[4] He also assumed responsibility for his mother's funerary monument at St Paul's Cathedral.

John Talbot's youngest daughter, Elizabeth, and his daughter-in-law, Jane (Humphrey's wife) seem to have been familiar with the London suburbs lying beyond the city walls, between Gracechurch Street and Whitechapel. They both retired, in later life, to the Convent of the Poor Clares near Aldgate.[5] There were other noble houses in this general area. The Nevilles once had their London home on what is now the site of Leadenhall Market.[6] It is entirely plausible, therefore, that John Talbot might have had a house in this part of the city or its suburbs. It is also possible that the Talbot family still from time to time made use of Furnival Inn in Holborn, which had been the former house of John's first father-in-law. It is said that the latter, as Lord Treasurer, had used Furnival Inn to accommodate the clerks of the Exchequer, who may have remained in occupation of at least part of the building. However, the property certainly belonged to the earls of Shrewsbury until the mid-sixteenth century.[7]

It was therefore probably either in a house off Gracechurch Street, or in Whitechapel, that John Talbot's reunion with Margaret and the rest of his family took place. This would have been the occasion of his first meeting with his daughter Eleanor. It is legitimate to wonder what the little girl (already nearly 6 years old) thought of this tall, dark stranger; the formidable man who was her father.[8] Had he remembered her birthday? Did he bring her a gift from France? And was it perhaps in this same house, later that night, or on one of the succeeding nights, that the last child of John Talbot's family was conceived, in that spring of 1442?

As usual, Lord Talbot spent little time in his native land. The situation in France meant that the Duke of York required reinforcements urgently. The king therefore commanded that the ships requisitioned to transport them to France should be at the port of Winchelsea by the last day of April.[9] For Eleanor, the unaccustomed presence of her long-absent father can have been only the briefest of interludes. Moreover, since the earl was much occupied with affairs of state, she probably saw very little of him.

Nevertheless, John Talbot does seem to have found time during this visit to discuss family concerns with his wife. Margaret was increasingly impatient with the pace – so slow as to be virtually indiscernible – of the legal resolution of her claim to part of the Berkeley inheritance. This claim had originally been asserted by her parents years before, upon the death of her grandfather. Then, the Earl and Countess of Warwick had occupied Berkeley Castle itself, as Margaret knew well, for in due course she was to repeat this action herself. However, Henry V had ruled against them and recognised as the new Lord Berkeley, the Countess of Warwick's cousin, James.

As a rather meagre compensation, Margaret's parents had been granted three of the Berkeley manors: Wotton-under-Edge, Simondshall and Cowley, for the Earl of Warwick's life only. In exchange, Richard Beauchamp had agreed to abandon his claim to the rest of the Berkeley inheritance – a considerable concession on his part. It is scarcely surprising, therefore, that when their father died, Margaret and her sisters were eager to hold on to these three manors, in spite of the condition of life tenure under which their father had received them.

Meanwhile, James, the new Lord Berkeley, repossessed the manors by force. Margaret's husband, and her brother-in-law, Edmund Beaufort, used their influence at court to have James imprisoned in the Tower, and the Earl of Warwick's inquisition post mortem ruled (somewhat surprisingly, in view of the terms of the original grant) that Margaret and her sisters were entitled to the disputed manors. Possession, however, has always proved nine points of the law, and James, Lord Berkeley was difficult to dislodge. There had been an attempt at arbitration by the husbands of Margaret's younger sisters in 1440, but Talbot (then serving in France) threatened to break off the siege of Harfleur and return to England if any decisions were made in his absence.

Margaret's son, young John Talbot III, next tried a legal approach, sending a subpoena to Lord Berkeley. This move was received with arrogant contempt. Gestures speak louder than words, and the haughty Lord Berkeley signalled unequivocally his uncompromising stance with a pantomime of theatrical provocation. He would make his detested rivals eat their words – literally! The unfortunate Talbot messenger was compelled to consume his master's subpoena, parchment, wax seal and all.

In 1441 Edmund Beaufort and Margaret's other brother-in-law, George Neville, Lord Latimer, were again disposed to compromise with Lord Berkeley. Talbot, however, still vigorously opposed any accommodation with the enemy, who, meanwhile, continued in defiant occupation. Legal moves aimed at ousting him dragged on, both in the courts in Gloucester and in Parliament. Meanwhile, Margaret and her husband, with their growing brood of children to provide for, refused to give up what they saw as their rightful claim.

No record has survived of their discussions in the spring of 1442, although such discussions must have taken place. This can be inferred from the actions taken by Margaret later that year, following John's return to France: actions in which she had the support of veteran men-at-arms who had served with her husband in France, and who must have been left at her disposal by him, for that specific purpose.

But before we get ahead of our story, let us continue with the events of early 1442, when we may conjecture that the Talbots also gave thought to the future domestic arrangements of their eldest son, John III, now 16 years old. Perhaps Lord Talbot deputed his wife to look out, in his absence, for a likely bride for the young man.

On Whit Sunday, 20 May 1442, King Henry VI acknowledged the growing importance of Lord Talbot by honouring him with an English earldom. He had already been created Count of Clermont by the English authorities in France (see above) but English contemporaries seem to have taken little account of this, for chronicles and in fact the Patent Rolls continue to call him Lord Talbot until the end of May 1442.

His new English title was officially *Comes Salopie*, which was perhaps intended to be read in English as 'Earl of Shropshire'. However, it was soon popularly rendered as 'Earl of Shrewsbury'. This form of the title became the norm, and it has continued to be borne by John Talbot's descendants, down to the present day, despite the fact that it was unusual in the fifteenth century for an earl's title to be derived from a town rather than a county. Talbot's new title meant that his little daughter was now unquestionably Lady Eleanor Talbot.[10]

On the following Friday, 25 May, commissioners were appointed by the king to take the muster of the new troops,[11] 'and the 25th day of May my Lord Talbot (*sic*) took his way toward the sea, for to pass into France with his retenue'.[12] By Friday 15 June they were all in Normandy and mustered at Harfleur. The new Earl of Shrewsbury had spent less than four months in England, but when he departed he left Margaret an acknowledged English countess. He also almost certainly left her pregnant yet again, carrying the child who was to be the last addition to their family.

Lord Shrewsbury's hard work on his king's behalf did not go unnoticed by Henry VI, who subsequently remarked on the earl's 'strenuous probity, even to old age'.[13] Nevertheless, the earl's return to France in the summer of 1442 may have been timely, in more ways than one. It had the distinct advantage that he was not on the spot to be asked awkward questions when violence subsequently erupted in connection with the Berkeley dispute (see below).

Before that, there was also a little matter of piracy accusations against the crew of a merchant ship belonging to the Earl of Shrewsbury. Apparently 'certain evildoers' from one of the earl's balingers had made off with six bales of cloth which merchants of the Hanse in London had been in the process of exporting, via Faversham and Dover, to Calais. The merchants, Robert Blitterswyk and Betrand Questenbergh, protested to the king, who instructed his sergeant-at-arms, Robert College, to track down the cloth and apprehend the 'evildoers'.[14]

This was not the first time that the king had found himself enquiring into the activities of one of the earl's ships. In December 1438 the then Lord Talbot and Furnival had made a formal complaint to the Lord Chancellor, the Bishop of Bath and Wells, that his ship the *Margaret of Portladown*, valued at 100 marks, was at sea bound for Rouen with a cargo of salt worth 13s 4d when a Cornish balinger, the *Jenot of Fowey*, had attacked her and made off with the cargo, with the knowledge of her owner, Thomas Jerard of Fowey.[15] On that occasion Lord Shrewsbury seems to have been the victim of a piratical attack.

There had also been another occasion (in 1440) when the king had been obliged to command the arrest of Thomas Williamson, master of one of the then Lord Talbot's balingers, for piracy: specifically, the plundering of a ship called *Le Crayer,* (master, Cornelius Brandson), containing the goods of the Hanseatic merchant John Dasse of Cologne.[16] What Lord Shrewsbury himself knew of such piratical activities by his own mariners, cannot, of course, be ascertained, but the fact that his ships should have been implicated in acts of piracy twice in two years looks a little suspicious.

Much more serious however – because it involved civil disorder – was the escapade upon which the Countess of Shrewsbury embarked later in the year. Finding that legal processes were apparently getting her nowhere, Margaret imitated the examples of her parents, and of her rival and cousin, James, and took the law into her own hands. She seized the manors of Wotton-under-Edge, Cowley and Simondshall. Having seized them, she kept them, and could not be removed. This bold exploit paid off, for not until several years later were the Talbots to enter into any kind of negotiation in respect of these three manors, and then the outcome was that they were allowed to keep them for life.[17] On this occasion, as on a similar, later occasion,[18] Margaret seems to have employed those men-at-arms provided by her husband: veterans of his French campaigns.

It was probably towards the end of this eventful year – in December, perhaps, or in January, that Margaret, Countess of Shrewsbury, gave birth to her last child and second daughter. As her time drew near, Margaret withdrew into her own chambers. The keyholes will have been blocked, and all but one of her chamber windows covered over in preparation for the coming event. For three or four weeks Margaret remained shut off from the rest of the world, surrounded only by her women. This was the first (and only) occasion on which Eleanor Talbot saw the complete withdrawal of her mother's powerful presence. It may have been a bewildering experience for the little girl.

When she had safely given birth, Lady Shrewsbury remained for some weeks in seclusion. At first, she would have been expected to remain in bed. Progressively she would then have risen, spending her time sitting, or exercising a little by walking around her rooms. Finally she would have reappeared in the rest of the house. Even then she would not, at first, go out of doors. Meanwhile the new-born baby would have been handed over almost at once to a nurse, as Eleanor and her brothers had been. Noble ladies did not normally breastfeed their own children. It would have slowed down their rate of reproduction: one of their principal *raisons d'être*. In theory, the fact that the new baby girl was in the hands of a nurse meant that she could be seen by her father, even though the mother was still confined to her chambers. In fact, of course, Lord Shrewsbury, as usual, was not even in the country when his last child was born.

Anxiety in respect of newborn infants meant that they were generally baptised as early as possible. Usually this ceremony was performed within a few days of birth. Since at that time Margaret was still lying in, she would have been unable to attend the new baby's christening herself. It is, however, possible that little Lady Eleanor attended her new baby sister's baptism, and it is highly probable that pride of place at the event was taken by one of Margaret's own sisters. For if Eleanor Beauchamp had stood godmother at little Eleanor Talbot's baptism six years previously, on this present occasion one can perhaps infer that Margaret's youngest sister, Elizabeth, Lady

Latimer, was the principal godparent. At all events, the new baby was certainly baptised Elizabeth.

For Margaret, the ritual of giving birth terminated in the ceremony of her churching, which marked her return to normal life. This was a short rite of purification and thanksgiving. Accompanied by her midwives and female attendants (possibly including Eleanor) the countess made her way to church bearing a lighted candle. She was received by clergy intoning psalms. An acolyte bore the holy water bucket and aspergillum, which the officiant took, sprinkling Margaret with holy water to cleanse her, while choristers chanted:

Asperges me, Domine, hyssopo, et mundabor;
Lavabis me, et super nivem dealbabor.[19]

4

Brothers, Sisters, Cousins

By the beginning of the new year of 1443, the family of John, Lord Talbot, first Earl of Shrewsbury, was complete, though the earl had yet to meet the latest recruit, the baby Elizabeth.

Next in age to Elizabeth, John and Margaret's only other daughter, Eleanor, was just turning seven. Eleanor's birthday fell in late February or early March, right at the year's end – for at this period the New Year in England began on Lady Day (25 March) rather than 1 January. Eleanor had been born under the sign of Pisces, and either by fate or by chance, she was to grow up with many of the characteristics traditionally ascribed to that star sign, for she was gentle, sensitive, idealistic and perhaps even somewhat passive. A girl who needed her own space, she would also ultimately develop a bent towards contemplation and mysticism.

Two years Eleanor's senior was Humphrey, now nearly 9 years old. Their ages meant that, to a large extent, these three youngest Talbot children grew up together as a little group. Their ages, which united them, also distanced them to some extent from their siblings, who were already almost adult when Elizabeth was born. Humphrey, Eleanor and Elizabeth were to remain close to one another throughout their lives.

John and Margaret's other two sons were both more than twice as old as Eleanor. Louis was fifteen in 1443, while at seventeen his elder brother, John III, was old enough for his parents to be thinking of his marriage, which took place later that year. It is questionable how well Eleanor really knew her two eldest full-blood brothers.

Relationships in the Talbot family were complicated not only by questions of age, but also by Lord Shrewsbury's two marriages. More than three times Eleanor's age were the members of the third and oldest group of Lord Shrewsbury's children: those born to his first wife, Maud Neville. Three of Maud's children had survived and were now grown up. The eldest of these, John II, was heir to the earldom of Shrewsbury – much against the wishes of his stepmother, Margaret, who felt that the earldom, bestowed on her husband so long after the death of his first wife, should have been the destined inheritance of her own children. She, after all, was the first Countess of Shrewsbury.

A few years later clear evidence would emerge that the relationship between the countess and her husband's eldest son and heir was strained. Such situations were by no means unusual in the fifteenth century. The antipathy between John II and his stepmother, coupled with a considerable age gap, may well mean that Eleanor had as little contact with her eldest half-brother as with her father. Even so, the relationship between the first Earl of Shrewsbury's two families was subsequently acknowledged. This is evident from the fact that Eleanor's brother, Sir Humphrey Talbot, who had been a Yorkist, left his property to Sir Gilbert Talbot, John II's Lancastrian/pro-Tudor younger son.[1]

John II was already a knight, having been given that honour by the young Henry VI the year after Margaret had married his widowed father. He had been serving with his father in France, on and off, since 1436. In fact he had gone to Normandy the previous summer, when his father had returned there with the reinforcements. John II, now 30 years of age, had married, a little more than a year earlier. His wife was Catherine, the young widow of Sir John Ratcliffe, and daughter and co-heiress of Sir Edward Burnell of Acton Burnell in Shropshire. She was several years older than her new husband. To the medieval mind both the partners to this alliance were well beyond normal marriageable age. As yet there were no signs of any children from this union.[2]

Maud Neville's third (and second surviving) son was Sir Christopher Talbot, also knighted by the king, and about 23 years old in 1443. Maud's only other living child was her daughter. Joan Talbot was around 21 years old in 1443, and it is possible that she too was by then married.[3]

The Earl of Shrewsbury also had at least one illegitimate son, Henry. It is not known whether he formed a normal part of the earl's household when at home in England, but in 1443 he may well have been serving with his father in France. Certainly a bastard son of the earl was in France in that year, because one was captured by the French army, commanded by the Dauphin, on 14 August 1443.

Noble children had to be educated, of course. Little girls had to be trained to be good future wives. They were also to be encouraged to form helpful social connections, first and foremost within their extended family. 'From the age of about seven, the education of boys and girls began to diverge. Mothers continued to be responsible for their daughters, although among the nobility a mistress might be put in charge ... Discipline for girls included physical punishment if this was thought necessary'.[4] Chastity and obedience were highly prized commodities in daughters, and a key feature of their education was their religious training.

It is very clear from their later lives that both Eleanor and Elizabeth Talbot grew up with a sincere and lively faith that transcended mere conventional observance. This must reflect their upbringing. Religious training for children began at a very early age, and by the age of 4 or 5 a little girl might be expected to be able to read the psalms in Latin.[5] In 1463 it was noted that Sir William Plumton's little granddaughter 'speaketh [English] prettily, and French, and hath near hand learned her psalter'.[6] This would probably have been mere rote-learning. While both the Talbot sisters could read (and probably also write) English, and possibly French as well,[7] their knowledge of Latin was probably confined to the reading of religious texts. There is no reason to suppose that either of them could write Latin. Such an accomplishment would have been very unusual for a noblewoman in the fifteenth century.[8]

There was, in fact, some debate in certain quarters regarding the advisability of teaching girls to read at all, but the majority of commentators seem to have been in favour of doing so, since 'in practice, reading was a useful skill for women who in adult life might find themselves taking over estate and business responsibilities'.[9]

On a practical level, aristocratic girls had to be taught to perform all the roles expected of successful wives. They needed to be literate in English, have some knowledge of arithmetic, receive hands-on training in household and estate management, and understand something about property law. Over and above specific skills, they had to learn to exercise authority over large numbers of people and take considerable initiative as mistresses of their households without violating their subordinate position.[10]

In addition to all this, 'reading ... freed the religiously inclined from the limitations of the rosary ... [and] permitted the frivolous to read aloud from poetry and romances when no one else was available to do so, an invaluable accomplishment on wet and windy days'.[11]

Writing, for girls, was a much rarer skill than reading. Even the women of the Paston family seem generally to have had their letters written for them by other people.[12] It is impossible to say whether Eleanor and Elizabeth Talbot acquired this skill. Almost certainly their surviving documents were written for them. Nevertheless, some aristocratic women did learn to write. Margaret of York was apparently able to do so, though she was brought up not as a king's sister, but as the daughter of a royal Duke.

In general there is a question mark over the degree of contact which normally existed between aristocratic children and their parents.[13] However, the Countess of Shrewsbury does seems to have been available to take direct charge of the upbringing of her daughters, and her subsequent relationship with them remained close, suggesting that she had been personally involved with them during their childhood. There is no evidence that the Talbot girls were sent away for training in another aristocratic household before their marriages; nor do either of them appear to have spent any part of their childhood at court, in the household of Queen Margaret of Anjou (although noble children were sometimes sent to court in this way).

Eleanor and Elizabeth Talbot could not have had a better teacher for some of the skills they required than their powerful mother. They may also have had a governess, or *maistresse*, but if so her identity is unknown. Since governesses were usually not appointed until girls had passed the age of 7, and Elizabeth Talbot, at least, was married by that age, it is quite possible that they had none.

The *Livre du Chevalier de la Tour*, penned as guidance for his three daughters by a French knight in the late fourteenth century, suggests priorities other than literacy, numeracy and languages, which the Countess of Shrewsbury might have had for her daughters' education. In this book, courtesy, deportment and a good reputation are all emphasised, as is obedience.[14] Girls and women should be suitably arrayed, certainly, but without immodesty or superfluity. Tinting the hair, or making up the face, was not to be encouraged.[15] Chaucer, on the other hand, seems chiefly to have valued dignity in a woman, together with religious devotion, French and good table manners.[16]

Among the female relatives with whom the little Talbot girls might have formed childhood associations were their various female cousins. On her father's side Eleanor had numerous cousins. Many of these, like some of her own siblings, were significantly older than Eleanor. Even so, there is clear evidence that these relationships were acknowledged.

Eleanor's paternal cousins were the children of her father's sisters. Of Lord Shrewsbury's brothers only one, his elder brother Gilbert, is known to have had a child. This was the heiress Ankaret Talbot, who had died before Eleanor was born. Lord Shrewsbury's sisters, in order of seniority, were Catherine, Mary, Elizabeth, Alice and Anne. Elizabeth (born *c.*1384) seems to have become a nun. The other four sisters all married (in several cases, more than once).

Catherine Talbot (born *c.*1378) married Thomas Eyton, of the Shropshire gentry. The Eyton family favoured the Yorkist cause, and Catherine Talbot's younger son, Nicholas (1400–*c.*1465), together with the latter's nephew, Roger (1420–*c.*1470) served as Members of Parliament. It is not clear whether Catherine also had daughters, but all her children will inevitably have been much older than Eleanor.

Mary Talbot (born *c.*1380) married Sir Thomas Green. She had several children, including a daughter, Joan. No evidence has so far been found as to whether Eleanor later maintained any kind of contact with the Greens, but they too seem to have been very much her seniors. Mary Talbot's eldest son, Sir Thomas Green II, was born in 1400 and died in 1461, while his sister, Joan, was reportedly born in 1396.

Alice Talbot (*c.*1390–1436) married Sir Thomas Barre of Burford. She had at least one son and three daughters. Alice's son, Sir John Barre (1412–1483) served as MP for Herefordshire. He was a Lancastrian. Despite this, his daughter, Isabel,[17] married Humphrey Stafford, whom Edward IV created Earl of Devon when the Courtenays forfeited that title by attainder. Sir John Barre's eldest sister, Elizabeth, and his youngest sister, Ankaret, both married and had families,[18] but most interesting is Sir John Barre's second sister, Jane (born *c.*1420?) who, like his daughter, also gravitated into the Yorkist camp. She became the second wife of Sir William Catesby I of Ashby St Leger (*c.*1408–1478), and thus the stepmother of William Catesby II (1440–1485), who has gone down in history as Richard III's 'Cat'.[19] It is clear that Eleanor knew Jane Barre (Lady Catesby) and her family. As we shall see, Jane's husband, Sir William, acted for Eleanor in matters of business. Jane had at least one child of her own, a daughter, Alice Catesby, born in 1447.

Anne Talbot (*c.*1395–1441) married Hugh Courtenay, Earl of Devon. Her son, Thomas (1414–1458), succeeded to his father's title and married Margaret Beaufort.[20] The Courtenays were Lancastrians, and Earl Thomas' two sons, who successively inherited the earldom, were both attainted and executed by Edward IV: Thomas (b. 1432) in 1461, and John in 1471.

In addition to his full-blood sisters, Eleanor's father also had a much younger half-sister, Joan Neville, born of his mother's second marriage with Lord Furnival. Joan Neville married Sir Hugh Lokesey (died 1445). It is not clear whether this couple had children.

On her mother's side were Eleanor's Beauchamp relatives. Her aunt Eleanor had many children, including five daughters by her second husband, Edmund Beaufort, Duke of Somerset. These Beaufort cousins were Margaret, Lady Stafford (the mother of Henry, Duke of Buckingham – and it is interesting to note his relationship with Eleanor), Eleanor, Countess of Wiltshire, Joan, Lady Fry, Anne, Lady Paston, and Elizabeth, Lady (Fitz)Lewis. These girls were close in age to Eleanor and Elizabeth Talbot. That fact, together with the affection existing between their mothers, the Beauchamp sisters (not to mention the fact that their fathers were comrades-in-arms and colleagues in government circles) more or less guarantees that Eleanor knew the Beaufort girls well during her childhood.

There is clear evidence that Anne Beaufort, Lady Paston, maintained contact as an adult with Elizabeth Talbot, Duchess of Norfolk. Indeed, she eventually married one of her own daughters into the Talbot family.[21] Aunt Eleanor's Beaufort sons, Henry, Edmund and John were the last Beaufort Dukes of Somerset.[22] The eldest, Henry, was almost exactly the same age as his cousin, Eleanor. These young male Beauforts were later to prove dangerous relatives to know, yet in spite of this, Eleanor's sister Elizabeth seems consistently to have acknowledged their kinship.[23] Aunt Eleanor also had a son and daughter by her first husband, Lord Roos.

There is also circumstantial evidence of a connection between Eleanor and Elizabeth Talbot and their mother's half-brother, Henry, Duke of Warwick.[24] It is possible, therefore, that they knew his little daughter, Anne Beauchamp, who died young. Of their other girl cousins on the Beauchamp side, Anne Neville (the future queen of Richard III) may have been too young to have had much to do with Eleanor and Elizabeth Talbot. However, they may have known her elder sister Isabel (the future Duchess of Clarence).

In June 1443 Eleanor's father returned once more to England to plead with the English Council, which, instead of reinforcing the Duke of York in Normandy, was proposing to send a separate force into France, under Shrewsbury's brother-in-law, Edmund Beaufort, Earl of Dorset.[25] Lord Shrewsbury had little success with this mission, and the council could not be persuaded to alter its plans. By August, he had returned to Normandy. However, he probably saw his younger daughter for the first time, during this visit, and he may have been in England long enough to witness the marriage of his son, John III, to Joan Chedder, the 18-year-old widow of Richard Stafford. The bride was a year older than the young Talbot, and her father, Thomas Chedder, was but an esquire. Although Joan was one of his co-heiresses, this was not a wonderful match for a son of the Earl of Shrewsbury, and either it reflects the reality of John's position as only the third surviving son of his father (with little hope of inheriting the earldom) or it must have been a *mariage d'inclination* on his part. The latter is a possibility, because at the time when he married, his mother was already working hard to have him raised to the peerage with a title carved out of her own maternal inheritance; an endeavour which bore fruit the following summer.

When the Earl of Shrewsbury returned to France, at the beginning of August 1443, his second surviving son, Sir Christopher Talbot, remained behind, and in circumstances which remain somewhat mysterious, the distance separating John Talbot III from his paternal inheritance was suddenly dramatically reduced. Sir Christopher was killed, soon after his father's departure, by one of his own men:

> Griffin Vachan of Treflidian in Wales, knight ... struck to the heart and slew with a lance worth 2s. Christopher Talbot, knight, then his master, on St Laurence the Martyr, 21 Henry VI [10 August 1443] at Cawce, Co. Salop.[26]

Christopher's death, at the age of only 23, brought John Talbot III one step nearer to the earldom of Shrewsbury. One wonders how the news of this stepson's death was received by Lady Shrewsbury. She may have brought this boy up from a very young age. Nevertheless, he was not her own son, and his unexpected demise potentially benefited her own children.

On 26 July 1444 Margaret succeeded in her attempt to have her own first-born son raised to the peerage. Henry VI acknowledged (or created) him Lord and Baron Lisle of Kingston Lisle in Berkshire.[27] By that time he had also received a knighthood. It was, however, probably not until the summer of 1448 that Joan, the new Lady Lisle, gave birth to John's son, Thomas (named, perhaps, after her own father).[28] Thomas was the Countess of Shrewsbury's first grandson, and was born less than five years after her own youngest child, Elizabeth. Indeed, he was to prove her only grandson, for of all her children only John, the eldest, and Elizabeth, the youngest (and still a baby in 1444) were ever to produce children, and all of Margaret's grandchildren except this first one were to be girls.

In France, meanwhile, another baby was baptised at about the same time as Thomas Talbot. Cecily Neville, Duchess of York had given her husband a daughter, who, in September, was christened Elizabeth at Rouen Cathedral. The Earl of Shrewsbury, who had been working closely with the Duke of York for some time now, was chosen to be this little girl's godfather.

Eleanor's Childhood

For Eleanor and her brothers and sister growing up in the Talbot house-hold, life would have been peripatetic. The Talbot family had a chain of estates 'from Marbury in South Cheshire through Whitchurch in North Shropshire, Corfham near Ludlow in South Shropshire, Credenhill near Hereford and Goodrich on the Wye in South Herefordshire to Painswick on the Cotswolds' edge in South Gloucestershire'.[1]

It is difficult to know whether the household moved around these estates in accordance with a regular set pattern, but there is evidence that on at least one occasion they spent October and November in London, January at Eccleswall, February and March in the region of Shrewsbury and Chester, which presumably took in Blakemere, April at Painswick, August at Painswick and Blakemere and September at Goodrich.[2] This gives an indication of their movements, but the pattern is incomplete, and is unlikely to have been rigidly followed. On one occasion Margaret Beauchamp is known to have spent Christmas at Blakemere, for she was entertained there on Twelfth Night by two actors from Shrewsbury, who presented an 'inter-lude' for her entertainment. The Blakemere household accounts for 1424–25 record a gift to these two men of half a gold noble (3s 4d).[3]

The houses and estates which the family and household inhabited as they moved from Gloucestershire to Cheshire were varied in style and size. Goodrich Castle was probably the most magnificent, although in the 1440s not perhaps the most convenient and up-to-date. The castle's substantial ruins reveal clearly the outline appearance of its great hall and of the solar block, where the members of the Talbot family would have lived, when in residence at the castle.

At Blakemere, nothing of their house survives. It is, nevertheless, possible to form a good impression of the building and its estate from surviving records, helped by a comparison with surviving structures elsewhere. Stokesay Castle, for example, in southern Shropshire, which also stands beside a small lake, gives some idea of the possible appearance of Blakemere. The park at Blakemere was enclosed by palings to keep in the deer, and it contained a watermill and a windmill. In the early 1390s a new garden, with a lawn of green turf, had been laid out. Such gardens were normally enclosed, to exclude the deer which wandered in the park, and to create a private space. An impression of the Blakemere garden's possible appearance may be gained from surviving instructions for the design of another fourteenth-century garden:

> Care must be taken that the lawn is of such size that about it in a square may be planted every sweet-smelling herb such as rue and sage and basil, and likewise all sorts of flowers, as violet, columbine, lily, rose, iris and the like. Between these herbs and the turf, at the edge of the lawn, set square, let there be a higher bench of turf, flowering and lovely; and somewhere in the middle, provide seats ... Upon the lawn, too, against the heat of the sun, trees should be planted, or vines trained; ... grapevines, pears, apples, pomegranates, sweet bays, cypresses and such like. [But] ... there should not be any trees in the middle of the lawn ... If the midst of the lawn were to have trees planted on it, spiders webs would entangle the faces of passers-by! If possible, a clean fountain of water in a stone basin should be in the midst.[4]

It seems likely that the garden at Blakemere will also have contained daisies (marguerites), the flowers emblematic of the first Countess of Shrewsbury's name. Margaret used paintings of them to decorate margins in her personal book of hours,[5] while her daughter, Eleanor, at the age of 17, had a signet ring engraved with daisies, which may have been a present from her mother. Eleanor used this ring to seal a letter of attorney on 10 May 1453.[6] Perhaps the garden also contained borage, the little blue flowers of which may later have been adopted as her badge by Elizabeth Talbot.[7] The garden at Blakemere must have made some impression on the Talbot children, for later, Elizabeth had a new private garden laid out for her pleasure in her park at Framlingham Castle, accessible by means of a cutting through the wall of the old great hall, and a new footbridge across the moat.

The walls of the house at Blakemere were of freestone, and it was roofed with wooden shingles, although the gatehouse was roofed in lead, and the outbuildings were thatched with reeds from the mere. Only the kitchen block had a roof of red tiles (to minimise the risk of fire). The outbuildings included a 'long stable' and also a 'great stable'. The latter was outside the gate, beyond the area enclosed by the moat. There was a kennel for the dogs, perhaps the white Talbot hounds which bore the family name. This breed is now extinct, but the dogs resembled the bloodhound except for the fact that they were pure white. The surviving Spanish Hound (*Sabueso Español*) is said to be descended from the Talbot, although it is not pure white, but has red or black patches.[8] A new wardrobe was put up at Blakemere in 1401. This was a free-standing building for the safekeeping of valuables. A new malthouse was built in 1403, and a new dovecote in 1408–09.

Within the house there was a great hall, a great chamber with a stone chimney which had a reredos plastered with lime, and a chapel leading off from the great chamber. The chapel and some of the other rooms had glazed windows. There was a 'middle room' and an 'inner room', and a 'lady's room', which had its own small chapel. The lady's room had wooden panelling. Possibly some of the rooms were hung with tapestries. The so-called 'Devonshire Hunting Tapestries', which are now in the Victoria and Albert Museum, and which were probably woven in the southern Netherlands,[9] may have been made for the first Earl of Shrewsbury.[10] There was a 'men-at-arms' room' and another room adjoining it; a 'knights' room', a 'seneschal's room' and a chaplain's room. There was an oriel, or gallery, a garret above the gate, and latrines either in or under the men-at-arms' room.[11]

The surviving buildings at Stokesay Castle give some idea of the former appearance of Blakemere. The area enclosed by the moat at Blakemere, which comprised the main dwellings and certain of the outbuildings, was about 48m by 52m.[12] This was a little larger than Stokesay Castle, which is irregularly shaped, but averages about 40m by 35m. Some household pottery has been recovered from the Blakemere site,[13] together with nails and everyday metal objects such as buckles and at least one pewter plate.[14] The whole estate at Blakemere comprised 32,000 acres, embracing the town of Whitchurch. This estate, a favourite with Lord and Lady Shrewsbury, must have been very familiar to Eleanor as a girl.

The Talbot household at Blakemere supplied much of its own produce, but also bought in goods from outside; 751 gallons of ale were brewed annually on the premises. In addition, nearly twice this amount was bought in every year from Whitchurch and other neighbouring towns. Some cloth was woven on the estate, but a great deal more, especially the green fabric needed for the Talbot livery, was purchased in Coventry and London. Pepper, saffron, cloves, mace, cinnamon and other spices could not be home produced, and were purchased in great quantities from John Glover in Shrewsbury. Salt came from Wyck, together with poultry.

Fishermen were brought in annually to fish the meres, but both freshwater and saltwater fish were also purchased in large amounts. The Talbots and their household ate cod, salmon, sprats, conger, plaice, whiting, halibut, whelks, shrimps, crabs, oysters and mussels, and also bream, pike, roach, dace, flounder and trout. As for meat, the warren at Blakemere produced rabbits, and the dovecote, pigeons. There was game from the park, although oxen, sheep and calves were also consumed. Most vegetables seem to have been home produced, but occasionally something more exotic was bought in, such as oranges.[15] Such a luxury item as this imported fruit must have delighted the children.

The Talbot household normally lacked the presence of its head, whom Humphrey, Eleanor and Elizabeth can have seen only rarely. As we have noted, for most of Eleanor's early life Lord Shrewsbury was absent, mainly in France. The children's life was therefore centred on their mother, Margaret. For girls of Eleanor's and Elizabeth's class this was, in any case, not unusual.[16]

Noble children, particularly sons, were often brought up away from their parents' home, in other aristocratic households. In the case of the Talbots, however, it is clear that the children were, at least sometimes, with their mother, whose household regulations took account of their presence. It is recorded that 'to the honour of God [she] made decree in her house, not her own children out set,'[17] that whatever person blasphemed our Lord by unlawful swearing he should lack that day all wine and chochyn [cooked food?] and only have but bread and water'.[18]

Direct responsibility for the children's education was presumably in the hands of one or more of the priests in their parents' service, and – in the case of the girls – of female attendants of their mother. What exactly they were taught, we cannot know, but Eleanor, Humphrey and Elizabeth, as well as Louis, were all certainly literate in later life. Also, these four young Talbots all later exhibited, in different ways, evidence of a strong and orthodox Catholic faith. Some writers have suggested that their father, in his youth, may have been slightly tainted with Lollardy, but there is no real evidence of heretical tendencies in the earl.[19] In any case, his frequent absences abroad mean that he can have had only a limited influence on his younger children.

As we have already seen, the little girls were certainly taught to read and write in English, and possibly also in French.[20] It was not normal to teach girls Latin, and there is no particular reason to suppose that either Eleanor or Elizabeth had more than a rote knowledge of that language, sufficient to enable them to recite liturgical texts such as those found in a book of hours. Religious and moral instruction was of course very important. Two generations later, Margaret, Countess of Salisbury, daughter of Eleanor's cousin, Isabel Neville, was exhorted by Henry VIII to place special emphasis in training his daughter, Mary, 'in all virtuous demeanour. That is to say, at due times to serve God'.[21] Lady Salisbury's education of the future Queen Mary I was, in this respect, a notable success, and it seems that the same could be said of Lady Shrewsbury's training of Eleanor and Elizabeth Talbot.

In addition to moral and practical instruction, aspects of the children's general cultural development will also have received attention. In the case of the girls, some appreciation of literature may have featured in their education, and it seems certain that an interest in music was cultivated. Elizabeth Talbot maintained a range of musicians in her household later, as Duchess of Norfolk.

Because the household accounts for Blakemere for the early fifteenth century have, in part, survived, we know more about this residence than about the other Talbot houses. One very important feature of the household at Blakemere, as of all noble households at this time, was the people who composed it, and who served the family. Often this service was hereditary. The Talbot children must have been familiar with the many members of the household: such names as Richard Kenleye, John Wylym, Robert Daykin and Richard Cholmely (whose father, Thomas, had also served the household at Blakemere in the 1390s). All of these men were important in the Talbot household, at least in the 1420s.

Later evidence clearly shows that one of the people that Elizabeth, Eleanor and Humphrey knew from their childhood was John Wenlock. Born, probably, near the end of the fourteenth century, he would have been about 20 years old, and was already the household steward, when, in 1419, following the murder of Henry Bykeley, he was appointed receiver at Blakemere. Subsequently he served both as receiver and as steward on further occasions, and was clearly a trusted administrator, well-known to the Talbot family, from whom he received an annual annuity of 48s for life. After the death of the Earl of Shrewsbury, John Wenlock was to continue to serve the dowager Countess Margaret until his own death, early in 1463. His land in Whitchurch was inherited by his son (another John) who was also in Margaret's service.

When the dowager Countess of Shrewsbury died, in 1467, John Wenlock the younger transferred to the household of her son, Humphrey. He also maintained links with Eleanor, as we shall see later. When he himself died, in London, in 1477, John asked to be buried near Margaret Beauchamp's tomb, and he left money for masses to be offered for the repose of the countess' soul. Like the Cholmelys, the Wenlocks provide an example of the loyal household members who served the Talbot family and their Lestrange ancestors for generations.[22] The testimony of John Wenlock's devotion proves that Margaret, Countess of Shrewsbury, who often comes over as a formidable and fearsome lady, could also inspire affection. Thanks to him, alongside the Amazon who fought the Berkeleys tooth and nail, we are also able to glimpse the devoted mother whom all her children seem to have loved and respected.

Not only men but also women served the Talbots. The children must have known their mother's women servants. The names of those who were serving her in the 1440s are not recorded, but twenty years earlier Maud Over and Eleanor Camvyle, both of whose husbands were also in the affinity, were mentioned in the accounts, as were also Margery Colchester and Margaret Lighbury. A woman called Alice worked in the dairy.[23]

The Countess of Shrewsbury cannot always have been with her children. She had many other duties and responsibilities. Early in 1445, when Elizabeth was 2 years old, Margaret journeyed to France where, with her husband, she participated in the ceremonies which surrounded the bringing to England of Margaret of Anjou, the chosen bride of Henry VI.[24] It is possible that some of the children, even perhaps Eleanor, then nearly 9 years old, might have been taken with their parents on this trip. However, the baby Elizabeth almost certainly remained at home in the nursery. If Eleanor went to France with her mother, she might perhaps have been allowed to see her father's precious and magnificent gift to the new queen: a very beautiful illuminated volume in French, which is now in the British Library. (Royal Ms. 15 E vi).[25] This book begins with dedicatory verses naming the donor, and probably composed by the earl himself:

> *Princesse tres excellente*
> *Ce livre cy vous presente*
> *De Schrosbery le conte.*[26]

At the end of this dedication, a *coda* sums up the loyalty of Eleanor's father to the king he served:

> *Mon seul desir*
> *au Roy et vous*
> *est bien servir*
> *jusqua au mourir*
> *ce sachant tout*
> *mon seul desir*
> *au Roy et vous.*[27]

Medieval childhood was a relatively short affair. Even if they did not accompany their parents to France in 1445, by the time they were in their early teens the Talbot boys were probably campaigning abroad with their father. As for the girls, they had to be married. 'The arranged marriage was the norm across medieval Europe'.[28] Plans for Eleanor's marriage may have been made while she was still a baby. The husband selected for her was Thomas Butler, only son and heir of Ralph, Lord Sudeley.

At the time of the marriage Lord Shrewsbury was a prisoner of the French king, waiting to be ransomed, so the leading role in Eleanor's marriage negotiations may have been taken by her mother. It is, of course, conceivable that the negotiations took place in France between Lords Shrewsbury and Sudeley. Lord Sudeley was certainly in France in the 1440s, but the fact that Lord Shrewsbury was a prisoner of the French makes this channel of communication problematic.

The marriage was concluded in 1449,[29] and the thirteen-year-old Eleanor bade farewell to her 7-year-old sister, Elizabeth. At the same time Elizabeth's own marriage negotiations were already underway. Indeed, by her sister's wedding day, she may already have been betrothed.[30] The exact date of Elizabeth's marriage is not known, but her father's will, written in 1452, refers to his youngest daughter, not by her Christian name, but by her new title. This indicates that her marriage had taken place by the time that the will was written, even though Elizabeth was then only 9 years old. Her new husband, who was about a year younger than she was, was a very splendid prize. John Mowbray, Lord Warenne was the only son and heir of the Duke of Norfolk.[31]

6

Lord Sudeley

So far we have explored Eleanor's early life within the context of her birth family, the Talbots. We have found her living in the Talbot family homes. We have got to know her father, her mother, her brothers, her sister, and her cousins. From the moment of her union with Thomas Butler the main focus of Eleanor's life naturally shifts away from her birth family, to the Butlers, her new family by marriage. In the next four chapters we shall be exploring the various connections which resulted from this alliance. We shall meet Eleanor's parents-in-law, her husband, and also some of the members of the wider Butler family.

In Thomas Butler, Eleanor Talbot was marrying a distant relative. She was also marrying a man more than twice her age, at a time when she herself was little more than a child. Whether she had ever met Thomas before her marriage; whether she had any say in the decision, it is impossible to know. We shall return to these points in due course. Incidentally, the modern spelling 'Butler' is convenient, but anachronistic. It is never attested in fifteenth-century documents relating to this family (where various different spellings of their surname are to be found).

Thomas Butler's ancestors had settled at Wem in Shropshire, which was at no great distance from the Talbots' home at Blakemere. The Butlers were related to Lord Shrewsbury twice over (on both his father's and his mother's sides). Rather like the Talbots, they had risen from the ranks of the gentry. In the case of the Butler family, their elevation had come about as a result of the marriage of Thomas' great grandfather, William le Botiler of Wem,

Shropshire, with Joan, the heiress of the de Sudeley family, a marriage which had raised the Butlers to the minor aristocracy.

Through his mother, Thomas Butler' grandfather and namesake had inherited the title Lord of Sudeley. This earlier Thomas Butler had died in 1398, but his wife, Alice Beauchamp, lived on until 1443. Eleanor's Thomas may well have known Alice, and her second husband, Sir John Dalyngrygg.[1]

Alice Beauchamp bore her first husband three sons, who held the Sudeley title in succession. Eleanor's father-in-law, Ralph, was the youngest son. Ralph's eldest brother, John, had died childless and unmarried in 1410. William, the second son, was then Lord of Sudeley for seven years, before he too died childless. William's widow, Alice, was a lady of some importance (although nothing is known of her family) because in 1424 she was appointed the governess of King Henry VI, with leave to chastise him when necessary. A right which she probably used sparingly, for Henry VI remembered her with affection and periodically made her gifts when he was grown up.[2]

In addition to his two elder brothers, Ralph Butler also had at least two sisters, whose marriages had provided Eleanor's new husband with several cousins. The most important of these was probably Sir Thomas Montgomery, but there were a number of others. We shall return to them later (see below: chapter nine).

Lord Sudeley was a little younger than Lord Shrewsbury, having been born in about 1393.[3] At the time of his son's marriage to Eleanor Talbot, Lord Sudeley would have been about 56 years old. Thomas Butler, his only child, was then probably 28, whereas Eleanor, the chosen bride, was only 13. However, such an age difference would not have been thought unusual at that period.

The marriage, in any case, would at first have been in name only. Consummation of a marriage where one or both parties were minors was deferred until the junior partner had reached the age of 16 years. Until she reached that age, Eleanor would have lived under the care of her parents-in-law (and most particularly, of her mother-in-law) and in their house. This means that Eleanor will have spent some, at least, of the next three years at Sudeley Castle.

This castle had been inherited by her father-in-law from his de Sudeley forebears. Illustrations exist which show Sudeley Castle in its pre-fifteenth century incarnation, as a simple motte and bailey construction. What condition it was in when Ralph took it over is unknown, but in the 1440s he rebuilt and refurbished it on quite a grand scale.[4] Perhaps because of the scale of the rebuilding, Ralph had to seek Henry VI's pardon for having crenellated it without licence.[5] Since Ralph Butler's time, there has been significant reconstruction at Sudeley, by Richard, Duke of Gloucester (Richard III) and other later inhabitants, but the fundamental layout of Ralph's work remains, as do parts of his castle building. Thus the outlines of the Sudeley Castle to which Lady Eleanor Talbot came, following her marriage to Thomas Butler, can still be discerned.

> The surviving buildings consist of the north or outer court, the south or inner court whose south side is missing, and the church east of the east range and the barn west of the approach to the house from the north. Boteler's buildings must have covered much the same area as the present house and ruins. The simple gateway from the north to the outer court is his work, *c.*1442, and there is much masonry in the west range of the inner court that is of this time, though the appearance of this range is now largely Victorian. Whether this masonry represents a mere curtain wall enclosing the court it is difficult to determine, as none of the masonry above the ground floor appears to be early. At the two ends of the former cross range between the courts the Portmare Tower at the west end and the Garderobe Tower at the east end, together with the fragment of the undercroft of an adjacent tower, are also Boteler's work. The most considerable remains of Boteler's buildings however are the church and the ruins of the great barn. The great barn, which stands almost to wall-plate level with gables complete at both ends, is mid-fifteenth century. On the east side there are two entrances with four-centred arches, and towards the south end a lower four-centred arch with windows above, where originally the barn must have had two storeys. It is buttressed all round and must have had eleven or twelve bays. The south gable has a curious finial like the ones on the tithe barn at Stanway.[6]

When Eleanor first saw Sudeley Castle, building work was probably still in progress. Indeed, the castle chapel (or St Mary's Church, as it is now known), had not yet been built.

Ralph Butler had been his parents' youngest son, and he only inherited the family title 'Lord of Sudeley' in 1417, when his second brother, William, died.[7] Ralph was then aged about 24, and may already have been a knight. (He is referred to as a knight in 1418, though confusingly in 1419 he is called 'esquire'.) Ralph may have been with the young King Henry V in France when he inherited his title. If not, he must have joined the king in France shortly afterwards. In 1420–21 he received grants of land in France. In 1423 he was captain of Arques and Crotoy, and in 1425 he took musters in Calais.

Ralph's service abroad was not uninterrupted, however. In 1419 he must have been in England at some point, for it was about then that he married the recently widowed Elizabeth Norbury, stepdaughter of his own sister, Lady Say. His new wife was about the same age as her husband. It was probably a year or two later that Elizabeth gave birth to the couple's only child, Ralph's son, Thomas.

Ralph was again in England in 1430, when he took muster of the troops going to France. He himself is not known to have returned to France until the following year. His commission to execute certain provisions of the will of Henry V might have been fulfilled either in France or in England, but his later roles of king's knight and chief butler sound superficially more likely to have been carried out in England. On the other hand his post as chamberlain to the regent of France, the Duke of Bedford, and his membership of the king's councils in France and Normandy must all surely have been performed on the continent.

The overall impression is that while Ralph clearly served in France throughout the 1430s and into the 1440s, he was probably in England rather more frequently than was Lord Talbot. In the spring of 1440 Ralph was made a knight of the Garter, and eighteen months later, on 10 September 1441 he was created first baron Sudeley. The following year he was charged with negotiating a treaty with the French. It was at about this time that his mother died. From 1443 to 1446 Lord Sudeley was employed in the treasury, and during 1445, was high treasurer of England. In 1450, probably soon after Eleanor's marriage to his son, Thomas, he was sent to take charge of the defence of Calais. It may be Lord Sudeley's absence on the Continent which in part explains his slowness in assigning property to his son and his new daughter-in-law (see below).

The Butlers had family links with East Anglia, and Lord Sudeley was certainly in the eastern counties on occasions. A recent (2005) metal-detector find from Great Tey in Essex consists of a harness pendant in gilt and enamelled bronze alloy, showing what could be the Sudeley arms. Unfortunately the coloured enamel is now lost, which makes positive identification of the arms difficult.[8] However, there is no doubt that Lord Sudeley was at Stoke-by-Nayland in Suffolk on 6 October 1466, for on that occasion he witnessed articles of agreement between Richard Wethermerssh (a gentle-man of Colchester and member of Sir John Howard's affinity) and Philip Mannok. This agreement aimed to protect Mannok's interests, together with those of Sir John Howard himself, Ralph Chamberleyn, John Tendring and the prior of Horkesley. The other named witnesses were local gentry: Sir Richard Waldegrave and Gilbert Debenham.[9]

Lord Sudeley and his second wife were also formerly commemorated in a stained-glass window at 'Chylton Cherche'.[10] The village of Chilton in Suffolk is now a suburb of Sudbury. It is probable that a little of the glass commemorating Ralph and Alice Butler, Lord and Lady Sudeley, has survived, for in the Crane Chapel 'the east window retains two lovely little figures of late fifteenth-century glass in its tracery lights. One shows St Apollonia bearing her emblem, the pincers, ... [in the other] St Michael is shown with raised sword vanquishing a blue demon'.[11] The Cranes, some of whose monuments are also in this chapel that bears their name, were cousins of Lord Sudeley, for Butlers had held the manor of Chilton from 1333 until 1400, when it passed to William Crane of Stonham as part of the settlement when he married Marjorie Butler. The Crane arms intimate a connection with Lord Sudeley's family.

As Lord Sudeley, Ralph seems to have consistently employed a circular seal matrix engraved with his arms and style. This was of relatively modest size, with no counterseal. The single-sided, red wax impressions produced from this matrix were attached to their documents by strips of parchment in the usual way. Impressions of Lord Sudeley's seal survive, in varying states of preservation, in the Warwick County Record Office (on L1/79, 80, 82 and 88). None is complete, but the best preserved is that on L1/82. The arms shown are quarterly 1 & 4 Butler, 2 & 3 Sudeley. The inscription is also incomplete, but appears to run:

sigillu]m radulphi buttiler d[om]ini [de?] s[u]del[ey
(The seal of Ralph Butler, Lord of Sudeley)

Elizabeth Norbury

An important influence in Eleanor's life after her marriage must have been her new mother-in-law. As we have seen, Ralph Butler married twice. However, his second marriage, to Alice Lovel, *née* Deincourt,[1] did not take place until 8 January 1463, by which time Ralph's son, Thomas, was already dead. Eleanor may well have known the second Lady Sudeley, but it was Ralph's first wife, Elizabeth, who was Thomas' mother and Eleanor's mother-in-law, and under whose care Eleanor lived between the ages of 13 and 16.

The first Lady Sudeley's name is often given as Elizabeth Hende.[2] Like Alice Deincourt (Lovel), however, Elizabeth had been married previously. Hende was therefore not her maiden name, but the surname of her first husband, the wealthy John Hende II, a draper of London from 1367, and at various times also sheriff, alderman and mayor.[3] Elizabeth already had two sons, born of her first marriage, when she married her second husband, Ralph Butler. These were John Hende III ('the elder'), and John Hende IV ('the younger'). The name of the latter certainly occurs in association with that of his stepfather, Lord Sudeley, and Eleanor must have known these elder half-brothers of her husband, who formed part of their stepfather's entourage.

The first Lady Sudeley's maiden name was Norbury. Her ancestors had once borne the surname Bulkeley, but, having for several generations held the manor of Norbury in Cheshire, they had eventually assumed the name of this estate. It had been Elizabeth's great grandfather, Roger, who had effected this change in the family surname. However, the arms granted to his Bulkeley forebears: 'sable, a chevron between three bulls' heads cabossed argent',[4] continued to be borne by Elizabeth's father, Sir John Norbury I, albeit with a *fleur de lis* sable on the chevron for difference.

Sir John Norbury inherited no manors to go with his coat of arms. He was thus obliged to make his own way in the world, which he did very successfully, becoming a wealthy man in the process.[5] The career of Sir John Norbury is well documented. He is first encountered as an esquire in the service of the house of Lancaster, where he was attached to John of Gaunt's son, the future King Henry IV. When Henry was banished by his cousin, Richard II, John Norbury accompanied him into exile in France, returning to England with Henry in 1399. Shortly before his abdication, Richard II was obliged to appoint Norbury Treasurer of England, a post which the latter retained throughout the reign of Henry IV. It brought Norbury into close contact with the rich businessmen in the city of London whose loans (together with loans from Sir John himself) financed the government of Henry IV. Prominent among the London businessmen with whom he had dealings was John Hende II, a rich widower to whom, in about 1408, Sir John Norbury was able to arrange the marriage of his young daughter, Elizabeth.[6]

Elizabeth Norbury had at least one sister, and also two half-brothers, for her father had also married twice. His first wife (who must have been the mother of both Elizabeth and her sister, Joan) was called Petronilla. Her surname is not recorded, although it may possibly have been Bostock.[7] Petronilla was still living in August 1401, when she and her husband were granted the manor of Cheshunt, in Hertfordshire, by the king. By 1412, however, Sir John Norbury had married Lord Sudeley's sister, Elizabeth Butler, and they already had two sons. Probably Petronilla died in about 1404 and Sir John's marriage with the widowed Elizabeth Butler (Lady Say) took place in about 1405.[8]

It was in about 1408 that Sir John Norbury's daughter Elizabeth (then probably about 15 years of age) married the much older but very wealthy widower, John Hende II, draper and former mayor of London, who was about 58 at the time. Hende's previous wife, Katharine Baynarde, had left him no sons.[9] Elizabeth, however, bore him two sons, in 1409 and 1412 respectively. As we have seen, both were christened 'John' after their father, and were later known as 'John the elder' and 'John the younger'.

John Hende II died in 1418, leaving £1,000 to Elizabeth and £1,500 to each of his sons. About a year later the widowed Elizabeth married Ralph Butler, who, on the death of his elder brother, had recently inherited the title of Lord of Sudeley. Ralph was already a connection of Elizabeth Norbury by marriage, since in about 1405 her widowed father had married Ralph's sister, Elizabeth Butler, by whom he had two young sons: Elizabeth's half-brothers. The elder of these half-brothers, Henry, was the godson of King Henry IV, after whom he was named.[10]

Sir John Norbury seems to have died about four years before his daughter's marriage to his brother-in-law. He was buried in the Church of the Grey Friars in London, beside his first wife, Petronilla. The epitaph upon his tomb described him as 'a brave knight, and a hardworking and honest man'.[11]

It was probably within a year or two of her second marriage that Elizabeth Norbury gave Ralph Butler a son and heir, the future Sir Thomas Butler. Elizabeth's Norbury arms can still be clearly seen, impaled by the arms of Butler of Sudeley, on the Sudeley pedigree roll which was later made to celebrate Sir Thomas Butler's marriage to Lady Eleanor Talbot.[12] Although Elizabeth's marriage to Ralph Butler lasted for more than forty years, Thomas was to be their only surviving child. If any other children were born they must have died young, but it seems quite likely that there were none, as Lord Sudeley spent the greater part of the 1430s and 1440s serving in France.

Although they were neighbours in England, it was possibly in France that Ralph first made the acquaintance of Eleanor's father, John Talbot. Lady Sudeley, meanwhile, probably remained in England, overseeing the management of the Sudeley estates and the upbringing of her three sons. When he returned to England, Lord Sudeley looked after the interests of his two Hende stepsons. We have already noticed that the name of the younger John Hende is not infrequently coupled with that of Lord Sudeley in surviving documents. Conversely (and curiously) there is scarcely any mention of the name of Lord Sudeley's own only son and heir. Possible reasons for this will be examined below.

Elizabeth Norbury was to outlive both her eldest and her youngest sons. John Hende 'the elder' died in 1461, and Sir Thomas Butler died in 1460. Elizabeth herself died in 1462. Following her demise, on 6 October of that year the chancery issued writs of *diem clausit extremum* to the escheators of the counties of Essex and Kent, where Elizabeth had held lands in her own right.[13]

Her middle son, John Hende 'the younger', outlived his mother, dying childless in 1464. Only Elizabeth's eldest son left descendants – via his daughter, Joan (or Jane). In Elizabeth's inquisitions post mortem this grand-daughter was recognised as her heir. Elizabeth was remembered, however, by her daughter-in-law, Eleanor, for under the terms of the endowment which Eleanor established at Corpus Christi College, Cambridge, matins of the dead and requiem mass were to be offered there for Eleanor's deceased relatives, amongst whom her mother-in-law, Lady Sudeley, was specifically included.[14] In the surviving indentures, however, Elizabeth Norbury's own name is not recorded. She is referred to only as the mother of Sir Thomas Butler.[15]

8

Thomas Butler

Thomas Butler was born in about 1421, at a time when Eleanor's father, John Talbot (who had not yet succeeded to his family title), was still married to his first wife, Maud Neville. In fact, Thomas was roughly of an age with the younger children of John Talbot's first marriage. He was, perhaps, two or three years younger than Sir Christopher Talbot, and about a year older than Maud Neville's daughter, Joan Talbot (who, from the point of view of age, might have been a better match for him than her much younger half-sister, Eleanor). By the time that Lord Talbot married Eleanor's mother, Margaret Beauchamp, Thomas Butler was already about 5 years old. He was six years the senior of Eleanor's oldest full-blood brother, John Talbot III (Lord Lisle), and probably about fifteen years older than Eleanor herself.

It was normal for a nobleman's son to be brought up in the household of another noble family from about the age of 7, and to receive his training there. Was it, perhaps, in the Talbot household that young Thomas Butler was placed? If so, he may have entered it in around 1428. He held no known offices in England in his youth, and his name is almost entirely absent from English records. It is possible that the reason for this is that, like Lord Talbot's own young sons, he was serving in France. His father, Lord Sudeley, certainly served in the French wars almost as much as did Lord Talbot.

As we have seen, Thomas married Eleanor in 1449–50, when she was still a minor, aged 13 or 14, he himself being then probably about 28 years of age. Eleanor's early marriage was typical for a girl of aristocratic family.

She was probably not consulted regarding the marriage plans, and need not have met Thomas before her marriage. We can assume that her bridegroom was the choice of her parents who, like most of their contemporaries, were doubtless interested first in the extent of Thomas' property, and second in his social status. His personal characteristics would have ranked low in their order of priorities.[1] It is a curious fact, however, that from the standpoint of the Earl and Countess of Shrewsbury, Thomas Butler's rank was but middling, so that in some ways their choice of him as a son-in-law is a little surprising. By 1449 one might have expected a daughter of the Earl of Shrewsbury to make a more advantageous marriage.

Nevertheless, it is possible to envisage a scenario which might help to explain why Eleanor Talbot's marriage represented, if anything, a somewhat retrograde step for her, socially. On the assumption that he may have been brought up partly in the Talbot household, Thomas Butler may have known Eleanor almost from the moment she was born. At the time of Eleanor's birth her father as yet held no English earldom, and the Talbot and Butler families were still on terms of social equality. Little Eleanor's betrothal in infancy to the heir of Lord Sudeley would have been seen as a good match for her at that time. Moreover, if Thomas was serving in her father's household it would have been an obvious alliance and one that was ready to hand. Indeed, whether or not Thomas Butler served in the Talbot household, it is extremely plausible, even likely, that his marriage to Eleanor was a plan agreed upon by their parents quite soon after she was born.

Later, of course, her father became an earl, and the Sudeley marriage may then have come to seem rather less advantageous from the Talbot point of view. Lord Shrewsbury certainly aimed much higher for his youngest daughter, Elizabeth, but probably Eleanor's Sudeley marriage contract had already been agreed. Since there was nothing actually against it, it was allowed to stand. On the basis of this reconstruction of events, Thomas Butler will have been a man whom Eleanor may have known all her life. Not well, perhaps, because, like her father and brothers, he had probably been serving in France, but still a man who was familiar to her; one whom she may have accepted in her mind as her future husband for as long as she could remember.

Nothing whatever is known of Eleanor's relationship with Thomas Butler. However, the fact that she had not chosen him does not in itself preclude the possibility that an amicable relationship developed between them. This seems to have happened in many (perhaps most) fifteenth-century arranged marriages. If Eleanor had indeed known Thomas all her life, such amicable relations may already have existed by the time they were married.

For couples of their class and culture, married love was generally regarded as synonymous with affection. (Sexual passion was regarded with some suspicion, as being potentially sinful and socially disruptive.) A married relationship for nobles at this period may have lacked some of the closeness of a similar modern relationship. There would have been little privacy, and the couple may have spent a significant proportion of their time apart. Nevertheless, after Thomas had died, Eleanor included him among those close family members for whose souls prayers were endowed. She certainly remembered him with duty, and possibly also with affection.

Thomas himself remains a shadowy figure. Only four facts seem to be known about him: his parentage, his marriage, his knighthood and his death. Indeed, only after his demise is his name unequivocally preserved in the public records – in connection with the death of his widow, Eleanor, and the ensuing confiscation by Edward IV of two manors which Thomas had once held.[2] Thomas' parents and marriage have already been considered. Let us turn now to his knighthood and his death.

A deed issued by Lord Sudeley, dated 15 January 38 Henry VI (1460), specifies that Thomas had been a knight at the time of his death,[3] and Eleanor's later inquisition post mortem confirms that this was the case. Since an earlier deed, issued by his father on 10 May 31 Henry VI (1453), accords Thomas no title, it appears that he must have received his knighthood between May 1453 and about December 1459 (when he died).[4]

This time period can be further narrowed by reference to negotiations between Lord Sudeley and the abbot of St Albans. The surviving record of these negotiations explicitly describes Thomas as a knight (in Latin, *miles*) on 15 May 1456.[5] It thus emerges that Thomas Butler was knighted at some point between 10 May 1453 and 15 May 1456. It is not currently possible to specify the date more precisely. It is conceivable that he was knighted following the first battle of St Albans;[6] a battle at which his father, at least, was undoubtedly present, in the entourage of Henry VI – receiving on that occasion an arrow-wound to the face.[7] However, it is equally plausible that Thomas was knighted quite soon after 10 May 1453.

Lord Sudeley's negotiations with Abbot John Wheathamsted of St Albans (who was a cousin of Lady Sudeley – though precise details of their relationship are lacking) frequently mention Thomas's half-brother, John Hende the younger (who, through his mother, was of course also related to the abbot). However, the St Albans archive does also provide a little additional information in respect of Thomas:

> Whereas Thomas Butler, knight, William Beaufitz and William Heynes hold of us (in the right of the aforesaid monastery) one messuage and various lands and tenements called 'Langeleys', with their appurtenances, in Rickmansworth aforesaid (late in the tenure of Roger Lynster) by fealty and by payment of ten shillings annually, … [they] have given, and by these presents granted to the aforesaid Ralph Butler nine shillings and eleven pence of the said rent of ten shillings.[8]

Three further references to a 'Thomas Boteler' (Butler) are extant, which could potentially throw further light on Eleanor Talbot's husband. We shall briefly look at these. However, we must remember that the person(s) named in these sources may or may not be identical with Lord Sudeley's son and heir.

A grant survives by a Thomas Boteler who is described as 'of Meridene', of lands, tenements, rents etc. in Meridene and Alspath in the county of Warwickshire. This grant is dated June 1443, and it was issued in favour of Ralph Boteler, Lord of Sudeley.[9] The mention of Lord Sudeley suggests some relationship, allowing for the possibility that this deed, like the St Albans grant, might have emanated from his son. The presence of the latter at Meriden (where the lordship of the manor was held by the Mowbray Dukes of Norfolk) is not otherwise attested. However, the neighbouring manor of Alspath was certainly held from the 1470s until 1523 by a family called Butler, who may have been relatives of Lord Sudeley.[10]

Confusingly, a modern calendar entry relating to this deed describes Thomas Boteler of Meriden as a knight. If he was a knight in 1443, Thomas of Meriden could not possibly be Lord Sudeley's son (who was not knighted until the 1450s). However, an examination of the original document has failed to confirm its use of the word 'knight'. The question of whether Thomas Boteler of Meriden was identical with the heir of Sudeley must therefore remain open.

Nine years later a reference survives to a 'Thomas Boteler, knight', to whom, (in association with others) certain lands in Buckinghamshire were entrusted on 25 September 1452.[11] Given that the heir of Sudeley apparently received his knighthood after 10 May 1453, this Thomas Boteler seems unlikely to be Lord Sudeley's son.

There is a further record that in the same year (1452) a Sir Thomas Butler, together with others, was granted land at Havering-at-Bower in Essex, which he subsequently released in 1457.[12] If the knightly rank accorded to this Thomas is to be understood as relating to 1457 (the date at which the record was written) rather than to 1452, this may indeed refer to the heir of Sudeley. In that case this reference of March 1457 might be our last glimpse of Eleanor's husband as a living man.

Eleanor's inquisition post mortem makes it clear that her husband died during the reign of Henry VI, and before Edward IV was proclaimed king on 4 March 1461.[13] The deed issued by Lord Sudeley (see above) provides an even earlier *terminus ad quem*. This document, dated 15 January 38 Henry VI (1460), specifies that Thomas was dead by that date.[14] It is therefore certain that the reference to a Sir Thomas Butler who was listed among the dead on the Lancastrian side at the battle of Towton cannot possibly relate to Eleanor's husband.[15]

The burial place of Eleanor's Thomas is also unrecorded. Meriden church houses the anonymous tomb of a fifteenth-century knight, of which the stone effigy depicts the deceased in armour with his head supported by angels. This tomb dates from about 1450–60. It might be the tomb of Thomas Boteler of Meriden, but even that is not certain. Coupled with the further uncertainty regarding the relationship (if any) between Thomas Boteler of Meriden and Thomas, heir of Sudeley, it leaves very questionable the possibility that the Meriden tomb might be our Thomas Butler's last resting place.[16]

Given that Sir Thomas Butler died before 15 January 1460, and probably during the latter part of 1459, it is conceivable that he died as a result of injuries sustained in battle, perhaps at Blore Heath. This, however, is speculation. Thomas and Eleanor left no surviving children and it appears certain that their marriage was childless. It was a normal part of a widow's duty to arrange, and pay for, her husband's exequies, and Eleanor may have done so for Thomas. There is no information on this point. Nor (as we have seen) can we say for certain where Thomas was buried, although one possibility could be St Albans Abbey, where his father had already endowed prayers for Thomas during his lifetime.

9

The Butlers' Wider Family

Like Eleanor, Thomas Butler also had a wider family. This included eight cousins, the offspring of his father's two sisters: Joan and Elizabeth Butler. By his aunt Joan, he seems to have had three Belknap cousins: John, William and Griselda, while his younger aunt, Elizabeth, provided Thomas with five more cousins: Henry and John Norbury, and Thomas, John and Alice Montgomery.

Aunt Joan Butler's marriage to Hamon Belknap must have taken place in about 1408 or 1409, when Joan would have been in her mid-twenties. The couple produced two sons, John and William. In February 1429 following Hamon Belknap's death, the care of his son, John, was committed 'to Ralph Boteler, knight, John Monngomery [sic], knight,[1] and Joan, late the wife of Hamon Belknap'. John Belknap is specifically stated to be Hamon's son and heir, so he must have been the elder son.[2] Nothing further is heard of him, however, so he presumably died childless, probably at an early age. The eventual Belknap heir was a younger son, William.

In addition to John and William it seems that there was also a third Belknap child, for when Alice, the widow of William Butler, Lord of Sudeley, was caring for the infant King Henry VI, she had amongst her ladies one Griselda Belknap.[3] The surname is unusual and it seems logical to suppose that Griselda must have been Alice's niece: a daughter of Joan Butler and Hamon Belknap, and the sister of John and William. It is not certain what became of Griselda Belknap but the fact that Lord Sudeley's elder stepson, John Hende III, married a lady called Griselda seems to be too much of a coincidence to be ignored. Probably John Hende's wife was his stepfather's niece, Griselda Belknap.

The remainder of Thomas Butler's cousins were the children of his younger aunt, Elizabeth Butler, who had three husbands: Sir William Heron (Lord Say), Sir John Norbury and Sir John Montgomery.[4] Some have argued that Sir John Norbury was Elizabeth's first husband, but this is chronologically impossible.[5] Elizabeth Butler must have been married first to Sir William Heron, from whom she derived her title of Lady Say. She can only have married John Norbury after Lord Say's death in 1404. There were no children from the Say marriage.

The relationship between the Butler and Norbury families is complex, reinforced by two ties of marriage: first the marriage between Sir John Norbury I and Elizabeth Butler, and then the marriage of Elizabeth Norbury to Ralph Butler. Sir John Norbury I's marriage to Elizabeth Butler must have taken place in about 1405. On 1 June 1412 the manor of Cheshunt was granted by Henry IV to the Norburys, who by this time had two sons, Henry (the king's godson) and John.[6] Henry Norbury had been knighted by 1434, and married Anne Crosier, the heiress of the manor of Stoke d'Abernon, in Surrey. The tomb of his wife, Anne, with her brass memorial, is still to be seen in Stoke d'Abernon church, where there is also a Norbury chapel, founded by Henry and Anne's son, Sir John Norbury III.[7]

On occasions, as in 1455, for instance, Sir Henry Norbury is found acting in association with his uncle (and half-brother-in-law), Ralph Butler, Lord Sudeley.[8] Possibly Henry survived his uncle to inherit the Sudeley estates.[9] However, the fact that Henry Norbury's wife, Anne Crosier (who died in 1464) is shown on her tomb as a widow suggests that Henry died in about 1456–1460, at about the same time as his cousin (and nephew), Sir Thomas Butler. Unfortunately there is scope for much confusion between Henry's younger brother, John Norbury II, and Henry's son, John Norbury III. John III could have been a knight by 1477, for in 1478 a Sir John Norbury occurs in association with Sir Thomas Montgomery, and thereafter was appointed the king's vice marshal by Richard III on 8 April 1484, and received various commissions from that king during 1483–85, the last one being dated 2 August 1485, a mere twenty days prior to the Battle of Bosworth.[10] Despite some confusion as to which John Norbury is meant, these facts suggest that at least one of Lord Sudeley's eventual heirs had no difficulty in accepting Richard III as king.

Another of Thomas Butler's cousins, Sir Thomas Montgomery, is well known as a prominent partisan of the house of York. The forebears of his father, Sir John Montgomery, had held land in various parts of England, but Sir John seems to have been the first Montgomery to make his home in Essex, settling at Faulkbourne, near Witham. Sir John served with distinction in the French wars, and received various titles and honours in the conquered lands, though of course these were lost later. He must have married Elizabeth Butler, Lady Say, widow of Sir John Norbury, in 1415, and their first child, a son, Thomas, was born in the following year.

Subsequently the couple had another son, John, and a daughter, Alice. All of these were first cousins of Sir Thomas Butler. Like his brother-in-law, Lord Sudeley, Sir John Montgomery eventually returned to England. This must have been after 1442, for in that year his wife, Elizabeth Butler (who was with her husband in France) stood as godmother to the Duke of York's new-born son – the future King Edward IV.

In 1445 and again in 1446 Sir John Montgomery was proposed for election as a knight of the Garter, although on neither occasion was he actually elected, and the Montgomery family had to wait until 1477 to attain this particular honour in the person of John's son, Thomas.[11] Sir John Montgomery died in 1449, and his widow, the much-married Elizabeth Butler, Lady Say, in 1465.[12]

As an esquire Sir Thomas Montgomery's name is found associated with that of Lord Sudeley's stepson, John Hende the younger. Both men were marshals of the king's hall and wardens of the mint in the Tower of London.[13] During the reign of Henry VI, Thomas was called upon to escort Eleanor Cobham, Duchess of Gloucester, from Leeds Castle in Kent (where she had been tried for sorcery) to London.

Thomas' brother, John, was executed by Edward IV in February 1462, for plotting against the Yorkist interest with Margaret of Anjou, the de Veres and Sir William Tyrell. However, this did not blight Thomas' career. He enjoyed Edward's favour, fighting for him against the Lancastrians at the battle of Towton, as a reward for which Edward had dubbed him knight bachelor. Thomas' loyalty to the house of York was so well-known that he was immediately imprisoned by the Earl of Warwick upon the restoration of Henry VI. He was released a few months later, in time to meet the returning Edward IV and to help persuade him to drop his pretence of returning only to reclaim his duchy of York.

As well as serving as the king's counsellor and virtually ruling Essex (receiving many of the manors of the exiled de Veres), Sir Thomas Montgomery enjoyed a distinguished diplomatic career. In 1474 he was sent to treat with the emperor for an alliance and subsequently he met also with ambassadors of the king of Hungary. He was much employed in negotiations with the Duke of Burgundy, and had been one of those who had escorted the wedding party of Margaret of York to Flanders in 1468.[14]

On this journey, if not before, he must have been much in the company of Elizabeth Talbot, Duchess of Norfolk, Margaret's principal lady-in-waiting. He must also have known Elizabeth's sister, Eleanor, who had been his cousin's wife. Elizabeth Talbot (and possibly also Eleanor) was a close friend of Sir Thomas Montgomery's sister-in-law, Anne, who, after the excution of her husband (Thomas' younger brother, John) lived under Sir Thomas' protection at Faulkbourne. Together with Lord Hastings and Lord Howard, Sir Thomas Montgomery negotiated the treaty of Picquigny. It was also Montgomery who was responsible, in the wake of this treaty, for returning the ex-queen, Margaret of Anjou, to France.

Richard III clearly trusted Thomas Montgomery, who is described in August 1484 as a 'knight of the body'. In April of the same year Richard III had granted 'for life to the king's counsellor, Thomas Montgomery, knight, the castle, lordship and manor of Hingham', and eleven other Essex manors, including Earls Colne, Hatfield Broadoak, Ongar and Harlow.[15] It is not known whether Sir Thomas took any part in the battle of Bosworth, but he survived Richard III's fall well enough to be called upon to hold the pall over Henry VII during the latter's coronation. Thereafter, however, he faded rapidly from public life. Many of his manors, together with the castle of Hedingham, were returned by the new king to their former owners, the de Veres.

In any case, Thomas Montgomery was growing old by this time. He died in January 1495, probably a little short of his 79th birthday, and he was buried in the new lady chapel which he had built at the abbey of St Mary Grace on Tower Hill, possibly to commemorate his brother who had been executed nearby. His two wives, Philippa Helion and Lora Berkeley were buried with him, or at least, commemorated on his tomb. Philippa had originally been buried at Faulkbourne, but her body may have been brought to London to lie beside her husband's remains. Certainly there is no extant memorial to her in the church at Faulkbourne. Sir Thomas' tomb, like the abbey which contained it, is long gone, but his image, together with representations of his mother, Lady Say, and his sister-in-law, Anne, the great friend of the Talbot sisters, can still be seen in the stained-glass donor portraits in the north aisle of Long Melford church, Suffolk. Sir Thomas Montgomery left no living descendants.[16]

Married Life

Eleanor's marriage was celebrated late in 1449 or early in 1450.[1] She was then 13 or 14 years old. What did she look like? Later, at the age of 24, her sister Elizabeth would be considered a beauty.[2] As for Eleanor herself, descriptions of her may be lacking, but in ten years time, she would command the attention of a king. There is therefore little reason to doubt that Eleanor too was attractive.

A hint of her appearance at about the time of her marriage to Thomas Butler can perhaps be glimpsed in a portrait by Petrus Christus of Bruges, now in the Staatliche Museen Preussischer Kulturbesitz, Gemäldegalerie, Berlin (no. 532). This portrait is not of Eleanor herself, but of one of her closest relatives. It was painted probably in 1468, at the time when Elizabeth Talbot, Duchess of Norfolk, with various members of her family, was in Flanders attending Margaret of York's marriage to the Duke of Burgundy. The sitter was identified as a member of the Talbot family by an inscription on the (now lost) original frame. The painting probably represents Eleanor's niece, Elizabeth Talbot of Lisle (the elder daughter of Eleanor's dead brother, Viscount Lisle). In 1468, Elizabeth Talbot of Lisle would have been about 16 – just a year or two older than Eleanor herself had been when she married Thomas Butler.[3] It is likely that in about 1450 Eleanor looked something like this portrait, although the skull in Norwich, which may possibly be Eleanor's (see below), exhibits more prominent cheekbones and a somewhat wider lower jaw.[4]

Young brides of aristocratic families, when they first married, 'usually lived with the groom's parents until they came of age',[5] and Eleanor, who was little more than a child bride, must presumably have done so. For the first three years of their marriage, therefore, she and Thomas probably lived in the Sudeley household, and had no separate establishment of their own. At least some of their time will have been spent at Sudeley Castle in Gloucestershire, which was the Butlers' main residence. At the time of Eleanor's marriage to his son, Lord Sudeley was in the middle of reconstructing this property in a grand manner. However, the Butlers also had other estates. They held manors in Warwickshire, which made them neighbours of the Talbots. They also controlled property in London, Hertfordshire and East Anglia (a part of the country which, in the long run, was to be significant for both Eleanor and her sister Elizabeth).

Not all of this property was intended for the family's habitation. Some was let, to provide additional income. The Butlers' London property included a messuage, or tenement in Wyndegoose Lane, which ran from Thames Street down towards the river, approximately where the north side of Southwark Bridge now stands. The property was in the parish of All Hallows by the Tower, and Lord Sudeley would later grant it to St Alban's Abbey. There were further London properties in the parish of St Mildred (Poultry).[6] In the 1450s Thomas Butler held (with others) a messuage, with various lands and tenements, known as 'Langeleys' at Rickmansworth in Hertfordshire (which he held of his maternal cousin, Abbot John Whethamsted)[7] and there is a record of a quitclaim from John, Lord Clinton and Say to Lord Sudeley in respect of the manor of Jovenellesburg in Hertfordshire[8] (in which the latter was enfeoffed with others, including his relatives, Sir Henry Norbury and Sir John Montgomery).[9] Also a number of manors in Norfolk, Suffolk and Essex came under the control of Lord Sudeley and various colleagues in their capacity as executors of the will of Sir John Fastolf.[10]

To mark the marriage of Thomas and Eleanor, the Butler family commissioned from an illuminator at Bury St. Edmunds in Suffolk, a splendid roll pedigree, showing Sir Thomas' ancestry and giving a parallel account of the kings of England served by his forebears.[11] This roll, commemorating the family which she was about to join, may have been intended as a gift to Eleanor. Her own arms were meant to figure on the pedigree, impaled by those of Thomas, above the entry of their names at the bottom of the scroll. In the event, however, the illuminator left Eleanor's half of the shield blank. Perhaps he was unfamiliar with the Talbot arms, or perhaps it was thought that it would be unlucky to paint them in before the marriage took place.

It may have been the intention that they should be added later, perhaps when children were born. If so, this was never done, and Eleanor's half of the shield remains blank to this day. Of course, if Eleanor and Thomas were betrothed soon after her birth, and the roll pedigree was commissioned at about that time, the blank shield may have been merely prudent economy. Children did not always survive, and if Eleanor had died in childhood the roll could have been reused for an alternative Butler bride.

Eleanor had been born and brought up during the final years of the Hundred Years War. As she embarked on her marriage with Thomas, this long war in France was drawing to a close, but another conflict, closer at hand, was about to start. There were stirrings of trouble in England in 1450, caused partly by the failure of Henry VI's government to hold his father's conquests in Normandy, and partly by the king's general incompetence. The murder of Henry's favourite, William de la Pole, Duke of Suffolk, was followed by a rising in Kent, led by the Irishman, Jack Cade. The rebels called for the return of the Duke of York from Ireland, where he was serving as lieutenant. In London, meanwhile, Eleanor's uncle, Edmund, Duke of Somerset, cousin of the king, had been seeking greater influence since the death of his uncle, Cardinal Beaufort. He had allied himself with the Duke of Suffolk and with Queen Margaret of Anjou, and now took the opportunity provided by Suffolk's murder to manoeuvre himself into a key position with, ultimately, the title of Constable of England.

These troubles at national level had echoes in the Talbot family, and also in Eleanor's extended family, including the Mowbray household of the Duke of Norfolk (into which Eleanor's sister Elizabeth was now married). The return of the Duke of York from Ireland and the rivalry between York and his cousin, Somerset, for power in the royal council confronted the Duke of Norfolk with a choice. In November he gathered men of his affinity around him at Ipswich, before riding to the Parliament at Westminster, where he chose to support his uncle, York, against the Duke of Somerset.[12]

Had he been in England, the Earl of Shrewsbury would have been faced with a similar, difficult choice of which side to support. It would have placed him in a grave dilemma, as he had long ties of comradeship and trust with both the Duke of York and the Duke of Somerset, arising out of their association in the French war. Fortunately, perhaps, under the circumstances, he was still a prisoner in France, and was thus spared from making any decision in the matter.

The Talbots, however, already had on-going conflicts of their own. Having seized by force the three disputed Berkeley manors of Wotton, Simondshall and Cowley, Eleanor's mother, Margaret, Countess of Shrewsbury, had had her possession of them confirmed (albeit for her life only) by a court at Cirencester in 1448. In 1450 Lord Berkeley, adopting Margaret's own tactics against her, seized them back. Apparently not expecting to be able to maintain his hold on them, he spent his time wreaking destruction on the manor house at Wotton. As Eleanor's mother herself later reported, Lord Berkeley and his son, William,

> which at that time kept within the Castle of Berkeley a great number of right riotous, unlawful and evil disposed people, … there assembled to them a great multitude of such misgoverned people arrayed in manner of war (the said Earl of Shrewsbury … then being in Normandy upon the safeguard of the duchy of Normandy), riotously came to the said manor of Wotton, and entered into the same, and the gates and doors of the said manor they brake, and all to hewe and cut the great and principal timber of the roofs and galleries, and other necessaries sawed and cut in two, the walls, vaults, quines of doors and windows they razed and tore a-down, the ferments of iron in the windows, hinges for doors and windows, gutters and conduits of lead, as well upon the houses as under the earth, they brake and beare away; And the said manor of Wotton in all that they could defaced and destroyed, insomuch that the reparations thereof cost the said earl, countess, John Viscount Lisle, and their servants then there being, to the value of four thousand marks.[13]

Margaret, furious, retaliated by sending her eldest son, Lord Lisle, to besiege her enemy in his castle at Berkeley. This conflict in Gloucestershire must have been particularly uncomfortable for Margaret's youngest daughter, Elizabeth, in her new home among the Mowbrays. It was, to say the least, awkward for Elizabeth to know that her mother Margaret was locked in combat with her father-in-law's aunt, Isabel Mowbray (Lady Berkeley), and the latter's husband and sons. We shall return to this conflict later, for the dispute continued for years to come.

Eleanor's eldest brother, John, Lord Lisle, was now in his mid-twenties. His family in 1450 consisted of his wife, Joan, and their 2-year-old son, Thomas. His elder daughter, Elizabeth – probable future subject of the Petrus Christus portrait – was born in about 1451. Lord Lisle had not recently served in France with his captive father. It was not that his life had been peaceable, but his battles had been fought not in Normandy but in Gloucestershire, where he kept up the family feud with Lord Berkeley. It seems likely that he was living chiefly, at this period, in the disputed (and recently wrecked) manor house at Wotton-under-Edge. It was probably there that he received the news from France that his father, the Earl of Shrewsbury, had been set free.

The same news will have reached Eleanor at Sudeley, Elizabeth at Framlingham, and their mother, probably at Blakemere. King Charles VII had demanded the Earl of Shrewsbury as a hostage when he finally took Rouen in 1449, and the Duke of Somerset had, perforce, acquiesced. From a window overlooking the cathedral, Lord Shrewsbury had watched the French king march into the city, the surrender of which marked the final English capitulation in Normandy. The earl had later been received by Charles VII, who, however, would not release him until the English fulfilled their undertaking to give up their remaining garrisons at Harfleur and other places. Only when Falaise finally surrendered, in July 1450, was Lord Shrewsbury set free.

Even so, it was to be many months before he saw his family in England. The French king had imposed certain conditions before releasing his noble hostage, for the name of Talbot had long been a thorn in his side. The earl was not to return home directly. First, he had agreed to travel to Italy, where he would make a pilgrimage to Rome. Lord Shrewsbury, in his own way a deeply religious man, was content with this. It was a good year for making a Roman pilgrimage, for 1450 was a Jubilee Year.[14] Pope Nicholas V, who had already restored the city walls of Rome, was celebrating the Holy Year with very great splendour.

It is probable that the pontiff received the earl during his pilgrimage. The Basilica of St Peter, however, may have been a disappointment to Lord Shrewsbury. The long Western Schism, which had only recently come to an end, meant that no repairs or rebuilding had been carried out either at the basilica or at the Papal palace for a very long time. The architect Leon Battista Alberti had recently reported to the Holy Father that St Peter's was in a dangerous condition, with the south wall leaning 6ft from the perpendicular, so that 'I am convinced that very soon some slight shock or movement will cause it to fall. The rafters of the roof have dragged the north wall inwards to a corresponding degree'. Plans for tearing down the old basilica and the building of an entirely new church had already been made, although the work was to advance only very slowly, and little progress was made before the death of Nicholas V. Nevertheless, the Earl of Shrewsbury must have been one of the last pilgrims to Rome to see the Emperor Constantine's old, fourth-century church before work started on the rebuilding of the east end. He may also have witnessed one of the disasters of the Jubilee when, because the crowds of pilgrims were so great, some 200 people were crushed to death on the Sant'Angelo Bridge.[15]

Lord Shrewsbury did not arrive back in England until 1451. Before leaving France, he had made a further promise to Charles VII, that he would never again bear arms against the King of France.[16] Having extracted this oath from his old adversary, and bearing in mind also the earl's advanced age (for by this time he was about 64) Charles VII must have believed that he had effectively safeguarded himself from any further encounters with '*le Talbot*'.

When Eleanor's father finally came home, the threat of domestic trouble still hung in the air. In March 1452 the Duke of York and his supporters nearly came to blows with the adherents of the queen and Somerset, at Blackheath. York withdrew, reassured by the promise of Somerset's arrest. In the event it was York himself who was detained and forced to forswear rebellion. During the summer, a summons came from the king for Norfolk and his uncle of York, to meet him at Canterbury. As a result the Duke of Norfolk took fright, distancing himself from his uncle's cause. Elizabeth Talbot and her Mowbray in-laws spent the winter at Framlingham, where they enjoyed a family Christmas, surrounded by their household, and by persons of the Duke's affinity, including, perhaps, John Paston, who certainly received an open invitation.[17]

Meanwhile a more lively time was being had in Gloucestershire. Bolstered by the return of her formidable husband, the Countess of Shrewsbury renewed her attack on her cousin, James, Lord Berkeley. In June, Lord Berkeley, still besieged in Berkeley Castle, had received the following letter from his wife, Isabel Mowbray (then working on his behalf in London) warning him that his adversaries were up to no good:

To my right worshipful and reverend Lord and husband be this letter delivered.

Right worshipful and reverend Lord and husband. I commend me to you with all my whole heart, desiring always to hear of your good welfare, the which God maintain and increase ever to your worship. And it please you to hear how I fare, Sir, squall and squall; Thomas Roger and Jacket have asked surety of peace of me, for their intent was to bring me into the Tower, But I trust in God to morrow that I shall go in bail unto the next term, and so to go home And then to come again; And Sir I trust to God and you will not treat with them, but keep your own in the most manliest wise, ye shall have the land for once and end: Be well ware of Venables of Alderley, of Thom Mull and of your false Counsell; keep well your place, The Earl of Shrewsbury lieth right nigh you, and shapeth all the wiles that he can to distress you and yours, for he will not meddle with you openly no manner of wise but it be with great falsedom that he can bring about to beguile you, or else that he caused that ye have so few people about you, then will he set on you, for he saith he will never come to the king again till he have done you an ill turn; Sir your matter speedeth and doth right well, save my daughter costeth great good; At the reverence of God send money or else I must lay my horse to pledge and come home on my feet: keep well all about you till I come home, and treat not without me, and then all things shall be well with the grace of Almighty God, who have you in his keeping.

Written at London the Wednesday next after Whit Sunday.

Your wife the Lady of Berkeley.'[18]

Faction fighting between the supporters of the Talbots and the supporters of Lord Berkeley, both of whom were maintaining private armies, continued throughout the year, terrorising the countryside, causing havoc, and making life generally uncomfortable for the local population (which either side claimed to be defending from the lawless molestations of the other).

Matters came to a head on 6 September 1451, when a party of men serving Lord Berkeley descended upon the home of a blind man called Richard Andrews, a tenant of the Earl of Shrewsbury. In Lady Shrewsbury's words: 'William Berkeley sent twenty of that same mischievous men to a tenant's house of the said Earl of Shrewsbury called Richard Andrews, which was a blind man, dwelling from the said castle [Berkeley Castle] ten miles, to rob the said Richard Andrews'.[19] As a Talbot tenant Andrews was evidently seen as fair game, and the men ransacked the house looking for valuables. They were disappointed by what they found, and since enquiry failed to persuade their blind captive to produce any significant sums of money, Lord Berkeley's men decided to resort to torture. Lady Shrewsbury takes up the story again: 'For cause they found but little good in substance, they took a brand iron and set it on the fire till it was glowing hot, and then they took the blind man and would have set him upon it, for he would be a know of no more good, And through that dread that they so put him in, he told then where his good was'. Fortunately for Richard Andrews, his neighbours, aware of his plight, had meanwhile sent in all haste to Lord Lisle to let him know what was afoot. Setting out at once, with a young army of his own, the viscount reached Andrews' house in the nick of time and caught Lord Berkeley's men off guard. They were apprehended without much of a struggle.

Now the tables were completely turned, and Lord Berkeley's men were put in fear of their lives. As a result, one of them, the oddly named Rice Tewe, turned coat, and offered, in exchange for his life, to give the Talbots entry into Berkeley Castle, a prize which Lady Shrewsbury had long coveted. We have two accounts of what followed. According to Lord Berkeley's eldest son, William:

the sixth of September in the said thirtieth year of Henry ye sixth, The said countess and her husband being then unjustly seised of their manors of Wotton, Simondshall and Cowley, the warth, newleyes, and Sagesland, by their subtle and damnable imaginations, laboured, entreated and hired one Rice Tewe, being then servant to the Lord James, to deceive and utterly to destroy him the said Lord James and his four sons, William, James, Maurice and Thomas, then being in the Castle of Berkeley with the said Lord James their father: which said Rice, having the keeping of the keys of the said castle, early in a morning let in the Lord Lisle, son to the said earl and countess, with great numbers of people warlike arrayed, and there took the said Lord James and his said four sons in their beds, and there kept them in prison in great duress by the space of eleven weeks, by the commandment of the said countess; they by all that time knowing no surety nor certainty of their lives, but ever waiting the hour of their cruel death.

Lady Shrewsbury's account, on the other hand, continues:

And straight they rode to the said castle. And when they come to the castle gate Rice called upon the watch, and anon the said watch went to the said Lord James who had the keys in his own keeping, and he them delivered to one Thomas Fleshewer [Fletcher?] then being yeoman of his chamber, who came and opened the wicket gate of the castle, and the servants of the viscount Lisle entered to take the said misgoverned men, and took the place without any hurt or misdoing to any person.

It is clear, at any rate, that Lord Berkeley and his four sons were captured, and that the Talbots took the castle. Lady Berkeley, however, seems not to have been present. Probably she was still in London, upon her husband's business, and thus escaped capture with the rest of her family.

What followed next is debatable, depending upon whether one chooses to believe the Talbot or the Berkeley account of events. Undoubtedly Lord Berkeley and his sons signed bonds in favour of the Talbots for enormous sums of money. Lady Shrewsbury insisted that they did so voluntarily; an explanation which possibly strains our credulity somewhat. Lord Berkeley and his sons, on the other hand, said that they only signed under duress, and in terror of their lives. Margaret, in any case, gleefully hauled the Berkeleys and their bonds before a court at Chipping Campden on 4 October, and subsequently a court at Cirencester ruled in favour of Margaret's rights to the Berkeley inheritance. As 1451 drew to a close there must have been a great air of celebration in the Talbot camp. At last, thirty-four years after the death of her grandfather, the Countess of Shrewsbury finally seemed to have secured possession of his entire inheritance. Her rival and his sons were in her hands, and in her power. Surely her victory was now complete.

Alas, there was one tiny flaw in her triumph. The absence of Isabel Mowbray from Berkeley Castle on the night of 6 September meant that she was still at large and free to act. Early in 1452, with great courage, not to say temerity, Lady Berkeley challenged Lady Shrewsbury in the courts at Gloucester. She was to pay dearly for this, for Margaret had her thrown into Gloucester gaol, where she languished for many months with no one to help her, finally dying there shortly before Michaelmas. Nevertheless, by her bold and decisive action Isabel had sown the seeds of Margaret's defeat.

In October 1452 the court at Cirencester confiscated to the crown the entire Berkeley estate, as the only means, for the time being, of putting an end to the violent disturbances which had troubled the area for so long. Thus the focus of attention moved to King Henry VI. Everything would now depend upon who had most sway with him. Margaret was probably relatively unconcerned at this stage, anticipating that, through the influence of her husband and her brother-in-law, the Duke of Somerset, her claims would soon be vindicated. She could not foresee the final, tragic twist of fate which would rob her of her chief support and undermine all her long endeavours.[20]

At Framlingham, meanwhile, the imprisonment and subsequent death of Isabel Mowbray at the hands of the Talbots can scarcely have been well-received. Unfortunately for his aunt, the Duke of Norfolk was in a rather weak position and therefore not well-placed to help her. His involvement with his uncle the Duke of York had undermined his credibility in the eyes of the king. In Holy Week of 1452, in London, he was glad to accept the amnesty which the king offered on Good Friday. After Easter he had returned to Framlingham Castle. In June he had been granted a royal pardon, but there were strings attached. Lady Shrewsbury's brother-in-law, the Duke of Somerset, objected to some of the members of Norfolk's council, in particular, Debenham, Lee and Tymperley. The Duke of Norfolk was forced to dismiss them. The Duchess of Norfolk and her servants were also apparently under suspicion for Yorkist sympathies. Since he and his household were viewed askance by the king and the Duke of Somerset during this period, Norfolk was not in a position to help his Aunt Isabel against Somerset's Talbot relations. The Mowbrays tried hard to keep out of the limelight for the rest of 1452, and spent their time quietly at Framlingham, occupying themselves not with national politics but with local issues.

Throughout this troubled period, Eleanor had been living quietly at Sudeley, under the care of her mother-in-law. On his return home, Lord Shrewsbury seems to have been perturbed to discover that Lord Sudeley had as yet made no provision to grant Eleanor and Thomas the estates which would comprise her jointure.[21] This failure is possibly explained by the fact that Lord Sudeley himself had been out of England, serving in Calais. However, a major change in Eleanor's life was now looming. Early in 1452 she celebrated her sixteenth birthday. Her marriage with Thomas Butler could now be consummated. Hopefully there would be children. With an eye to the future, Lord Sudeley began making plans for the young couple to set up a home of their own.

Some documents relating to this phase of Eleanor's marriage are preserved in the Warwickshire County Record Office, where they survive as part of an archive relating to the manor of Fenny Compton. They deal with transfers of this and other Warwickshire manors, together with certain properties in Wiltshire. The first document in the series is a deed of gift from Lord Sudeley, issued in Burton Dassett, and dated 10 May 31 Henry VI (1453). By this document he enfeoffed his son and daughter-in-law (together with their still hypothetical issue) with the manors of Burton Dassett, Griff and Fenny Compton, all in Warwickshire, together with the lands and tenements called 'Shipleys Thing' in Griff.[22]

Two related documents are associated with Lord Sudeley's deed of gift.[23] Both are letters of attorney, bearing the same date as the deed itself. The first emanates from Lord Sudeley and carries instructions to give seisin of the three manors to Thomas and Eleanor. The second is from Thomas and Eleanor, instructing their attorney, Thomas Throckmorton, to accept livery and seisin from Lord Sudeley.

Given their letter of attorney, it is not necessary to assume that either Thomas or Eleanor was present in person in Burton Dassett on 10 May 1453, and their whereabouts at that time remain unknown. Their letter of attorney bears the seals of the young couple. Unlike his father, Thomas Butler did not employ a heraldic device. His seal matrix almost certainly comprised the bezel of a signet ring. The red wax impression shows a hart, impressively antlered, partially surrounded by what may be intended as an elaborate letter 'T'. The seal is circular, and ropework borders the design.

Eleanor's seal is also not heraldic. Again, a signet ring was clearly used. This is evident from the fact that the scalloped shoulders of the ring have left impressions in the wax. These marks show that, like the contemporary signet ring of the Earl of Northumberland (found on the battlefield of Towton, and now in the British Museum) the design on Eleanor's signet ran horizontally across the ring, and not vertically, as on a modern example. The bezel was oval, engraved with a daisy, or marguerite, bearing ten petals and flanked by sprigs of leaves. While not a particularly appropriate symbol for Eleanor herself, this flower was undoubtedly used by Margaret, Countess of Shrewsbury, as her name emblem.[24] It therefore seems likely that Eleanor's ring had been a gift from her mother.

Of the property granted to Thomas and Eleanor by Lord Sudeley, Griff lies just to the south of Nuneaton (of which, in the 1920s, it became a suburb). As early as the reign of William the Conqueror, the adjacent manor of Chilvers Coton had already been held by Harold, son of Earl Ralph, Lord of Sudeley. Harold held eight hides (960 acres) in Chilvers Coton;

land which subsequently descended in the de Sudeley family. When a later Ralph de Sudeley founded Arbury Priory in the twelfth century at Chilvers Coton, and also granted land there to the order of Knights Templar, the focus of his own estate moved to the adjacent hamlet of Griff, where a new manor house for the de Sudeleys was established in about 1185.

After the death of the last male member of the de Sudeley family in 1367, the manor of Griff passed (1380), like the other Sudeley lands, to his nephew, Thomas Butler. The descent of the manor of Griff to Ralph Butler, Lord Sudeley, is fully set out in a patent of 1469.[25] The manor of Griff, as held briefly by Thomas and Eleanor, had a total area of 508 acres, under various kinds of cultivation. The least valuable land was the woodland, valued at less than 1d per acre. Most profitable was the small quantity of meadow land, which brought in 1s 3d per acre. There were 200 acres each of arable and of grazing land, valued respectively at about 8½d and 7¼d per acre. Thomas and Eleanor presumably stayed from time to time at the manor house at Griff, the origins of which dated back to the late twelfth century. Of this manor house nothing now remains.

The couple's second Warwickshire manor, named in the deed of gift as Cheping Dorset, and in Eleanor's inquisition post mortem as Great Dorset, is now called Burton Dassett and is situated in the south of the county, a few miles to the east of Stratford-upon-Avon, and south east of Warwick. Burton Dassett was known, from the thirteenth to the seventeenth centuries, by a range of names, such as Magna Dercet (or Derset), Derced Major, Dassett Magna and Great Dorcestre, to distinguish it from its smaller southern neighbour, now called Avon Dassett, but formerly known as Parva Dersete.

The more recent history of this manor has been very different from that of Griff. Whereas the latter is now a busy suburb, Burton Dassett is now almost deserted. Ironically, while neighbouring Avon Dassett has become quite a large and prosperous village, the once greater Burton Dassett now houses only a church, a beacon tower and a few scattered farm houses among fields of sheep, the whole comprising a country park famed for its scenic views. In Thomas and Eleanor's day, however, the manor was well populated, its tenants providing an annual income of £18 in rents; more than half of the revenue from the manor. Its present depopulated state is due to the enclosures of the Belknap heirs of Ralph Butler, Lord Sudeley, who, having inherited the manor, drove off the 350-strong population in Tudor times to make way for the sheep.

The large and beautiful church of All Saints still houses medieval wall paintings, but the stained-glass windows in the chancel which once displayed the Sudeley arms, and which survived into the eighteenth century, are now no more. The nearby hilltop, where the sixteenth-century beacon now stands, once also housed Eleanor's windmill. This was ruined by a storm in 1655, but was reconstructed and then survived until it was finally destroyed by another storm in 1946. Early twentieth-century photographs exist which show the windmill standing beside the beacon tower.[26]

Burton Dassett was a good deal smaller than Griff, comprising only 204 acres. The area is hilly, so it is not surprising that in the fifteenth century only 125 acres of the land were in use for arable farming, although the exposed hilltop made an ideal site for the windmill where grain could be brought from elsewhere to be milled. Most of the land was in use as meadow, though the hay produced at Burton Dassett apparently commanded a lower price than the hay at Griff – only 1s an acre, as opposed to 1s 3d. There was a small amount of grazing land and, given the hilly nature of the terrain, this was probably used in the fifteenth century, as it is today, for sheep. This may account for the fact that it too brought in less money per acre than the grazing land at Griff – 6d instead of about 7¼d. The grazing land at Griff was perhaps used for cattle. The comparatively poor terrain of the hilltop at Burton Dassett may also have been the site of Thomas and Eleanor's rabbit warren. There is still a manor house at Burton Dassett, but the present building was erected long after Eleanor's day. It is likely, however, that Burton Dassett was Thomas and Eleanor's principal residence from 1453 until 1459.

By the time Lord Sudeley made his grant to Thomas and Eleanor, the latter's father was once again active on the international scene. Following the loss of Normandy, the English government was concerned to preserve the Aquitaine from the incursions of the French king. Its mind turned naturally to that great national champion of the French wars, Lord Shrewsbury. Despite his promise to Charles VII, Lord Shrewsbury was now sent to fight in the Aquitaine.[27] This time his son, Lord Lisle, accompanied him. It is not, of course, impossible that, among other considerations, the English government saw this as an opportunity to calm the situation in Gloucestershire by getting Shrewsbury and Lisle out of the country.

The Earl of Shrewsbury made his will in Portsmouth on 1 September, and set sail with his son for Bordeaux.[28] With them they took two of their prisoners, the younger sons of Lord Berkeley. Subsequently, on 12 February

1453, possibly simply as a reward, possibly with the idea of giving Lord Shrewsbury an increased personal stake in the defence of the province, Henry VI granted 'for life, to Lewis Talbot, knight, son of John, Earl of Shrewsbury' rents and revenues in the Aquitaine.[29]

When he rode into battle at Castillon, early in 1453, Lord Shrewsbury left off the armour which he had sworn never again to wear in the field against King Charles' forces, despite the fact that this left him highly vulnerable. Although one might think that the spirit of his promise not to bear arms against France should have precluded Lord Shrewsbury from fighting at all, it seems clear that he himself thought that he was adhering to his oath by this dangerous compromise. Predictably, perhaps, he was either dragged from his horse or the animal was killed under him, and he was then dispatched by a blow from a battle axe to the back of his skull, which no helm protected.[30] Lord Lisle, and one of Lord Berkeley's sons, died with him. Lord Berkeley's other son was captured by the French. Lord Shrewsbury's face was disfigured, and his body was no doubt stripped by those who picked over the field after the battle. Only by his missing left molar was one of his squires able to identify the old earl's body for the French victors on the day after the battle.

This time, then, Eleanor's father did not return home. The French buried him with honour on the battlefield, erecting a little chapel on the site.[31] Not until forty years later, towards the end of the fifteenth century, was his grandson, Sir Gilbert Talbot, to fetch Lord Shrewsbury's remains back from France, to lie, as the earl had requested in his will, in the church at Whitchurch, near his beloved Blakemere. When the remains of the first Earl of Shrewsbury were examined in 1874 the cause of his death was still readily apparent. 'Immediately behind the right parietal eminence of the cranium was a perpendicular fracture, evidently caused by a sharp instrument'.[32]

By dying at his father's side, Lord Lisle provided Shakespeare with the basis for the moving (but chronologically misplaced) episode in *Henry VI*, part 1, act 4, scene 7, where the body of his son is placed in the arms of the dying father. Eleanor's brother left a very brief will, which gives no details of either property or beneficiaries. However, it is of interest for its accompanying grant of probate which, most unusually, emanates not from some diocesan official, but from the Cardinal Archbishop of Canterbury in person. It seems likely that this circumstance is due to the fact that Eleanor's half-brother, the second Earl of Shrewsbury, had contested his father's testamentary dispositions, thus embroiling the Talbot heirs in litigation.

The death of Eleanor's father completely undermined the position of his widowed countess. The new Earl of Shrewsbury was Margaret's stepson, John II, with whom she was on bad terms. Her husband had tried to secure her position, and at the same time, provide for the children of his second marriage, by dividing up his inheritance, hiving off the Lestrange portions (which were not entailed) for his second wife and family. Naturally, this was not well received by his heir, who at once prepared to do battle for this property which he considered rightfully his.

To free his hands for the conflict with his stepmother, the new Earl of Shrewsbury had every incentive for bringing all other conflicts which might have involved him, to a rapid conclusion. The Berkeley inheritance dispute fell within this category. As he was not himself a Berkeley descendant, the second earl had no personal interest in the matter, and with all possible speed, he made peace with Lord Berkeley, agreeing to some financial compensation. In token of their accord, the elderly James, a widower since the death of his wife, Isabel, in Gloucester gaol, now married the new Earl of Shrewsbury's sister, Joan Talbot.

Towards the end of the year an inquisition post mortem on the late Earl of Shrewsbury confirmed his eldest surviving son's inheritance of his titles, and in due course a court of law adjudicated to him all his father's inherited lands in Shropshire and Gloucestershire except for the manor of Corfham in Shropshire, which his stepmother held in dower. This was only the beginning of a new battle between the dowager countess and the second earl. While it continued, Margaret was to have no leisure to pursue her earlier battle with the Berkeleys, whom her stepson was now openly befriending.

Not only had Margaret been robbed of her strongest prop, her husband; her influence at court was further seriously weakened in 1453 by the decline in her brother-in-law's fortunes. In August 1453, Henry VI suffered a complete mental breakdown which left him unaware of who and what was around him. The queen and the Duke of Somerset attempted, for a time, to conceal his sad condition, but the birth of a son to Queen Margaret on 13 October led to the holding of a Great Council.

Attempts by Somerset to exclude the Duke of York from this council meeting were unsuccessful, and once present, York rallied support among the peers. Warwick, Salisbury, Worcester, Pembroke, Richmond and Norfolk combined to back him, and on 27 March 1454, York was named 'Protector'. Somerset now found himself imprisoned in the Tower. With her powerful brother-in-law eclipsed at this key moment, Eleanor's mother saw that the Berkeley inheritance, which had seemed to be within her grasp at last, had eluded her once again. All her dreams had evaporated into thin air.

In the country as a whole, the noise of the conflict between the Duke of York on the one hand, and the Duke of Somerset and the queen on the other, echoed through the great noble households as Lords held aloof, or began to espouse one of the competing causes. What side Eleanor's father would have taken, had he lived, must remain a matter for speculation. He had, it is true, long served the house of Lancaster, and had close ties to the Duke of Somerset, who was married to his second wife's sister. On the other hand, he had also worked closely with the Duke of York in the vain defence of Normandy, and the two men clearly had respect for one another. The earl had stood godfather to one of the Duke of York's children. In the dead earl's absence, the surviving Talbots took various directions in the incipient conflict.

Eleanor's half-brother, the second earl, had held no great offices during his father's lifetime, and in 1453 he continued to stand aloof, viewing the Duke of Somerset, husband of his step-mother's sister, with suspicion. In fact it was in the council of the Protector, York, that he first appeared close to the centre of government. Although he was never a regular member of the Protector's council, he attended meetings from time to time. When the king recovered his senses, towards the end of December 1454, and when Somerset, released from the Tower, was restored to power, the latter was soon seen once again to be favouring his sister-in-law, Margaret, rather than her stepson. Nevertheless, when hostilities broke out, and despite his then rather Yorkist associations, the second Earl of Shrewsbury took no part, on either side, in the first battle of St Albans, on Thursday 22 May 1455. From 1456, however, and for reasons which are not perfectly known, he became a moderate member of the court party, being subsequently awarded various honours and appointments by Henry VI (or those who acted for him).

Meanwhile, Eleanor's father-in-law had also come out in favour of the reigning king. Lord Sudeley was at Henry VI's side at St Albans,[33] and it is reported that when Somerset led the king's loyal Lords out into St Peter's Street to face the Duke of York's men, Lord Sudeley bore the royal standard before his sovereign:

> Then came the king out of the abbey with his banner displayed, into the same street, and Duke Edmund [Somerset] with him, and the Duke of

Buckingham, the Earl of Northumberland, and the Lord Clifford, and the Lord Sudeley bearing the king's banner.[34]

It is possible that Thomas Butler was with his father on this occasion, and it may have been at about this time that Thomas received his knighthood. Meanwhile, in addition to espousing the cause of Henry VI, Lord Sudeley was making other plans for the future. In 1456 he acquired the manor of the Moor, in Hertfordshire, which he held of the abbot of St Albans, who at that time was Lady Sudeley's kinsman, John Wheathamstead (a fact which may have facilitated the Sudeleys' acquisition of the manor). This seems to have been part of a scheme for the aggrandisement of his dynasty, which at that time he no doubt hoped shortly to see consolidated by the birth of grandchildren. It was a hope which was fated to be disappointed.

While her family by marriage was now openly supporting the Lancastrian cause, Eleanor's closest blood relatives were increasingly evincing Yorkist sympathies. As a result of her Norfolk marriage, Eleanor's sister, Elizabeth, had, of course, firmly entered the Yorkist camp. The Mowbrays, the Bourchiers, and the Mowbrays' Howard cousins all supported the Duke of York. However, for the dowager Countess of Shrewsbury the real choice was not between the rival royal houses. As her stepson moved progressively towards the Lancastrian side, so Lady Shrewsbury moved in the opposite direction, though this process was a gradual one, and Thursday 16 June 1457, for example, still saw both Margaret and her stepdaughter-in-law, the new Countess of Shrewsbury, attending Queen Margaret of Anjou at the Corpus Christi celebrations in Coventry.[35]

Margaret's father, the Earl of Warwick, had, in his day, supported the house of Lancaster, but Margaret's change of direction was opportunistic, and more concerned with her own affairs than the issue of who wielded power in the country. It clearly arose out of her conflict with her stepson. She did not so much choose to be a Yorkist as reject the Lancastrian cause because this came to be espoused by the second Earl of Shrewsbury. Many other choices of sides in the dynastic conflict were decided, perhaps, by similarly personal motives.

Eleanor's two surviving brothers, Louis and Humphrey, are not known to have taken any part in the ensuing conflict. Indeed, it is possible that Sir Louis Talbot was already sick with an illness which, in another year or so, would carry him off to an early grave.[36] In so far as they shared the aims and ambitions of their mother, however, (for upon this their fortunes depended), and opposed their half-brother, the second earl, who had deprived them of the inheritance which their father had tried to leave them, Eleanor's brothers must, like Margaret, have inclined towards the house of York.[37] Always uppermost in their minds, however, were their own best interests.

So far as is known, no member of the Talbot family took part in the first battle of St Albans. Elizabeth Talbot's father-in-law, the Duke of Norfolk (who, had he taken part in the battle, would have been on the opposite side to Eleanor's father-in-law) did assemble his men and march to the aid of his uncle, but he did not reach St Albans until Friday 23 May, the day after the battle. Consequently he took no part in the engagement. However, Margaret's brother-in-law, the Duke of Somerset, was killed there, fighting in the market place. He had long feared a 'fantastic prophecy' that he would die under a castle, and had even avoided going to Windsor because of it. As the Yorkist swords cut him down, he saw that he had reached the place of his doom, for 'at Saint Albans there was an hostelry having the sign of a castle, and before that hostelry he was slain'.[38] York, for the moment victorious, now succeeded his adversary as Constable of England.

Meanwhile in Warwickshire Eleanor was quietly occupied with the domestic routine of her manor house. Doubtless the eyes of the Butler family were also watching closely for some sign that she was about to perform her other principal duty, but if so, they were disappointed. Lord Sudeley's hoped-for grandson did not materialise. It is not known whether Eleanor simply failed to conceive, or whether she conceived but miscarried. The pelvis of the skeleton in Norwich which may be hers shows no evidence that its owner had ever experienced childbirth, but the attribution of this skeleton to Eleanor is not certain. Moreover, it is now questioned whether childbirth leaves discernible signs on the skeleton, and in any case the miscarriage of a very immature foetus might well leave no trace on the pelvic bones. For whatever reason, however, Thomas and Eleanor remained childless. There may have been some congenital problem, since similar difficulties were apparently experienced by Eleanor's sister, Elizabeth.[39] In fact, far from increasing, Eleanor's family circle was shortly to lose yet another member.

In 1453, while the first Earl of Shrewsbury and Lord Lisle still lived, Henry VI had granted to Eleanor's brother, Sir Louis Talbot, 'all places, lands, lordships possessions, rents and revenues in the duchy [of Aquitaine] now held by the Lord of Pons and Pouton ... to the value of 200 marks a year'.[40] This may well have been at Lord Shrewsbury's request – a first move to augment the status of the second son of his second marriage – though it was also part of the pattern of grants of Gascon lands to Englishmen, by means of which the government of Henry VI sought to create an English vested interest in the reconquest of the Aquitaine.[41] The subsequent loss of English-held territory in France means that Sir Louis is unlikely to have derived any long-term benefit from this grant. It is also doubtful whether, in the end, Louis derived any great benefit from his father's will. As we have already noted, the curious grant of probate relating to the will of his brother, Lord Lisle, reflected the conflict of interests which existed between the dowager Countess of Shrewsbury and her children on the one hand, and the second Earl of Shrewsbury on the other.

It is possible therefore that Louis was largely left to make his own way in the world, and he may have attempted to secure for himself by force of arms, either some part of the Berkeley inheritance, or lands which had belonged to his father. In September 1457, there is the record of a 'pardon to the king's serjeant, Lewis Talbot, knight, of all treasons, offences, felonies, mis-prisions, murders, forfeitures and contempts before 29 August last, and all actions, suits, quarrels and demands which the king could have against him'. This seems to imply that Eleanor's eldest surviving brother might then have been involved in disputes of some kind in England.[42]

Subsequently, in 1458, the 'declaration of Nicholas Alderley concerning variances and troubles between Sir Louis Talbot, Knight, and John Botlere of Badminton co. Gloucester, [e]squier, for lands and tenements in Tresham and Kilcote', indicates that there had been further disturbances.[43] Tresham, in Gloucestershire, is in the vicinity of Nibley, Wotton-under-Edge and Kingswood and seems likely to have been part of the Berkeley lands. Kilcote, on the other hand, is about twelve miles north of Tresham and three miles east of Ross-on-Wye, at no great distance from the Earl of Shrewsbury's seat at Goodrich Castle. Sir Louis' claim to it may therefore possibly have been inherited from his father.

Sir Louis Talbot died in 1458. His will was proved in October of that year, though it had been drawn up several years earlier. In it Louis describes him-self as 'of sound mind but sick in body'.[44] The phrase is conventional in this context, yet it suggests that the young man may have been in poor health during the final years of his life. On the other hand his recent involvement in 'troubles' means that the possibility that he was injured in some conflict with John Butler, and then died of his wounds, cannot be discounted.

Louis left practically everything to his mother, and declared that his burial should be 'according to the wishes of my mother, the Lady Margaret, Countess of Shrewsbury'.[45] Where he was ultimately buried is not known. Wrexham church and Gresford church are both obvious contenders, but no monument to him survives in either.[46] By the end of 1458, of Eleanor's immediate birth family, only her mother, her sister and one brother now remained alive. A further and even more significant bereavement was shortly to befall her.

Widowhood

In 1459, and probably towards the end of that year, Eleanor, then aged 23, became a widow. How Sir Thomas Butler died is unknown, though it is possible that he was either killed or injured at the battle of Blore Heath. It is equally possible that he died of some illness. The earliest surviving mention of his death is in a deed issued by his father on 15 January 1460.[1] It was at about this time that Ralph, Lord Sudeley, built the beautiful chapel (St Mary's Church) at Sudeley Castle. No doubt a new chapel was already planned, as part of the overall rebuilding of the castle, but possibly this chapel was in part conceived as a memorial for Ralph Butler's only son.

Seen today from the outside, the building survives substantially as Lord Sudeley left it, 'all with embattled parapets. The (renewed) windows are Perpendicular, with carved stops to the hood-moulds, those of the west doorway representing Henry VI and Queen Margaret (Boteler supported the Lancastrians), though the figures in the niches are nineteenth century'. The interior, however, damaged during the Civil War, 'is now the creation of Sir George Gilbert Scott, c.1859–63. The church comprises a nave and chancel without structural division'.[2]

This chapel at Sudeley would make a fitting commemoration of the lost hopes of the Butler family, for the death of Sir Thomas had put an end to Lord Sudeley's dynastic ambitions. He now lost interest in his recently-acquired Hertfordshire manor of the Moor which, in 1460, he conveyed to trustees: John Eure, Thomas Clopton and others. These, in turn, conveyed the Hertfordshire manor back to the abbot.[3] We shall meet John Eure and Thomas Clopton again, later. Lord Sudeley's return of the Moor was accompanied by an agreement, whereby the abbey of St Albans undertook to pray for the good estate of Ralph and his wife, and for the repose of the soul of their dead son.

On 28 August 1462, Ralph and Eleanor suffered a further bereavement, when Elizabeth Norbury, Lady Sudeley, followed her son into the grave. Eleanor had lived under Lady Sudeley's care during the first three years of her marriage, and must have come to know her mother-in-law well. As for Lord Sudeley, he and Elizabeth had been married for more than forty years. Though there had perhaps been frequent separations during that time, Ralph had always had a wife and family to come home to. Now he was left entirely alone.

Probably he felt lonely. At all events, a little over a year after Elizabeth Norbury's death, on 8 January 1463, he married the widowed Alice Deincourt (Lovel), who was to outlive him. This second marriage cannot have been in the hope of a replacement Sudeley heir, for Alice Deincourt was about 60 years old when Ralph married her.[4] Perhaps she was an old acquaintance.

Eleanor also seems to have known the second Lady Sudeley. It was at about the time of Ralph Butler's second marriage that Eleanor initiated her endowment at Corpus Christi College, Cambridge. While her original documentation does not survive, the later (extant) indentures specifically require prayers for the souls of Eleanor herself, of her parents, of Sir Thomas Butler, 'of Ralph Butler, Lord of Sudeley, and of his wife, and of the parents of the said Thomas Butler'. This wording, which at first sight seems strange, becomes intelligible when Lord Sudeley's two marriages are taken into account. The prayers for 'Lord Sudeley and his wife' were clearly intended for Ralph and Alice Deincourt, while the prayers for 'the parents of Thomas Butler' were for Ralph and Elizabeth Norbury. Thus both Lady Sudeleys were included in Eleanor's commemoration.

While the details of Eleanor's relationship with the new Lady Sudeley remain obscure, the fact that they were apparently acquainted is interesting, for Alice Deincourt was (by her first marriage) the grandmother of Francis, Lord Lovel. We have already noted, through Eleanor's relationship with the Catesby family, her connection with the future King Richard III's 'cat'. We now perceive that she also had a connection with his 'dog'.

Following the death of Thomas Butler, the widowed Eleanor had automatically retained, in dower, the manors which Lord Sudeley had granted to her and her husband on 10 May 1453.[5] These comprised the three Warwickshire manors of Griff, Burton Dassett and Fenny Compton.[6] There was no obvious reason why any change should have been made to this arrangement, and in the normal course of events, Eleanor would have held these three manors for the remainder of her life, and upon her death they would have reverted to Lord Sudeley or his heirs.

In the thirty-ninth year of the reign of Henry VI (1460/61), however, for reasons which are unclear, Eleanor returned Griff to her father-in-law.[7] It is difficult to understand why Eleanor should have surrendered one of her manors in this way, although such a surrender is not unique.[8] The clear implication in her inquisition post mortem is that the initiative for this transfer was Eleanor's, for we are told that Lord Sudeley 'agreed' to it. Since, in so far as one can judge, both Eleanor and her sister, Elizabeth, subsequently remained on good terms with members of Lord Sudeley's family, they cannot have harboured any resentment, and the transfer must therefore have been amicable. The surrender cannot be dated very precisely, but it seems highly likely that Eleanor's return of Griff to Lord Sudeley was linked to, and in fact, immediately followed, another transaction which took place at about this time.

On 15 January 38 Henry VI (1460), Lord Sudeley had issued a quitclaim to Lady Eleanor in respect of the manor of Fenny Compton.[9] By this quitclaim he resigned all title to this manor, in Eleanor's favour. From this point onwards the 23-year-old Eleanor held Fenny Compton absolutely, in her own right, and not in dower.

The reason for Lord Sudeley's action likewise remains a matter for conjecture, but it may argue a degree of regard and affection for Eleanor on the part of her father-in-law, which Eleanor probably reciprocated.[10] 'Coresidence gave women an opportunity to develop a warm relationship with their husband's parents'.[11] It is possible that the transactions between Eleanor and Lord Sudeley in respect of Fenny Compton and Griff also parallel the contemporary agreement between Lord Sudeley and St Alban's Abbey in respect of the manor of the Moor (see above). In the case of the Hertfordshire manor, Lord Sudeley – now without direct heirs to provide for – traded landed property in exchange for prayers for the souls of himself, his wife and his son. It is possible that his agreement with Eleanor was along similar lines, for it must have been at about this time that Eleanor was planning her endowment at Corpus Christi College, Cambridge, and it can be no accident that this endowment mentioned not only Eleanor's birth family, but also her relatives by marriage. Nor can it be accidental that Eleanor ultimately gave Fenny Compton to her sister Elizabeth, who bore the responsibility, as Eleanor's executrix, for maintaining the Corpus Christi endowment.

The total value of Eleanor's jointure as a widow is difficult to assess. The value of Fenny Compton is not precisely recorded,[12] and it is unclear what other lands Eleanor held, and when she acquired them. Nor is it entirely clear which of Eleanor's lands (other than Burton Dassett) were strictly speaking part of her jointure.

English aristocratic widows' jointures during the period 1450–1490 seem to have ranged in value from £10 a year to well over £1,000 a year. Daughters and wives of knights tended to have the smaller incomes, as might be expected, generally less than £50. Daughters and wives of peers were expected to be better off than this (though to have a jointure which produced an income of more than £500 a year was quite exceptional).[13] Eleanor's manor of Burton Dassett produced an annual income of just over £30. The surrendered manor of Griff had yielded an annual income of about £20.[14] Assuming that Fenny Compton brought in at least as much as Griff, Eleanor's annual income from her two Warwickshire manors must have surpassed £50 in total. Since Eleanor held, in addition, a manor in Wiltshire, together with adjacent rents and other sources of income, her total annual revenue may well have amounted to £75 or more.[15] This was a reasonable sum – though not lavish. As a total income, it approached the 10 per cent of the value of Eleanor's dowry which would normally have been expected to constitute her annual revenue from her jointure alone.[16]

It was not unusual for noble widows to hold property above and beyond what constituted their jointure. Usually any such property was a gift or legacy from a husband. Occasionally the woman herself purchased land. Fenny Compton was not the only manor which Eleanor held in her own right during her widowhood. At some stage she also acquired the above-mentioned property in Wiltshire, which we must examine in some detail, since it may be connected to Eleanor's relationship with King Edward IV.

The Wiltshire property comprised the manor of Oare-under-Savernake, together with 'divers messuages, lands, tenements, rents, reversions and services in Draycote, Coldecot and Chikeladerigg', all in the same county (or counties).[17] There are various difficulties in respect of these Wiltshire properties, not the least of which is the fact that neither in the Wiltshire archives, nor in the national archives does any record appear to survive of Eleanor's tenure of them. It is also not entirely clear what is meant, in this case, by 'the manor of Oare-under-Savernake'.

Oare and the nearby forest of Savernake are situated about ten miles west of Newbury, a little to the south of Marlborough, in north east Wiltshire (near the Berkshire border). 'Draycote' is clearly Draycot FitzPayne, which neighbours Oare. 'Chikeladerigg' (Chicklade Ridge) refers to Chicklade, a tiny hamlet in south west Wiltshire, now transected by the A303. Chicklade seems too small to have qualified as a village in the Middle Ages. It has no medieval (or later) parish church. It lies about ten miles west of Stonehenge and five miles south of Warminster, near the county boundary with Dorset. The 'Great Ridge', where Eleanor's land lay, rises up steeply on the northern side of the hamlet. 'Coldecot' is more of a puzzle. It may be Calcutt in Wiltshire, or possibly Caldecote in Warwickshire (north of Nuneaton).

How and when had Eleanor acquired her holdings in Wiltshire? There is no clue in the Fenny Compton archive in the Warwickshire County Record Office, which is the only surviving source to mention these holdings. There seem to be three possibilities. The Wiltshire lands might perhaps have come to Eleanor from her own family. Alternatively they might have been a gift from the king, designed, perhaps, to help to maintain Eleanor – or to keep her quiet. The third possibility is that Eleanor herself purchased them.

The last of these options is difficult to evaluate. Did Eleanor have sufficient income to purchase land and manors? As for the other possibilities, for Eleanor to have brought landed property from her natal family to her Butler marriage would have been highly unusual, given that she was not an heiress.[18] Rather, Eleanor would have been expected to bring a cash dowry to her marriage. Indeed, we have already seen that she did so. 'A woman's dowry constituted her inheritance and forestalled her making any further claim on the family estates, although fathers could, and often did, leave their daughters additional legacies in their wills'.[19] Eleanor would have had no claim on family lands, and is extremely unlikely to have acquired any unless by any chance her father chose to leave some to her.

In point of fact, however, no bequest to Eleanor is mentioned in the first Earl of Shrewsbury's will, nor in the wills of Lord Lisle or Sir Louis Talbot, the two brothers who predeceased her.[20] As for the possibility that Eleanor might have been left the Wiltshire property by her mother, the dowager Countess of Shrewsbury, who died on Sunday 14 June 1467,[21] there is a major difficulty with this explanation. Following Margaret's death, writs of *diem clausit extremum* were almost instantly dispatched to the escheators of the numerous counties within which she had held lands. These comprised Gloucestershire, Somerset, Staffordshire, Berkshire, Oxfordshire, Devon, Worcestershire and Warwickshire. Writs were also sent to the mayors of Lincoln and London in their capacity as escheators of those cities.[22] No writ was dispatched to the escheator of Wiltshire. The clear implication is that Margaret held no lands in that county. She cannot, therefore, have left any to her daughter, Eleanor.

The lack of clarity as to what exactly Eleanor held in Wiltshire complicates the discussion. The Forest of Savernake itself seems to have been under the control of Edward IV's great uncle, Edward, Duke of York, earlier in the fifteenth century. There is a record of a grant made by him in favour of the Carmelite friars, giving them the right to collect fuel there.[23] Subsequently the forest was certainly in the hands of the crown and was conferred on the royal consort. In 1452 Henry VI granted it to his queen, Margaret of Anjou, and in 1466 Edward IV gave it to Elizabeth Woodville.[24] If Eleanor's Wiltshire property included any part of the forest, such a gift can only have come to her from the king.

As for her manor of 'Draycote', by a very curious coincidence the manor of Draycot FitzPayne was held by the Skillings, the family to which the stepmother of Edward IV's mistress, Elizabeth Wayte (Lucy) belonged.[25] However, there was also a second estate at Draycote, in addition to the one held by the Skillings. By 1242 this second estate was in the hands of the Berkeley family 'and was still part of the lordship of Berkeley in 1401. Although said to be in Draycot until at least 1442 it became part of Oare tithing and the base of the reputed manor of Oare'.[26]

It is tempting to conclude that this second Draycot manor formed part of Eleanor's holdings, and was an inheritance which came to her from her mother's Berkeley ancestors. Eleanor's choice of words when referring to her Wiltshire property, while in itself proving nothing, could be consistent with such a conclusion.[27] In fact, however, as we have seen, it seems impossible that Eleanor acquired any land in Wiltshire from her mother. Moreover, there are other difficulties about this explanation, which relate to the identities of the sub-tenants of the Wiltshire lands.

The sub-tenants of the Berkeleys' manor of Oare were the Cotel family in the thirteenth and fourteenth centuries, and the lease was inherited by the Paultons in the fifteenth century. 'Before 1442 ...William Paulton (d.1450) settled Oare on his daughter Gillian when she married John Cheney'.[28] Subsequently the Berkeleys' manor of Oare remained in the hands of the Cheney family as sub-tenants until at least the late seventeenth century. However, the Fenny Compton archive contains a clear and unequivocal statement that all Eleanor's Wiltshire lands had passed, by 1474, into the hands of one Thomas Rogers.[29] This implies that whatever land Eleanor held in Wiltshire cannot have included the manor once held by the Berkeleys.

It would, of course, be extremely helpful if any confirmatory material in respect of Eleanor's Wiltshire tenures survived in the Wiltshire archives. Sadly, nothing of the sort has been found there, though there is certainly corroboration of the existence of John Cheney, and of his family's connection with the manor of Oare.[30] Until and unless further information comes to light, mysteries will remain in respect of Eleanor's Wiltshire land holdings.

One interesting question requiring consideration is where Eleanor resided, following the death of Sir Thomas Butler. Even if she already held the Wiltshire property at that stage (which seems unlikely), clearly she cannot have lived there, since there was a sub-tenant in residence. During her marriage, Eleanor and Thomas may well, from time to time, have visited the de Sudeley manor house at Griff, but after 1461, at the latest, the surrender of Griff to Lord Sudeley would have ruled out this possibility. This leaves only the manor houses at Burton Dassett and Fenny Compton, either or both of which might have been used by Thomas and Eleanor during their marriage.

Neither of these medieval manor houses is now extant,[31] but it is probable that Eleanor was living in one of them at the time of her husband's death, and presumably she remained in residence, for a time at least. It is apparent, however, that fairly soon after Thomas' death, Eleanor's main focus of attention shifted from Warwickshire to East Anglia.

The Butler family had links of its own with East Anglia, where, at various times, Lord Sudeley had held portions of a number of manors.[32] The pedigree roll which had been commissioned to mark Eleanor's marriage to Thomas was of East Anglian manufacture. Also, Lord Sudeley and his second wife were formerly commemorated in a stained-glass window at Chilton

Church, near Sudbury (Suffolk).[33] It is conceivable, therefore, that Eleanor's initial move to the eastern counties was undertaken in the company of her father-in-law. There is no indication, however, that Eleanor herself ever held any of the Butler family's manors in this part of the country. It is therefore likely that quite soon, Eleanor sought shelter with her younger sister, Elizabeth, who, in 1461, had become Duchess of Norfolk.

It is very probable that Eleanor first joined her sister's household at Framlingham Castle, a building which is still standing. The modern visitor, gazing at the castle across the fields and over the mere, or approaching it from the town, could be forgiven for thinking that this chief dwelling of the Mowbrays (and of the Bigods before them) has survived the centuries intact, for the outer curtain walls and towers, built of flint, are remarkably well preserved. Alas, when one crosses the now dry moat and takes the path that John Mowbray and Elizabeth Talbot must often have taken, through the gateway,[34] the illusion is shattered. Inside the walls almost nothing now survives of what they would have known. Nevertheless, the scene that would have presented itself to their eyes can be reconstructed.

The gatehouse itself was a substantial building, containing two chambers. To the right, just inside the gateway, the all-important castle well stood then as now, but in their day it was covered by a small building with accommodation above. Against the wall to the left (west) stood domestic service buildings (footings of which remain), including the kitchen, distinguished by its tall, pointed roof with louvres through which the smoke and heat could escape.

Further to the north, but still on the left-hand side, on the site now occupied by the later poor house, stood the thirteenth-century great hall, adjoined by two chambers at its northern end. An inventory, taken in 1524, calls these 'the chamber at the hall end' and 'the inner chamber at the hall end'.[35] At the southern end of the great hall, between the hall and the separate building which housed the kitchen, were 'the great chamber', 'the dining chamber', 'the chamber at the great chamber end', and another 'inner chamber'.

Opposite this thirteenth-century block, abutting the right hand (eastern) wall, stood the castle chapel, next to which was the original great hall, dating, like the chapel, from about 1150. Replaced by the newer, thirteenth-century great hall on the opposite side of the enclosure, the old great hall had been converted to other uses, and housed the 'wardrobe' (which was a sort of storehouse) and probably the armoury, as well as a room known as 'the chapel chamber' which was perhaps used for guests. One of the windows in the outer wall of the old great hall had been recently enlarged to form a doorway, through which the duchess and her ladies could pass, by a little footbridge, across the moat to reach the new private garden in the deer park. Between the chapel and the gatehouse, against the eastern curtain wall, ran timber buildings, housing the stables.

The main residential block, where the chambers of the Duke and duchess were to be found, was freestanding within the open space enclosed by the curtain walls. It was probably located between the chapel and the main gate, for an aerial photograph of the site shows signs of what could be the rectangular foundations of a building towards the western end of the castle precinct.[36] This block probably dated from the late fourteenth century or later. It may even have been erected by the first Mowbray Duke. It was described in the seventeenth century by Leverland. 'Between the hall and the chapel, fronting the great gate of the castle, was a large chamber with several rooms and a cloister under it'.[37]

The 'several rooms' which were on the first floor of this block are probably those listed in the 1524 inventory as 'the Lord's chamber', 'Lady Oxinford's chamber', 'the inner chamber to Lady Oxinford's chamber', 'the young ladies chamber' and 'the inner chamber there'. The Lord's chamber was doubtless the room used by the fourth Duke of Norfolk in his day, and Elizabeth Talbot's room was probably the one which the inventory calls (after its most recent inhabitant) 'Lady Oxinford's chamber'.

The 1524 inventory helps us to picture the interior furnishings of the castle in John and Elizabeth's time. After all, the second Howard Duke, who died in 1524, was born in the same year as Elizabeth Talbot, though he outlived her. Also, the inventory specifies that many of the furnishings were old, which implies that they had been at Framlingham for a long time, so that John and Elizabeth may well have owned them, and Eleanor may well have seen them when staying at Framlingham.

The whole castle was extensively hung with tapestries, some of which the inventory describes as 'counterfeit Arras'. The tapestries in the great hall were of the kind which the inventory calls 'verders': rich tapestries ornamented with representations of trees or other vegetation. This kind of tapestry was hung in many rooms of the castle. The tapestries in the great hall, in addition to verdant foliage, also had many animals depicted, while in the great chamber were tapestries with depictions of the labours of Hercules. The dining chamber was 56ft long by 26ft wide. This room is known to have had glazed windows (as no doubt many of the other rooms did too) and a tiled floor. Its walls were hung with tapestries depicting one of the Sybils, and on one wall hung a large mirror, perhaps a convex glass, intended to reflect the light, similar to that shown on the rear wall in Van Eyke's *Arnolfini Marriage* portrait. The dining chamber also housed a chair upholstered in tawny velvet, fringed with red, white and green silk, with a cushion of black velvet and blue satin.

Many (perhaps all) of the chambers had fireplaces. We know that this was the case in the Lord's chamber, because 'anderons' (fire dogs) are mentioned there. No doubt Eleanor's brother-in-law, John Mowbray, slept here in the 1460s. There was no bed in this room in 1524, but the 'large bed of state' stored in the wardrobe probably belonged here. It was hung with curtains of cloth of gold, white damask and black velvet, and had a valence of yellow, green and red silk. The Lord's chamber had 'verders' on the walls and curtains at the windows.

The room which was probably once Elizabeth Talbot's chamber was also hung with 'verders'. The bed was of wood panelling. Like most of the great beds of the period, it was not a 'four-poster'. Instead, it had a suspended canopy (the 'seler') from which the curtains hung. At the head of the bed the area between the bed itself and the seler was also covered in fabric. This part of the bed was known as the 'tester', from the French word for 'head'. In this case the tester and seler were of black and purple velvet and the bed had a counterpane to match. The underside of the seler was lined with green satin, and there were panels of matching green satin in the centre of the counterpane and forming the middle panel of the tester. The bed curtains were of yellow and purple sarcenet, and the bed had the usual valence of green, yellow and red silk. There were carpets in the window embrasures, and cushions, perhaps on window seats.

The chapel and the old great hall had Norman windows, small, with rounded arches. The east window of the chapel partly survives, as it cut through the outer walls of the castle. It was flanked by two smaller, arcaded recesses. The chapel had a high pitched roof with lead guttering.[38] The interior of the chapel was hung with Arras-style tapestries. The high altar had a reredos of tapestry, showing the crucifixion, and over it hung a baldichino of blue satin powdered with gold (perhaps in the form of stars), with a valence of white, red and green silk. On the altar stood a jewelled crucifix of silver parcel gilt, and two pairs of matching candlesticks. Before the altar was a carpet of English manufacture. There were two side altars, with silver gilt statues of the Virgin and of St John. Both side altars had silver gilt candlesticks. The chapel had 'a pair of organs with four stops', and all the necessary equipment for its functioning, including many sets of rich vestments, altar frontals, altar cloths, silver gilt chalices, pattens, a processional cross, censers, a silver incense boat, silver cruets, a silver holy water bucket and sprinkler, a silver sanctus bell and valuable illuminated antiphoners, plainsong books, missals bound in crimson or purple velvet, and books of the gospels, bound in silver gilt. There were eight albs for children – either altar boys or choir boys.

In all, Framlingham Castle had some twenty-nine rooms. There were only eight bedsteads in the castle, but in addition there were 'livery featherbeds' and 'mattresses for men and grooms' providing beds for a total of ninety-five people. At the time of the 1524 inventory the stables at Framlingham contained thirty-three horses, with three more stabled at Earl Soham Lodge, a few miles away. The castle's scullery contained a cauldron and an assortment of cooking pots and pans, made of brass, together with household vessels of pewter, but there was also tableware of silver or silver gilt. Some of this was clearly old, however, and the inventory records that the gold on the silver gilt spoons was worn away, which indicates that they may well have dated from fifty years previously, when John Mowbray and Elizabeth Talbot inhabited the castle. Some of the tapestries and carpets were also said, in 1524, to be old and worn. This inventory, taken at a time when the castle was about to be abandoned and enter its long decline, thus evokes the Framlingham of the 1460s, which Eleanor Talbot will have known.

Edward IV

During the 1450s, as we have seen, the Talbot family had become increasingly split between the rival factions of Lancaster and York. Eleanor's half-brother, the second Earl of Shrewsbury, had become a moderate supporter of the Court Party. Her mother and her brother, Humphrey, by a kind of magnetic repulsion, moved slowly but surely in the opposite direction.

Of the members of Eleanor's family by marriage, Lord Sudeley, at least, remained a Lancastrian. The Butlers, however, like the Talbots, were awkwardly poised between the dividing loyalties of the age. Lord Sudeley (and perhaps also his son) may have borne arms for Henry VI, but Lord Sudeley's sister, Lady Say, was godmother to the Duke of York's eldest son, Edward, Earl of March. One of Lady Say's sons, Thomas Montgomery, was to be knighted in 1461 by Edward (by then, King Edward IV) as a reward for his strenuous exertions on the Yorkist side at the battle of Towton. Unfortunately the same king was also obliged to execute Thomas Montgomery's younger brother, John, at about the same time, for his exertions in the opposite direction.

Perhaps Lord Sudeley and his son were with the royal army which marched from Nottingham into Shropshire in 1459 to prevent the union of the Neville forces from the north with the army of the Duke of York. As things fell out this force was not engaged in battle, for another Lancastrian army, under the nominal command of the young Prince of Wales (and actually led by Lord Audley) encountered the Earl of Salisbury's men first, at Blore Heath, and was defeated by them. It is possible that Sir Thomas Butler was killed, or fatally injured at Blore Heath. At all events, he died at this time or fairly soon after.

Meanwhile, as a result of the battle of Blore Heath, Salisbury's men were able to join up with the Duke of York's army at Ludlow. Nevertheless, York was deserted by his strongest contingent, the men from the Calais garrison, who refused to fight against the king. Consequently the Duke of York fled back to Ireland while the Nevilles, together with York's eldest son, the Earl of March, took ship for Calais.

From all these events John Mowbray, third Duke of Norfolk (the father-in-law of Eleanor's sister, Elizabeth) held aloof. He attended the Parliament held by Henry VI at Coventry towards the end of the year, and, when required, took the oath to the Lancastrian succession. It was perhaps to persuade Norfolk to this oath that, on 11 December, Henry VI made him a grant of £50 a year for life.[1] When the Yorkist Lords returned in 1460, the Duke of Norfolk kept a fairly low profile.

In any case, the weather, that summer, was not such as to inspire anyone to take the field. Like Eleanor, the heavens were in mourning. It rained incessantly, flooding mills and sweeping away bridges. The sodden crops rotted in the fields and roads were deep in mire.[2]

By July, however, when the Yorkists entered London, the Duke of Norfolk may have bestirred himself to greater activity in his uncle's cause, though he took no part, apparently, in the battle of Northampton, on 10 July 1460, a battle in which Eleanor's half-brother, the second Earl of Shrewsbury, was killed fighting for Henry VI. Fortunately for him, Norfolk was also nowhere near the battle of Wakefield at the end of December, when the Duke of York, his son the Earl of Rutland, and the head of the Neville family, the Earl of Salisbury, were all killed by Queen Margaret's men. At the time of this battle Norfolk was safe in London with Eleanor's uncle, the Earl of Warwick.

In the meantime, York's eldest son, Edward, had been in the eastern counties. In August 1460 he seems to have been staying with the Duke of Norfolk's cousin, John Howard esquire (as he was at that time) at Stoke-by-Nayland in Suffolk. On 27 August, Edward, as Earl of March, was named as a feoffee, together with Howard and well-attested members of the latter's household such as Thomas Moleyns and Robert Cumberton, in respect of a messuage and land at nearby Higham and Stratford-St-Mary.[3]

Although the Mowbrays' ducal title related to Norfolk, the principal Mowbray seat of Framlingham Castle was, in fact, also in Suffolk, and it is intriguing to speculate whether Edward could have met Eleanor some-where in that county during the summer of 1460. She had already been a widow for more than seven months by that time. Unfortunately the pre-cise date of her move to the eastern counties is unknown. We shall return to the possibility of such an early meeting between Edward and Eleanor shortly.

Following the death of the Duke of York in December 1460, events in England moved with bewildering speed. While the new Yorkist leader, the nineteen-year-old Earl of March, won a victory at Mortimer's Cross, the Duke of Norfolk, still with the Earl of Warwick, now had the misfortune to fight instead at the second battle of St Alban's, on Tuesday 17 February 1461, when the Yorkists were defeated. Norfolk escaped from the battlefield and made his way safely back to London. There, a fortnight later, on Tuesday 3 March, he and his brother-in-law, the Archbishop of Canterbury, attended a council of Yorkist Lords held at Baynard's Castle. This meeting supported the proclamation of the Earl of March as King Edward IV. Norfolk also attended the new king's enthronement at Westminster on the following day. Thereafter the duke marched north with the new king, and on Palm Sunday, 29 March, fought bravely at the bloody battle of Towton, which secured Edward's position. In the wake of this Yorkist success, the Mowbrays were riding high. On his way back to London from the north, Edward passed through Norwich. There, he was perhaps attended by members of the Duke of Norfolk's family, including his daughter-in-law, the beautiful young Elizabeth Talbot, Countess Warenne.

More than a year had now passed since Sir Thomas Butler's death, and at some point during this time the widowed Eleanor had apparently joined her sister's household in East Anglia. By March 1461 Eleanor would have been out of mourning for two or three months. In spite of the Lancastrianism of her father-in-law (and perhaps also of her dead husband), Eleanor would have encountered no difficulty in being presented to the new king. Thanks to her connection with the Duke of Norfolk, Eleanor's sister, Elizabeth, would certainly have been *persona grata* at Edward's court. In addition, Eleanor's uncle, the Earl of Warwick, was very much in Edward's favour. So too was her late husband's cousin, Sir Thomas Montgomery. Any one of these people could have assisted in bringing about the fateful encounter between Edward and Eleanor which took place, at the latest, in the early spring of 1461. Nor need we assume that either the person who presented her to the king (or indeed, Eleanor herself) necessarily foresaw any particular purpose in this meeting, for 'the scope of accident in human affairs is always far greater than can be ascertained'.[4]

We may try to picture the two young Talbot sisters – Eleanor now just 25 years old, and Elizabeth aged 18. No known portrait of Eleanor now survives (though she was once depicted, with her brothers and sister, on her mother's lost tomb at old St Paul's Cathedral) and the only extant representation of her sister, Elizabeth, dates from a later period. However, it seems likely that Elizabeth had her father's dark colouring rather than her mother's fair hair. This colouring was also exhibited by others of John Talbot's descendants, and Eleanor probably shared it.

We may therefore imagine Eleanor and Elizabeth with dark brown or black hair, and brown eyes. Both girls probably also had aquiline noses, a combination of the genes inherited from their father and mother. As we have already noted, Elizabeth is reported to have been beautiful.[5] Probably Eleanor was too. At all events, her appearance was sufficiently striking to attract the king. The skeleton in Norwich which may be Eleanor's is that of a healthy young woman, who in life stood some 5ft 6in tall.

Edward was 19 years old. Six feet two inches in height, he had brown hair which in 1461 was still cut short in the 'Henry VI' style.[6] At this stage of his life he may have been drawn to women older than himself. Possibly he also preferred brunettes. Both Eleanor Talbot and Elizabeth Woodville were slightly older than Edward (though Elizabeth Wayte [Lucy] may have been younger). Moreover, despite a persistent legend that she was fair, the portrait of Elizabeth Woodville at Queen's College, Cambridge, shows dark auburn hair under the front edge of her headdress.

At all events, it seems that Edward was attracted to Eleanor, who reciprocated. Tudor writers entirely omitted her from their histories,[7] but since Eleanor's existence was once again generally acknowledged in the seventeenth century, no historian has ever questioned her association with Edward IV, so we may confidently assert that a relationship of some kind did exist between them. The chronology of the king's love affairs means that his association with Eleanor must have begun either in the summer of 1460, when he was still Earl of March, or early in 1461, very soon after he attained the throne. By the autumn of 1461 the king was already moving on to pastures new, taking as his mistress the young Elizabeth Wayte (Lucy), who bore him a daughter the following year.[8]

The nature of Eleanor's relationship with Edward cannot now be proved beyond all question, but both her high rank and her notable piety militate against the notion that she would willingly have accepted the role of royal mistress. At the same time Edward's subsequent conduct in respect of Elizabeth Woodville (with whom he undoubtedly contracted a secret union) makes it entirely plausible that he would have pursued a similar course earlier, with Eleanor. Moreover, fifteenth-century sources exist which report that he did so.[9] The great nineteenth-century historian, James Gairdner, considered that 'no sufficient grounds' have been brought forward for regarding such a secret marriage between Edward IV and Eleanor Talbot as 'a mere political invention',[10] and this assessment is still valid.

It may also be as well to state very clearly at this point that the relationship which was alleged between Edward IV and Eleanor Talbot in the fifteenth century was neither more nor less than marriage. The Act of Parliament of 1484 is quite explicit on this point (see Appendix 1). The widespread use of the term *precontract* in relation to this union is not particularly helpful, since its meaning is very frequently misunderstood. It is often taken to mean something like 'betrothal', but this is emphatically not what *precontract* means. It is, in fact, a legal term which can only be applied retrospectively, the *contract* to which it refers being precisely a contract of marriage. Such a contract could, of course, only become *pre-* with hindsight, when viewed in relation to a subsequent, second (and necessarily bigamous) contract of marriage with a third party.

In the case of Edward IV the second and bigamous contract of marriage was with Elizabeth Woodville. It was not possible to actually enter into an agreement called a *precontract*. Thus at the time when it was made, any contract between Edward IV and Eleanor Talbot would simply have been a contract of marriage. To refer to it from its inception as a *precontract* is, therefore, both misleading and inaccurate. Indeed, it is tantamount to implying that, at the time of his relationship with Eleanor, Edward IV already envisioned a subsequent second contract of marriage with Elizabeth Woodville: an implication which is certainly unjust to all three of the people involved.

Given the essential nature of a secret contract, together with Edward IV's later behaviour, and Eleanor's subsequent decisions in respect of her own life (see below), it is not surprising that the sources available to us are not precisely contemporary with the event. They date from twenty years later, when both parties to the contract were dead. Nevertheless, given that during the second half of the fifteenth century Edward IV's marriage with Eleanor Talbot was asserted; that the reality of this marriage was accepted as a fact by Parliament, and that no evidence to disprove its existence has ever been produced by anybody (either in the fifteenth century or subsequently), it is reasonable to accept that such a marriage existed.

Historians have frequently accepted working hypotheses which rest on less solid evidence than three almost contemporary written sources, one of which is an Act of Parliament. This is particularly so in the case of secret royal marriages. For example, the documentary evidence of a marriage between Henry V's widow, Queen Catherine, and Owen Tudor is both less full, and later (in relation to the alleged event) than is the case for Edward IV's Talbot marriage. Indeed, in respect of Catherine's union with Owen it has been observed that 'the potpourri of myth, romanticism, tradition and anti-Tudor propaganda surrounding this match is rarely borne out by historical fact'.[11] Actually the chief evidence for the Tudor / Valois union seems to be the existence of offspring – a circumstance lacking, of course, in the case of Edward IV and Eleanor Talbot.

Whether secrecy was initially seen as an essential element of Edward's contract with Eleanor is not clear. It is conceivable that, in his haste to consummate his infatuation, Edward simply dispensed with ceremony. There are other possibilities, however. If Edward and Eleanor met in the summer of 1460, before Edward became king, and while the Duke of York was still living, and if their marriage took place at that stage, it is possible that the element of secrecy arose from the fact that Edward had not had the opportunity to discuss the matter with his parents. If, on the other hand, the marriage took place after Edward's accession, it is conceivable that a deliberately secret marriage was Edward's dishonourable way of making a promise which Eleanor believed to be honourably meant.

In theory, the fifteenth-century chivalric code placed a high importance on the keeping of one's word. In general it was held that 'an honourable man was bound to be true to his word – so long as it was publicly and honestly given, not made in secrecy, nor extorted, and in harmony with the true intention of the speaker'.[12] In the present instance, however, we are dealing with a clandestine promise, possibly made under a degree of pressure (at least in Edward's eyes), and where the king's true intentions are a matter for speculation.

Edward IV was undoubtedly capable of telling lies and squaring such behaviour with his honour. He was to do so famously on his return from exile in 1471. On that occasion it was considered that 'the lies that he told were mere "noysynge", necessary to fulfil his true intention, which was in itself validated … by his true claim to the throne'.[13] It is perfectly conceivable, therefore, that Edward would not have regarded himself as bound by any promise he may have made to Eleanor if he later found it inconvenient.

Wherever and whenever the young couple met, it is related that Edward played out with Eleanor a scene that was probably quite similar to the one he would subsequently enact with Elizabeth Woodville. According to Commynes, he 'promised to marry her, provided that he could sleep with her first, and she consented'. Edward 'had made this promise in the Bishop [of Bath]'s presence.[14] And having done so, he slept with her'.

Stillington's reported presence tends to imply that the actual marriage must have post-dated Edward's accession to the throne. This does not, however, preclude the possibility of an earlier initial meeting. Elsewhere, Commynes goes further, stating explicitly that Stillington 'had married them',[15] although a priestly officiant was not essential for a valid marriage, and in theory, at least, 'priests were forbidden to participate in any clandestine marriages'.[16] Stillington was essentially a man of the world, whose career was first and foremost that of a servant of the government. He had several illegitimate children, and during the course of his episcopate seems to have visited his diocese very rarely.[17] Nevertheless, in dealing with a devout lady, as Eleanor clearly was, it was clever of Edward IV to choose a priest (albeit a somewhat worldly one) to be present at their exchange of vows, in whatever capacity.

In point of fact, a private marriage required neither a priest nor any third party to be present, but in this case Stillington, as reported by Commynes, claimed that he had witnessed Edward's contract of marriage with Eleanor, and this would certainly explain how Stillington came to be aware of the existence of the marriage, and was later able to publicise it. In addition to Commynes' evidence, both Mancini and Vergil (neither of whom mentions Eleanor by name) refer to Edward IV's involvement with a member of the Earl of Warwick's family, and Mancini speaks specifically of a promise of marriage.

It is quite possible that Edward had initially expected to make Eleanor his mistress. Doubly armoured in her strong religious principles and in her multiple noble and royal descent, however, she clearly considered herself far above this dubious honour. This outcome may well have surprised Edward, but since both she and the king were unattached, from Eleanor's point of view no impediment stood in the way of a more honourable resolution.

In the face of Eleanor's rejection of his initial advances, the king had only two choices: either to accept defeat, or to accept her terms. Perhaps duplici- tously, he accordingly offered her marriage if she would sleep with him. For a young widow of her social class a second marriage would be entirely normal. More than 45 per cent of such women remarried.[18] Nor was there any legal impediment to prevent an English monarch from marrying a widow. An earlier fifteenth-century instance of such a royal marriage was that of Henry IV with Joanna of Navarre.

In the Middle Ages a promise *per verba de futuro* – that is to say, marriage by means of a promise couched in the future tense, as in 'I will marry you' – consolidated by subsequent sexual intercourse, constituted a valid marriage. Such a marriage came into effect when it was consummated, which in this case was apparently almost at once. Such marriages were recognised (if not greatly favoured) by the Church, and had been formally acknowledged, for example, by decretals of Pope Alexander III.[19]

It has always been the Church's teaching that marriage is a self-conferring sacrament, which is effected by the free consent of the parties, confirmed by consummation. In the Middle Ages (when marriage had not yet become a civil contract) the logic of this argument led ineluctably to the conclu- sion that no form of public ceremony was therefore essential. The Church, nevertheless, strongly recommended public marriage ceremonies, pre- cisely in order to avoid consequences such as those which arose in the case of Eleanor Talbot's relationship with Edward IV, and in 1215 the Fourth Lateran Council had generalised throughout Europe the system of publica- tion of banns before marriage.[20] It remains the case, however, that if Edward IV acted as Commynes reports, then by virtue of his future tense promise of marriage to her, followed by sexual intercourse, he was unquestionably married to Eleanor Talbot.

The marriage remains hypothetical only in that, while it is entirely plau- sible that Edward behaved as Commynes stated, it is not absolutely certain that he did so. On these grounds only, and on no other, is the sceptic able to argue that there is no conclusive proof of a valid marriage between Edward IV and Eleanor Talbot. Yet what proof could there possibly have been, other than a public acknowledgement of the marriage? In the fifteenth century marriage licences did not exist. In the nineteenth century, as we have seen, James Gairdner, by no means a credulous historian, wrote that there were no grounds for dismissing this marriage as 'mere political invention'.[21]

The marriage remains entirely credible. Moreover, in addition to the explicit written sources, there is also clear circumstantial evidence that it existed, or at least, that some people believed it to exist. Why else, for example, should Elizabeth Woodville herself have later expressed doubts concerning the validity of her own marriage with the king? When the Duke of Clarence appeared to be a threat to her sons, Elizabeth is said to have been particularly anxious because of 'the calumnies with which she was reproached, namely that according to established usage she was not the legitimate wife of the king'.[22]

Moreover (as we have also seen) there was even, ultimately, a public acknowledgement of the marriage, though not by Edward IV, nor in his lifetime.[23] No one, either at the time of that public acknowledgement or later, ever came forward with evidence that the account of the Talbot marriage was a fabrication. No member of the house of York or of Eleanor's own family spoke against the Act of Parliament of 1484. Some readers may consider that during the reign of Richard III this was scarcely surprising. However, the situation changed entirely in 1485. Henry VII would have welcomed evidence undermining the marriage claim. Yet despite the fact that some members of the Talbot family were prominent amongst Henry's supporters, no evidence was forthcoming. In these trying circumstances Henry could only seek to suppress all mention of Eleanor and her relationship with Edward IV.

In making a promise of marriage to Eleanor, Edward may simply have been lying, cynically, in order to get her into bed with him. Indeed, Philippe de Commynes, commenting on these events from a continental perspective, some years later, was of precisely that opinion:

> King Edward had promised to marry [her] ... because he was in love with her, in order to get his own way with her ... and having done so he slept with her; and he made the promise only to deceive her.[24]

However, even if Edward did not really mean what he promised; even if he was deliberately attempting to deceive Eleanor; that is immaterial. By virtue of the words uttered, together with the fact that both parties were free to make such promises, and their subsequent consummation of their union, they were married.

Nor need we assume, with Commynes, that Edward's intentions were nefarious from the outset. It may be that he meant his promise at the time, and only changed his mind later. As we have seen, it is possible that he gave Eleanor estates in Wiltshire.[25] We must remember that Eleanor was an earl's daughter and a lady of royal descent. By birth she was the equal in rank of Edward's own mother, Cecily Neville. She was therefore by no means a non-starter for the *rôle* of queen. She was at least as well born as Elizabeth Woodville, whom Edward subsequently (and bigamously) married – also in secret.

Eleanor's story and that of Elizabeth Woodville have obvious similarities. Both were widows from Lancastrian backgrounds, both were attractive, both were a little older than the king. And in both cases, apparently, Edward's solution was the same. He went through a clandestine form of marriage and initially kept the affair quiet. Only the final outcomes differed.

One key distinction between Eleanor Talbot, (who failed to get the king to honour his contract with her) and Elizabeth Woodville (who succeeded), was the latter's proven fecundity, which Edward is said to have considered a great point in her favour. Although Buck suggested that Edward and Eleanor may have had a son, there is absolutely no evidence to support this contention.[26] In fact, the wording of Richard III's Act of Parliament of 1484 explicitly rules out the possibility that Edward had children by Eleanor (see below, Appendix 1, note 20). It seems unlikely that Eleanor ever conceived by either of her husbands (and her sister, the Duchess of Norfolk, also seems to have had some difficulty in conceiving). Another key difference was Elizabeth Woodville's great determination and strength of character. It is plausible that a third difference may lie in the possibility that Eleanor herself ultimately decided that marriage with Edward was not what she wanted. This possibility will be explored in greater depth shortly.

Let us now briefly look forward in time, to June 1483, when the question of Eleanor's marriage at last became a public issue. In respect of the actions of Richard, Duke of Gloucester at that time, the objection has been raised that he should have referred the dispute in respect of Edward IV's marriage to the church courts. As the present writer has pointed out previously, however, Richard himself was not a party to the marriage dispute, so that his right to bring such a case would probably have been questionable.

Moreover, it is apparent that in instances where some other legal outcome (in Richard's case, the succession to the throne) was contingent upon a disputed marriage, but where the validity of the marriage itself was not the main point at issue, civil courts unhesitatingly passed judgement without referring the marriage dispute to canon law.[27]

Many records do survive of medieval women in Eleanor's situation who successfully sought legal remedy in the church courts to substantiate their married status. For Eleanor, however, such an action was probably never a realistic and practical possibility, given that she would have been challenging her sovereign. Noblewomen 'were at a particular disadvantage when they disagreed or quarrelled with their husbands'.[28] If the man in question also happened to be the king the disadvantage would, of course, have been considerably increased. It is also difficult to see *when* Eleanor might have taken action. For some months, at least, she probably expected Edward to keep faith with her. A further indeterminate period of doubt and confusion may then have followed.

Meanwhile, in the summer of 1461 another and much more immediate matter was preoccupying the minds of the nobility of England. Early in June the Duke of Norfolk and his family set out from Framlingham for Westminster, to attend Edward IV's coronation. The young Earl and Countess Warenne were presumably members of the party,[29] and it is feasible that Countess Warenne's widowed sister, Eleanor, also attended the ceremony. It was the Duchess of Norfolk's brother, Archbishop Bourchier, who set the crown upon Edward's head, while the Duke of Norfolk officiated at the ceremony as earl marshal. After the coronation the Mowbrays returned to Framlingham Castle, although the Duke came up to London again in October, to attend the king at Greenwich Palace. By the end of that month at the latest, however, he was back at Framlingham again, and there, suddenly, on Friday 6 November, he died. It was not quite two months since he had celebrated his 46th birthday. His son and heir, John Mowbray, now fourth Duke of Norfolk, was still a minor, only a few weeks past his 17th birthday. 1461 had brought significant changes: a new king; a new dynasty ruling in England. Now Elizabeth Talbot had assumed the coronet of a duchess. Before the year ended would her sister Eleanor be wearing the queen consort's crown?

13

Disillusion

Whatever part he may have played in the fighting of 1455–61, at the end of 1461 Ralph Butler, Lord Sudeley was summoned to, and attended the first Parliament of the reign of Edward IV. He was by then in his late sixties, and possibly in indifferent health. The loss of his only son and heir had probably been a considerable shock to him. Subsequently, on 26 February 1462 Edward IV granted 'exemption for life of Ralph Botiller, knight, Lord of Sudeley, on account of his debility and age, from personal attendance in council or Parliament, and from being made collector, assessor or taxer of tenths, fifteenths or other subsidies, commissioner, justice of the peace, constable, bailiff or other minister of the king, or trier, arrayer or leader of men-at-arms, archers or hobelers. And he shall not be compelled to leave his dwelling for war'.[1]

When this exemption was granted, Ralph's former daughter-in-law, Eleanor, was probably still intimately involved with the king. Indeed, it may well have been Eleanor who obtained the exemption for Lord Sudeley. She may also have been responsible for the royal grant, three months later, of 'four bucks in summer and six does in winter within the king's park of Woodstock'.[2] It was perhaps also at about this period that Eleanor received her mysterious grant of property in Wiltshire, which may have been a gift from Edward. The case for Eleanor's involvement in Edward IV's grants to Lord Sudeley is strengthened by the fact that, after she withdrew from her intimacy with the king, Ralph's exemption was treated as a dead letter. Lord Sudeley was again appointed to commissions on a regular basis from the end of 1462.[3] Though this may undermine one's perception of the king's kindliness, at the same time it also suggests that at that time he did not mistrust Lord Sudeley's loyalty.

Previously, there have been varying interpretations of the significance of Edward IV's apparently contradictory actions in respect of Lord Sudeley. This offers just one small example of the kind of problems which arise when one tries to explain the events of this period without taking account of Eleanor. Unfortunately, no earlier writer had noted the significance of the fact that Edward's kindliness dated from the period when Ralph's daughter-in-law was the king's partner. Some therefore speculated that the king may simply have been seeking a pretext for removing Ralph from Parliament. However, the *Complete Peerage* refuted this: 'The suggestion that Edward IV was hostile to him is weakened by this exemption, and by a grant in 1462 for life of bucks from Woodstock, and a general pardon for trespasses and debts in 1468'.[4] We shall return later to Lord Sudeley's pardon of 1468, which is incontrovertibly connected with Eleanor.

Edward IV's actions in respect of Lord Sudeley imply that the king's relationship with Eleanor lasted into 1462. While their secret seems to have been very well kept by both parties, and even though Eleanor seems to have very successfully avoided (or been kept out of) the limelight, clearly there were rumours. Only thus can one explain the currency of vague references to a relationship between the king and a relative of the Earl of Warwick which were reported later by both Mancini and Vergil. Nor is it surprising that Eleanor should have been referred to, and later remembered, in this oblique way. Although her dead father had been famous, she herself was a virtually unknown figure in 1461–62. Of her close living relatives the highest in rank was her sister, who had just become Duchess of Norfolk. But, at this time, by far the best-known of Eleanor's living relatives was undoubtedly her uncle, Warwick.

It is possible that it was through Eleanor that Edward met Elizabeth Wayte (Lucy), who was to be Eleanor's immediate successor in his bed. Eleanor's land in Wiltshire was contiguous with a manor belonging to the family of Elizabeth Wayte's stepmother. At the same time, Lucy's figured in the affinity of Lord Sudeley. What part the king's growing interest in Elizabeth Wayte played in the ending of his relationship with Eleanor must remain guesswork. However, since Eleanor herself had been unwilling to accede to an illicit relationship with Edward, she is not likely to have readily condoned such a relationship between the king and another woman, particularly if that woman was married.

Edward and Eleanor were both fourth and fifth cousins once removed, owing to their common descent from Roger Mortimer, first Earl of March (see illustration 11). At an earlier period this would have meant that they should not have married without a papal dispensation. However, at the Fourth Lateran Council in 1215, Pope Innocent III had restricted the impediment of consanguinity to the fourth degree of kinship (third cousins).[5] The fact that no dispensation seems to have been provided for the marriage of Eleanor's maternal grandparents, the Earl and Countess of Warwick, (who were more closely related, and whose alliance *did* fall within the prohibited degrees of kinship) suggests that Eleanor and Edward's families may well have been unaware of their common Mortimer descent. It is doubtful whether a church court would have considered the impediment of consanguinity sufficient to invalidate even the Warwick marriage. In the thirteenth century, for example, when the marriage of Sir Walter de Beauchamp had been called into question because he was related in the fourth degree to his wife, the Bishop of Worcester had 'decreed that their marriage was lawful ... as they were ignorant at the time they contracted the marriage that there was any impediement between them'.[6]

The king certainly never tried to take advantage either of consanguinity or of any other grounds to seek an annulment. To do so would, of course, have required acknowledging the marriage in the first place. While this might conceivably have been a possibility from 1461 until 1463, once Edward had compounded the complexity of the situation by contracting a second secret marriage, any formal acknowledgement of the first was out of the question. He was then committed to a policy of silence. Indeed, in respect of the Talbot marriage Buck asserts, very credibly, that 'he held them not his friends nor good subjects which mentioned it'.[7]

Eleanor, for reasons of her own, also seems to have elected to maintain a dignified silence, at least as far as the world in general was concerned. Being a rather private person, she shunned any publicity, lived in retirement and cultivated religion.[8] How much Elizabeth Talbot knew at this time of the relationship between her sister and the king is uncertain, but later, when Eleanor had been abandoned by Edward, she may have spoken of the affair, both to Elizabeth and to their mother.[9] Elizabeth's subsequent relationship with her sister shows, perhaps, a protective streak which may have arisen out of some sense of responsibility for what had befallen Eleanor. Theirs was a relationship which lasted well beyond the grave, for when Elizabeth was in her fifties, Eleanor (already thirty years dead) was still very much on Elizabeth's mind. This is proved by Elizabeth's touching concern in the 1490s to make an endowment for the good of her sister's soul; an endowment which, by that time, she could not really afford, and for which, in the end, she had to pay by instalments.

But Edward and Eleanor were not the only people who knew of what had passed between them. There was at least one other. Canon Robert Stillington was Keeper of the Privy Seal in 1461, and held a number of ecclesiastical appointments,[10] but he was not yet a bishop. Edward, however, favoured him towards the end of 1461 to the extent of awarding him an annual salary of £365,[11] and it will be instructive at this point to consider the circumstances of Stillington's subsequent appointment as Bishop of Bath and Wells.

As we have already noted, essentially 'Stillington's career is that of a politician rather than that of an ecclesiastic'.[12] Nevertheless, 'bishoprics were frequently used ... to reward officials without depleting the limited supply of crown lands.'[13] Despite this, it is noteworthy that when the see of Carlisle became vacant a few months *before* the Woodville marriage was made public, Stillington was not nominated for that post. Edward IV only seems to have marked Stillington for episcopal preferment from mid-September 1464 – the time when the king's subsequent Woodville 'marriage' was brought into the open (see Chapter 16). Although the Archbishop of York had then recently died,[14] the king had probably already earmarked this appointment for Warwick the Kingmaker's brother, George Neville, Bishop of Exeter. In any case, since Stillington had not previously held a bishopric, the metropolitan see of York would have been a considerable promotion for him.

No English bishoprics fell vacant in the last months of 1464 (though there were vacancies in several Irish sees and one Welsh see). In fact the next English bishopric to fall vacant after the announcement of the Woodville alliance was that of Bath and Wells, which became available following the death of Bishop Thomas Bekynton on 14 January 1465. Royal licence for the election of a successor was issued on 19 February.[15]

It seems evident that Edward IV had been waiting for such a vacancy in the episcopacy in order that he might award it to Stillington. He clearly intended this appointment for Stillington from the outset, for as soon as news of Bishop Bekynton's death reached him he granted Stillington custody of the see's temporalities. It was about four months after the announcement of the Woodville 'marriage' when this grant was made, on 20 January 1465.[16]

When the king's proposed choice was communicated to the Holy See, however, a difficulty arose. During the lifetime of Thomas Bekynton the pontiff had explicitly reserved to the papacy the nomination of the next Bishop of Bath and Wells. Accordingly Pope Paul II now proposed to appoint to this vacant see John Free, a learned English divine, resident in Rome.[17] When the pope was confronted with the king's counter-proposal there must have been a small diplomatic crisis. Delicate negotiations doubtless ensued, though no record of them survives.

Meanwhile the bishopric remained vacant in theory, although in point of fact Robert Stillington was already making appointments in the diocese of Bath and Wells as though his episcopal elevation had already received papal confirmation.[18] The *impasse* was ultimately resolved by the untimely death of the pope's candidate, whereupon Paul II accepted Edward IV's nominee. On 30 October 1465, by the bull *Divina disponente clemencia*, the sovereign pontiff at last formally provided Robert Stillington to the vacant bishopric, and the following day, granted faculty for his episcopal consecration.[19] Thenceforward Robert Stillington was acknowledged as Bishop-elect of Bath and Wells. The following spring he was finally consecrated by George Neville, the new Archbishop of York.

The Woodville 'marriage' was yet another big mistake on Edward's part, because, like the marriage with Eleanor, it was conducted in secret. In canon law as interpreted in England in the fifteenth century, only a subsequent marriage *in facie ecclesiae* (i.e. in public) could have had any effect in the face of Edward's existing contract with Eleanor – and even then only to the extent that the children of the subsequent, public (but still bigamous) marriage could arguably have been regarded as legitimate.[20] The church courts would then have contended that Eleanor or her representatives should have objected to the second marriage when the celebrant asked if anyone knew just cause why it should not proceed. Failure to object at that stage would have meant that the second marriage, albeit bigamous, would have been capable of producing offspring who could be recognised as legitimate. However, since Edward's Woodville marriage had been secret, neither Eleanor nor anyone else had had any opportunity to object to it. The Woodville marriage was therefore invalid and all the offspring of it, bastards.

Although Eleanor did not appeal to the church courts to uphold her marriage, records of appeals made in other, similar cases do exist. One example is the case of Muriel de Dunham against John Burnoth and Joan, his 'wife'.[21] On Monday 21 June 1288 Muriel appeared before the Consistory Court of Canterbury 'seeking to have the marriage between John Burnoth of Chartham and Joan, whom he keeps as his wife, annulled and John and Joan separated and John adjudged her husband because, before John made a marriage contract with Joan, he contracted marriage with Muriel by words *de presenti*'.[22] This case took more than six months, and was prolonged by the contumacy of Joan, the allegedly bigamous wife, who refused to appear in court for four months, despite repeated citings to do so. One can imagine that, had Eleanor brought her case to court, Elizabeth Woodville might well have proved at least equally contumacious. When judgement had finally been delivered in Muriel's favour, John and Joan, who were clearly happy living together, appealed against the decision, and although their appeal was eventually quashed and the court pronounced 'the *de facto* marriage between John and Joan null and void, and … [adjudged] John to Muriel as her husband and Muriel to John as his lawful wife',[23] it is difficult to believe that John and Joan simply accepted this after fighting so hard against it, or that John and Muriel can have lived together thereafter in contented conjugal bliss, whatever the church court may have ruled.

Had Eleanor dared to cite the king of England before the ecclesiastical courts, it is equally difficult to believe that Edward would have passively submitted his matrimonial affairs to public scrutiny, or that (if things had ever been allowed to reach the unimaginable stage of judgement being given against him and in Eleanor's favour) he would simply have accepted this, dutifully parted from Elizabeth Woodville and set up home with Eleanor. Had Eleanor even so much as attempted to bring the case to court she may well have been putting her life in jeopardy. Fighting the case in the church courts was therefore not an option. Eleanor had no realistic alternative but to accept the *fait accompli* and live quietly in retirement, well away from public life.

While she remained silent, Edward IV apparently treated her with consideration, and showed some regard for her wishes. Nevertheless, rather than living alone, on her own manors in Warwickshire, Eleanor preferred East Anglia, and the protection of her sister, the Duchess of Norfolk. Although it was not unusual for a single woman to live in the household of a married relative, Eleanor's choice may suggest that she felt safer in a protected environment.

One other significant factor helps to explain why Eleanor made no attempt to substantiate her marriage through the courts. Indeed, if we can understand it, this factor will perhaps bring us as close as one can now come to understanding something of Eleanor Talbot's character. It concerns her religious beliefs.

14

Corpus Christi

During the 1460s Eleanor Talbot was an active patroness of Corpus Christi College, Cambridge, where, towards the end of 1461 or early in 1462, she endowed a priest-fellowship. It is possible that her interest in the college was in some way inherited, for her uncle, Henry Beauchamp, Duke of Warwick, is also believed to have patronised Corpus Christi, and his arms were displayed in the College Hall.[1] If Eleanor's interest in Corpus Christi College was not, in a sense, hereditary, then the precise motive for her association with the college is unknown, but 'provision for education was … considered a work of charity, and the growth of the universities was fostered … with both women and men acting as patrons'.[2] It is also important to bear in mind that at this period such colleges were essentially religious foundations.

Corpus Christi College was originally established for a master and six fellow-chaplains.[3] In 1460–61 the college was headed by 'that efficient and somewhat dictatorial master',[4] Dr John Botwright, with whom Eleanor must have negotiated her endowment. John Botwright had been born at Swaffham in Norfolk in about 1395, and was thus in his late sixties at the time of his negotiations with Eleanor. He was a man of her father's and her father-in-law's generation, who had been a fellow of the college since 1416-17, and had been elected master on 25 April 1443.[5] Among other benefices, he was rector of his native town, and from 1447 he had also been chaplain to Henry VI.

Throughout the period 1454–59 the college did indeed have six fellows in addition to the master, at least, judging from the library lists which record the loan of college books.[6] On the basis of the same evidence, in 1459–61 the number of fellows fell to five, but in 1461–62 two new fellows joined the college, Cosyn and Shotesham. This increased the number of fellows beyond the statutory six, to a total of seven. Of the two new fellows, it seems certain that Thomas Cosyn (who was a protégé of the Talbot sisters) held a new fellowship, endowed by Eleanor. His history is examined in greater detail below.

The other college fellows at the time of Eleanor's endowment were Robert Baker, Richard Brocher, Robert Fuller, Ralph Geyton, Thurstan Heton, and Robert Shotesham.[7] Baker was born about 1420, and had become a fellow in 1445. Brocher, perhaps a few years younger, was admitted in 1452. Fuller and Geyton were probably about the same age as Richard Brocher. Fuller obtained his fellowship in 1454–55, having studied abroad. Geyton had entered Corpus Christi in 1452. Heton was educated at Eton. He must have been among its first students. He was probably of about the same age as Robert Baker, and became a fellow of Corpus Christi in 1445. Shotesham, probably the youngest of the fellows, had first come to the college as a bible clerk. He obtained his fellowship only in 1461. The master and the fellows were not the only college residents at this time. Thomas Fisher, for example, who had been a fellow of Corpus Christi from 1437 to 1451, was again in residence at the college at the time of Eleanor's endowment, despite having resigned his fellowship.[8]

No document relating to Eleanor's original endowment at the college is now extant. The surviving accounts for the 1460s are somewhat fragmentary, but in this case there is probably a specific reason why Eleanor's indentures were not preserved, which we shall consider shortly. Nevertheless, it is clear from later references to Eleanor as a benefactress of the college, and from the fact that the new priest-fellowship was consistently and specifically designated as being *ex fundatione Helionore Butler*,[9] that the endowment was Eleanor's initiative.

There is possible further evidence of Eleanor's patronage of the college in a letter, which refers to an unnamed 'gracious Ladi ... our most bountous Lady' who was financing building work at the college. It is possible that this refers to Eleanor.[10] What survives is not the actual letter, which was dispatched to an unnamed recipient who might possibly have been Sir John Howard, but a draft or a duplicate 'file copy' of it in Dr Botwright's own handwriting.[11] This is now bound as part of his *Liber Albus*. The letter is dated 2 August but no year date is given.

The letter mentions a gentleman called Cotton who has been acting as a go-between. This surname does not figure in the surviving affinity lists of the Mowbray Dukes and duchesses of Norfolk,[12] which may tend to suggest that the lady referred to is not Elizabeth Talbot, Duchess of Norfolk (despite the use of the title 'Highness'). Sir John Howard did, however, have a gentleman with this surname in his entourage during the 1460s.[13]

John Botwright was master of Corpus Christi College from 1443 to 1474. However, mention in the letter of master Thomas Cosyn, who only became a fellow of the college in 1462, indicates that it must have been written between 1462 and 1474, while the implication that Cosyn was still a young man suggests a date in the 1460s.[14]

Thomas Cosyn's birth is not recorded, but probably occurred in about 1440, making him a member of the same generation as his patronesses, Eleanor and Elizabeth Talbot. He came from Norfolk, and his family (like Corpus Christi College itself) probably had historic connections with Eleanor's family, for her grandfather, Richard Beauchamp, Earl of Warwick, had presented a Simon Cosyn to the living of 'Bichemwell All Saints' in Norfolk in 1435, which living Simon exchanged for that of North Elmham in 1449.[15] It may also be that Canon John Cosyn, Augustinian Canon Regular (and from 1467, Prior) at Great Massingham Priory, Norfolk, was another member of the same family, for Prior John Cosyn was in residence at Corpus Christi College in 1470.[16]

Nothing is known of Thomas Cosyn's early education, but he gained his MA in 1460–61, and in 1462 he became a fellow of Corpus Christi College. As we have seen, his admission increased the number of the college fellows by one, and it seems certain that his appointment was to the new fellowship endowed by Eleanor. It is likely that his duties initially included keeping the obits of the first Earl of Shrewsbury, and of Sir Thomas Butler and his mother. Doubtless he was also required to pray for the good estate of Eleanor herself, of her mother, the dowager Countess of Shrewsbury, and of Lord and Lady Sudeley, during their respective lifetimes, with provision for these prayers to be transformed into additional anniversary commemorations after their demise. It is possible that Eleanor's brother, Lord Lisle, was also included in the endowment from its inception, although if so, it is, perhaps, a little strange that her other brother, Sir Louis Talbot (who had died four years earlier, in 1458), was not also mentioned.

In addition to his college post, from 1468 to 1490 Thomas Cosyn was appointed to a series of East Anglian livings which he held in plurality. In

1487, he was elected master of Corpus Christi, despite the fact that he was not, at the time, the most senior fellow. His elevation was almost certainly on the strength of the patronage of the Duchess of Norfolk, who was funding building work at the college in the 1480s, and whose chaplain he then was. Cosyn was later named as one of the executors of the Duchess of Norfolk's will (1506) so his association with the affairs of the Talbot sisters was a long one.

From the moment of his arrival at Corpus Christi he seems to have been accorded extraordinary privileges and prominence. He was 'apparently given the master's quota of borrowable books as soon as he arrived', being listed in the Markaunt Register for 1462 next after the master of the College, despite the fact that he was then the most junior fellow.[17] Thomas Cosyn's particular prominence in the Corpus Christi records in 1468, the year of Eleanor's death (when he again figures prominently in the Markaunt Register), may perhaps confirm that he was then serving as her priest under the terms of her endowment.

However, it is probable that in 1487 Eleanor's new fellowship effectively lapsed (remaining in abeyance until it was revived by her sister in March 1496). This would have been as a direct result of Thomas Cosyn's promotion. When Cosyn was elected as master of the College in October 1487, apparently no one was nominated to replace him in his tenure of Eleanor's fellowship. For a time this irregularity seems to have escaped the attention of the Duchess of Norfolk, but in 1496, she took notice, and decided to remedy the situation. Elizabeth Talbot's extension and confirmation of Eleanor's original endowment, which post-dates the latter by about thirty-five years, took the form of a new agreement with the master and fellows, thus superseding Eleanor's original indentures. It was probably as a consequence of this that Eleanor's redundant original documents were discarded.

Thomas Cosyn must have known Eleanor well, and he appears to have held her in particular esteem. Many years after her death, in 1496, in the Corpus Christi College agreement concluded with her sister, Elizabeth, he recalled Eleanor in warm terms, referring to her sincere religious faith and to the close and friendly relationship which had existed between her and the college.

Dr Cosyn also applied to his erstwhile patroness, the word 'renowned'. It is difficult to conceive of anything which would have justified the use of this adjective during Eleanor's lifetime, when she seems generally to have

1. Goodrich Castle, Herefordshire, where Eleanor spent part of her childhood.

2. The site of the Talbots' manor house at Blakemere, where Eleanor may have been born.

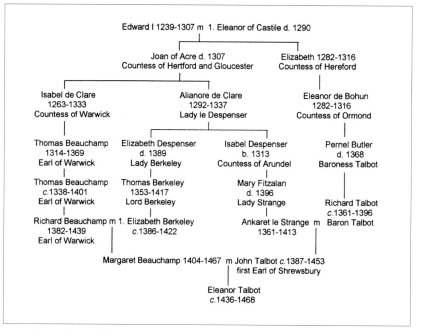

Above: 5. Eleanor Talbot's descent from Edward I and Eleanor of Castile.

Below: 6. The two Talbot families.

Maud Neville (1) m	John Talbot Lord Talbot & Furnival Earl of Shrewsbury	m (2) Margaret Beauchamp
John Talbot II, 2nd Earl of Shrewsbury Sir Christopher Talbot Joan Talbot		John Talbot III, Lord Lisle Sir Louis Talbot Sir Humphrey Talbot Eleanor Talbot Elizabeth Talbot

Opposite above: 3. Sudeley Castle, Gloucestershire, home of Lord Sudeley. Eleanor lived here in the early years of her first marriage.

Opposite below: 4. Framlingham Castle, Suffolk, from the site of the Duchess of Norfolk's private garden. Elizabeth Talbot and her ladies would cross the moat by means of a vanished wooden bridge supported on the stone piers in the foreground.

Above left: 7. Eleanor's mother, Margaret Beauchamp, Countess of Shrewsbury: a determined lady, but her children were devoted to her.

Above right: 8. Eleanor's aunt, Anne Beauchamp, Countess of Warwick: wife of the 'Kingmaker', and mother of Richard III's queen.

Above left: 9. Eleanor's aunt, Eleanor Beauchamp, Duchess of Somerset, who was perhaps also her godmother.

Above right: 10. Eleanor's uncle, Edmund Beaufort, Duke of Somerset. The Beaufort connection was dangerous in Yorkist England, but was always acknowledged.

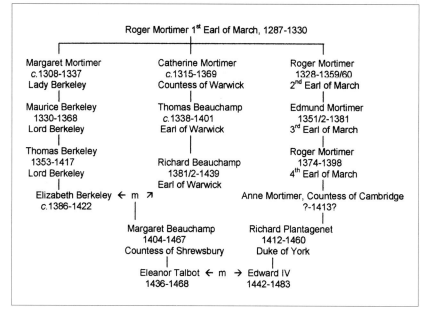

11. The Mortimer descent of Edward IV and Eleanor Talbot.

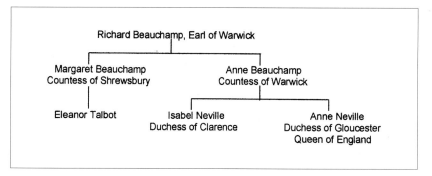

12. Eleanor's relationship to the wives of Edward IV's brothers.

Above left: 13. Eleanor's father, John Talbot, first Earl of Shrewsbury, was a great national hero – the 'Sir Winston Churchill' of his day.

Above right: 14. Eleanor's sister, Elizabeth Talbot, Duchess of Norfolk, was also her greatest friend and protector.

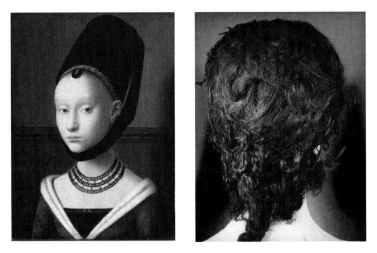

Above left: 15. Eleanor's niece, Elizabeth Talbot, Viscountess Lisle. This portrait, probably painted in Flanders during Margaret of York's marriage celebrations, may suggest the possible appearance of Eleanor herself at the age of about sixteen.

Above right: 16. Hair of Eleanor's niece, Lady Anne Mowbray. The colour is genuine, but was probably darker in life. Eleanor's mother had fair hair, but Eleanor herself, like most of her family, was probably a brunette.

```
              Joan, heiress of Sudeley m William le Botiler
                                |
                 Thomas Butler 1355-1398 Lord of Sudeley
                                |
   ┌──────────────┬──────────────┴──────────────┬──────────────┐
Two daughters    John Butler          William Butler      Ralph Butler
 See Fig. 19     c.1381-1410          c.1383-1417          1389-1473
     ↓           Lord of Sudeley      Lord of Sudeley      Baron Sudeley
                    d.s.p.               d.s.p.                 |
                                                          Sir Thomas Butler
                                                            c.1421-1459
```

17. The descent of the lordship of Sudeley.

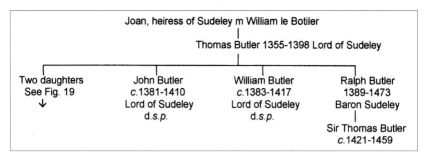

18. The family of Elizabeth Norbury, Lady Sudeley.

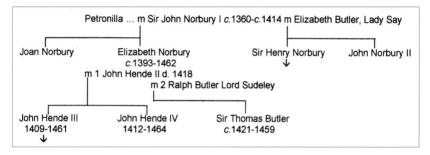

19. Sir Thomas Butler's cousins.

Above left: 20. The tower of Burton Dassett Church. Eleanor and her first husband, Thomas, lived in the nearby manor house.

Above right: 21. The Old Court, Corpus Christi College, Cambridge. Building in this courtyard was financed by Eleanor and her sister.

Left: 22. The great west doorway of the Carmelite Priory Church, Norwich, now re-erected in the Norwich Magistrates' Court. Eleanor's coffin must have passed beneath this archway.

Right: 23. Eleanor's hearse, displaying her arms as Lady Butler, at the office of Lauds for the Dead, celebrated for her at Norwich Cathedral, 1999.

Below: 24. The conjoined arms of Eleanor's parents, from the tomb of her grandfather, Beauchamp Chapel, Warwick.

25. The seal of Eleanor's father-in-law, Ralph Butler, Lord Sudeley. (*Warwickshire County Record Office, L1/82.*)

26. Impression of the signet ring used as a seal by Eleanor when married to Thomas Butler. The ring bore her mother's emblem: the daisy, or marguerite. (*Warwickshire County Record Office, L1/81.*)

Above left: 27. Eleanor's
memorial plaque at the
Norwich Whitefriars site,
with her arms as Lady
Butler

Above right: 28. The young
Edward IV in about 1461.

Right: 29. Eleanor in about
1462? A reconstruction
based on the skull of CFII,
and portraits of Eleanor's
close relatives. (*Watercolour
and gouache by Mark
Satchwill.*)

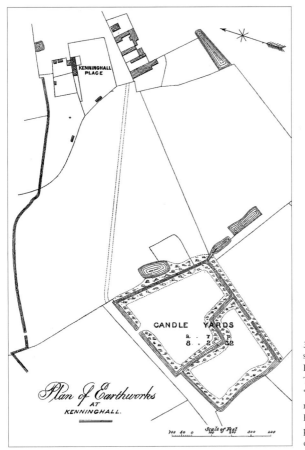

30. Plan of the site of East Hall, Kenninghall, Norfolk. The site marked 'Candle Yards' is the moated site of East Hall, whose three fish ponds survive to the east of the moat.

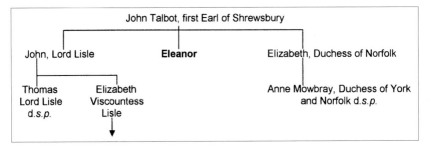

31. Eleanor's heirs (simplified).

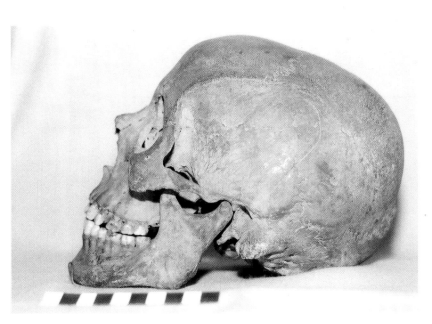

32. Eleanor? The skull of CFII, Castle Museum, Norwich. (Remains of a medieval noblewoman found at the Whitefriars site in Norwich in 1958.)

33. The ruins of the Norwich Carmel *in situ*. This archway led to an anchorite's cell.

34. The Guild Hall, Henley-in-Arden. Eleanor's inquisition post mortem was probably held here.

35. Tomb effigy of Eleanor's niece, Viscountess Lisle (died 1487). Eleanor's tomb in Norwich may have borne a similar effigy.

36. The ancient icon of Our Lady of Mount Carmel at the fourteenth-century church of *San Niccolò al Carmine*, Siena. According to tradition, the early Carmelites brought it with them from the Holy Land when they fled to Europe.

37. Eleanor's signet depicting this icon. Her ring became stuck in the hot wax. Dragging it out blurred the image of the Christ child. (*Warwickshire County Record Office, L1/86.*)

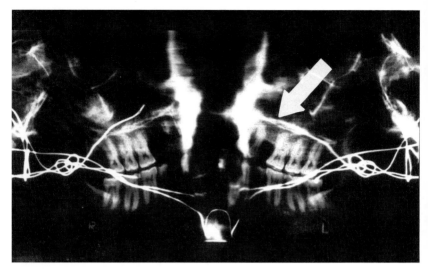

38. Evidence of congenitally missing Talbot teeth? Dental X-ray of the skull of CFII (Eleanor?). The arrow indicates the possible congenital absence of an upper left premolar.

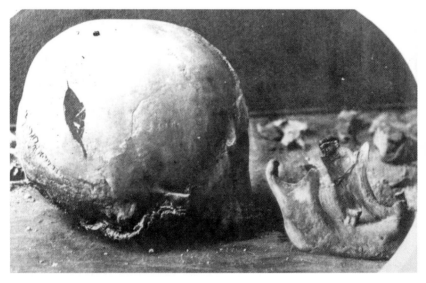

39. The skull of Eleanor's father, John Talbot, Earl of Shrewsbury, showing the wound which killed him. The earl's body was identified on the battlefield by his missing back tooth.

lived very quietly, shunning publicity. However, his description dates from 1496 and perhaps recalls the period in 1483–84, when the *titulus regius* of Richard III had made Eleanor's name much more widely known, both in England and abroad, than it had ever been while she was alive.

Eleanor's pious endowment at Corpus Christi College was not the only indication of her developing interest in works of charity and religion in the early 1460s. At about the same time as her foundation in Cambridge, she also associated herself with a religious house in Norwich. It is quite likely that other works of charity were also undertaken by Eleanor at this period, details of which have either not survived, or not yet been brought to light. Her association with the Carmelite friars in Norwich, however, was to develop into a serious commitment on Eleanor's part, and one which was to have quite a considerable impact on her lifestyle. Precisely how Eleanor's relationship with the Norwich Carmel began is unknown. However, it may be connected in some way with the fact that she had now taken up residence in Norfolk, probably in the village of Kenninghall.

Mount Carmel

East Hall, a mile or two to the east of Kenninghall, was a large, moated property, trapezoid in plan, with a bridge across its moat located on the longest, north-western side. Natural springs on the north-eastern side fed both the moat and a series of three fish ponds. The enclosure within the moat was of ample dimensions. The longest (north-western) side measured some 444ft in length, while the shortest (south-western) side was about 225ft.[1] The dwelling, being defended by a moat, was almost certainly also crenellated, and if it survived today, we should probably be inclined to call it a castle.

In reality, like the Talbot and Lestrange family home at Blakemere, which Eleanor had known in her childhood, it was actually a fortified manor house rather than a true castle. East Hall, however, was a good deal larger than Blakemere. It was of flint construction, as was common with stone buildings in this part of the country, and the flints which once composed its walls still liberally sprinkle the ground upon its now devastated and empty site. Only the outline of the moat – not so deep, today, as it once was, and filled with bushes and small trees – now defines the site, for the house was destroyed in the sixteenth century by the third Howard Duke of Norfolk when he built a new residence, Kenninghall Place, a short distance to the east of the old site.[2]

East Hall probably dated from the thirteenth century. The first recorded mention of it occurs in 1276, when the manor of Kenninghall was held by the d'Aubigny family. In 1282 both manor and hall had passed by dowry to the Fitzalans. Just over 100 years later, Richard II confiscated Kenninghall from Richard Fitzalan, Earl of Arundel, and granted it to Thomas Mowbray, first Duke of Norfolk.

When Thomas became the second husband of the Earl of Arundel's daughter, Elizabeth, he gave her East Hall as her dower house.[3] Elizabeth Fitzalan was a long-lived lady. 'She or her husbands held Kenninghall until her death in 1426 when it reverted to the Montagus. The Nevills, who inherited the manor with the Hundred of Guiltcross two years later, returned them once again as a marriage portion to the Fitzalans', when Joan Neville married William Fitzalan, ninth Earl of Arundel.[4] In or soon after 1450, William sold Kenninghall back to the Mowbrays as part of the jointure to be settled on Elizabeth Talbot at the time of her marriage to the third Duke of Norfolk's son and heir.[5]

Visitors to East Hall in the 1460s would have ridden from the triangular square at the centre of Kenninghall, where the road from Thetford to Norwich passes through the middle of the village, up Church Street, passing the parish church on the left. They would have left the route of the modern road where it bends right towards the village of Fersfield, to continue up what is now a private road. This led to the flint-built outer walls fringing the inner edge of the moat. Crossing the latter by means of what was probably originally a drawbridge, one would have passed through the gatehouse into the large courtyard, containing stables, kennels, garderobes, a kitchen block and the main residential quarters, centred on a great hall with an adjacent solar block which contained more private family rooms, and a chapel.

There is clear evidence that Elizabeth Talbot lived at East Hall, for she left her mark on Kenninghall Church, reglazing the east window with Talbot and Mowbray heraldry, surrounding a huge white *rose-en-soleil*, emblem of the house of York. Some of this glass survived until the 1780s although all is now gone.[6] Elizabeth also rebuilt the church tower which she likewise bedecked with the arms of her own and her husband's families.[7] The remains of her east window were removed early in the nineteenth century, and the shields at the base of her tower are now blank, but high up on its south western buttress can still be seen a carved Talbot hound, and on the south eastern buttress is a lion, emblem of both the Talbots and the Mowbrays. Curiously this lion, which should by rights face towards the left, is actually reversed, and faces to the right. This heraldic puzzle is perhaps to be explained by the fact that the lion, high up on the church tower, thus faces across the fields of Kenninghall, gazing towards the moated site of East Hall in the distance.

Elizabeth's residence at the hall, and her work on the church probably date from the 1470s and 80s, when she was a widow. In the 1460s, however, it seems likely that the house was occupied by her sister, Eleanor, who probably also died there.[8] During this period of her life, Eleanor's character was developing in very particular ways, and it is important to attempt to understand what was happening to her. Eleanor's religious beliefs must have been formed initially in childhood, the germs being inculcated by her mother, Lady Shrewsbury. Her faith was probably never superficial, though there is reason to believe that it grew deeper with the passage of time. All Eleanor's siblings seemed to have shared a real and lively religious faith. This is evidenced in different ways by the wills of Sir Louis and Sir Humphrey Talbot, and by the lifestyle chosen by the dowager Duchess of Norfolk in her declining years.

Probably for Eleanor (as, much later, for the nineteenth century Carmelite, St Thérèse of Lisieux) 'the family into which she was born was deeply imbued with a spirituality of … good works and merit [and] … a standard of behaviour befitting the devout christian was scrupulously adhered to'.[9] A picture thus emerges of a girl brought up with a degree of religious commitment that went deeper than the average, and with a clear sense of right and wrong. Eleanor's father is reputed to have 'had an inborn sense of justice and fair play'.[10] Incidentally, it would, of course, be naïve to imagine that any of this assures freedom from sin, particularly the sins of the flesh. Eleanor's religious beliefs certainly do not guarantee that she could not possibly have consented to be Edward IV's mistress. Rather, it is the surviving sources which tell us that she would not consent to this, for they explicitly state that it was Eleanor's refusal which caused Edward IV to agree to a marriage.

Early in the 1460s, and for reasons which we cannot discern, Eleanor's religious faith seems to have grown more profound. This may have been either a gradual development, or more in the nature of a *coup de foudre*. In general terms, this development in a spiritual direction was ultimately shared by her sister, the Duchess of Norfolk, and the principal surviving source stressing Eleanor's religious motivation is her sister's indenture of 1495 with Corpus Christi College, Cambridge.[11]

After her husband's death the Duchess of Norfolk chose to further her own spiritual life mainly under the guidance of the Franciscan order and of her friend Anne Montgomery (cousin by marriage of Sir Thomas Butler). Together with Anne Montgomery and a small circle of other ladies, the duchess eventually formed a spiritual community associated with the prestigious Abbey of the Poor Clares ('the Minories') at Aldgate.[12] Eleanor, on the other hand, seems to have elected to pursue her religious development under Carmelite guidance. Evidence for this is supplied by Eleanor's seals, by the possible negotiations conducted on her behalf with the Whitefriars, and by her eventual burial at the Norwich Carmel. In the case of the Duchess of Norfolk her degree of spiritual commitment was ultimately to be profound, and there is no reason to doubt that this was also true in the case of Eleanor. It will scarcely be possible, therefore, to understand the person Eleanor was to become in the last five years of her life, without taking account of this development.

As we have seen, when she was married to Thomas Butler, Eleanor had sealed her documents using a signet ring possibly given to her by her mother. The bezel of this ring bore the impression of a daisy, the Countess of Shrewsbury's name-flower.[13] Later, as a widow, Eleanor acquired new signets. One of these was a ring with the bezel in the form of an elongated trapezium, somewhat irregularly shaped, and wider towards the top.[14] The design engraved on this is at first difficult to interpret. It appears to represent a piece of cloth. On the lower part of the bezel a rectangular area is clearly marked with a criss-cross design indicating woven fabric. A larger, bunched shape towards the top of the design, while somewhat worn in the surviving seal impression, appears to bear the same criss-cross pattern. In the centre (between the two areas representing fabric) there is a pointed oval shape, resembling an eye or a mouth. It seems that what is intended is a representation of the Carmelite brown scapular, the rectangular length of cloth, with a hole in the middle through which the head and neck pass, which is worn by members of the order, hanging down over the wearer's chest and back, as part of their religious habit.

Carmelite friars wear a brown habit and over this, on formal occasions, the white choir cope which gives the order its nickname of 'Whitefriars'. They also wear, over the habit and beneath the choir cope, a brown scapular. This is a special token of the Carmelite order, believed to have been delivered by the Blessed Virgin (Our Lady of Mount Carmel) to the Carmelite saint, Simon Stock, in a vision. When Pope Nicholas V established the second and third orders (Carmelite nuns and tertiaries) he extended to them the wearing of the brown scapular. As a lay member of the order (tertiary) Eleanor would have been required to wear the scapular, even if only in symbolic form. Wearing a representation of a scapular on the bezel of her signet ring would have been one means of fulfilling this obligation.

On Eleanor's seal impression the lower rectangular area of fabric represents that portion of the garment which hangs down in front, over the wearer's chest, while the larger bunched portion towards the top of the design is the part of the garment which covers the wearer's back. The eye-shaped gap in the centre would be the hole to accommodate the wearer's head and neck. It seems indicative of Eleanor's devotion that she should have chosen to represent this simple garment on one of her seal rings.

Eleanor also had a further seal ring. Only one impression of this appears to survive, and it is imperfect, for the signet ring was evidently dragged slightly to the right as it was extracted from the wax, thus blurring the impression, which now appears somewhat oval in shape.[15] The matrix was, nevertheless, probably circular, or nearly so. It depicted the bust of a woman, veiled, and facing three-quarters right. This probably represents the Virgin Mary, holding the Christ child on her left arm (though the child's image is very blurred). In fact this signet appears specifically to depict the ancient icon of Our Lady of Mount Carmel, brought from the Holy Land when the Carmelite hermits fled before the tide of Islam, and now preserved at the church of *San Niccolò al Carmine*, Siena (see illustrations).

The meagre surviving documentary evidence suggests that it was probably in March 1463 that Eleanor became a tertiary, associated with the Carmelite Priory in Norwich, her commitment to the Carmel being apparently negotiated on her behalf by her brother-in-law, the Duke of Norfolk, through the intermediary of his cousin, Sir John Howard.[16] As a key member of the Mowbray affinity, there is no doubt that John Howard was well acquainted with members of the Talbot family. Elizabeth Talbot, Duchess of Norfolk, is mentioned on several occasions in Howard's accounts.[17] He lent money to her, bought and sold horses and wine on her behalf, and had the loan of her minstrels. Later he was associated with her in projects such as the rebuilding of Long Melford Church in Suffolk. Howard also knew Elizabeth's only surviving brother, Sir Humphrey Talbot, and her nephew, Thomas Talbot, Viscount Lisle, to both of whom, in May 1465, he delivered gifts from the Duke of Norfolk in the form of valuable crimson cloth, the livery colour of the Mowbray Dukes.[18]

Given these contacts, it is not surprising that Sir John Howard should also have had connections with the Duchess of Norfolk's sister, Eleanor, particularly since the latter seems to have become permanently resident in East Anglia. Howard may, indeed, have known a very great deal about Eleanor's affairs. We have seen already that he was Edward IV's host in Suffolk when the latter was still Earl of March, in the summer of 1460, and that he may have been Dr John Botwright's correspondent in the matter of Eleanor's patronage of Corpus Christi College, Cambridge.[19]

On 23 March 1463, Howard paid Thomas Yonge, sergeant at law, 13s 4d 'for his two days labour at the White Friars for my Lord's matter'.[20] The editor of the Howard accounts assumed that this was a reference to the Carmelite Priory in London. This may indeed be the case, although there is no justification in the text for such an assumption. It is true that both Howard and the Duke of Norfolk seem to have been in London at about this time, but there is nothing to indicate where the lawyer, Thomas Yonge, had been, while carrying out his errand, and his messages could equally well have been delivered to the Norwich Carmel.

Whichever priory was Yonge's destination, it seems likely that the business which Howard was conducting with the Whitefriars on the Duke and Duchess of Norfolk's behalf, was connected with Eleanor's oblation. A few months later, in July 1463, Sir John Howard was again acting as an intermediary for the Duke of Norfolk. On this occasion he paid John Davy 16d 'to ride on my Lord's errand to Kenehale [Kenninghall]'.[21] While the Whitefriars' errand may or may not have been to the priory in Norwich, in this case there is no doubt regarding the destination of the messenger. Given Eleanor's probable residence at Kenninghall at this time, it is not fanciful to suggest that the Duke of Norfolk's message on this occasion was addressed to his sister-in-law, and may once again have been connected with the ongoing negotiations in respect of Eleanor's oblation to the Carmelites.

Eleanor's involvement with the Carmelite order may have arisen in some way out of her residence at East Hall, for the village of Kenninghall had apparently already produced two noted Carmelites, the late John Kenyngale, former chaplain to Edward IV's parents, prior of the White Friars in Norwich and Father Provincial of the Carmelite order in England until his death in 1451, and Peter Keningall, prior of the Carmelite Priory in Oxford and noted preacher.[22] This suggests that a Carmelite presence had already, in some way, made itself felt in Kenninghall before Eleanor arrived there. It is also possible that Eleanor had met Prior Peter before she came to East Anglia, either during her own residence in Warwickshire, or through her stepmother-in-law, the second Lady Sudeley, whose previous home, at Minster Lovell Hall, was not far from Oxford.

The master of Corpus Christi College, Cambridge, Eleanor's friend and protégé, Dr Thomas Cosyn, would later describe her as *Deo devota* ('vowed to God').[23] Nevertheless, Eleanor never 'entered religion' in the sense of becoming a nun. It is essential to state this unequivocally because there is a widespread popular misconception on the subject, which seems to have become particularly firmly embedded in historical novels. However, 'the number of laywomen living a life of religious devotion and piety in the later Middle Ages blurred the distinction between the lay and religious worlds',[24] and there were various alternative options available to fifteenth-century English women who wished to be 'vowed to God'. The term 'vowess' which became established in the late fifteenth century, describes the vocation of laywomen – often (though not invariably) widows – who adopted a way of life which contained elements of both the religious and the lay state. For such women:

> the significant vow was one of perpetual chastity. Like nuns, vowesses were clothed and veiled at an episcopal ceremony; unlike nuns, these women did not promise either poverty or obedience. Indeed their state remained formally a lay one, with physical freedom to come and go, and economic freedom to dispose what were sometimes considerable holdings of land or goods. The vow did not imply a rule of life, like that of a third order, and no particular spiritual regimen was specified.[25]

There was an established ceremony for becoming a vowess, which is preserved in several pontificals. The ceremony took place before the reading of the gospel at mass. The vow was made to the local bishop, who presided from his throne or chair, received the written vow, and blessed, clothed and veiled the woman, giving her a ring. The making of the vow was recorded in his episcopal register.[26] The motivation of vowesses was varied, and not always exclusively religious. Some vowesses made their vows in obedience to the terms of their late husbands' wills, and in many cases economics and social and legal status seem to have been significant factors in their decision-making process. In the case of Eleanor's religious oblation, however, religious motives seem to have been a serious consideration. Both the words of her friend, Cosyn, and the design of her seals imply a serious religious commitment.

But Eleanor did not become a vowess. The episcopal register of Bishop Walter Lyhart of Norwich is unpublished. The original, which is in a rather decrepit state, is not easy of access, and the available microfilm version is of poor quality and difficult to read for some folios. However, an examination of both the microfilm and the original register has revealed no record of Eleanor's profession as a vowess before Bishop Lyhart,[27] though the bishop, a Lancastrian by inclination,[28] would doubtless have been intrigued by Eleanor's story had she chosen to reveal it to him.

As we have already seen, there is evidence which suggests that Eleanor's association was specifically with the Carmelite order. This, of course, makes it certain that she remained a laywoman, since there were no nuns of the Carmelite order in England in the fifteenth century. The Carmelites did, however, have an established third order. That fact, together with the evidence of Eleanor's seals, and the possible evidence of negotiations undertaken with the Whitefriars on her behalf suggests that Eleanor became not a vowess but a Carmelite tertiary. Her profession as a tertiary would have been recorded not in the episcopal register but in the records of the Norwich Carmel, which are not extant. It would have been made to Prior Richard Water, the superior of the Norwich house,[29] or possibly (if he were on hand) to the provincial of the Carmelite order in England.

The only reference to the Norwich Carmel in Bishop Lyhart's register for the 1460s appears to be a record of the appointment of 'Andrew Fysshman of the order of Carmelite friars of Norwich' to the living of Beston juxta Norwich as vicar, in February 1461/2.[30] But while the appointment of a Carmelite friar to a living within his diocese was a matter for the bishop, in respect of its internal affairs a religious order would certainly have kept its own records, and the profession of a tertiary would have fallen within this category.

As Erler has stated (above) joining a third order was distinct in certain essentials from the way of life adopted by most vowesses. Being a tertiary implied both a rule of life and religious obedience. As a tertiary, Eleanor would have been committed to the recitation of the Divine Office according to the Carmelite usage. Following an earlier Carmelite tradition which is examined in more detail below, it is possible that she may also have volunteered (or been required) to dwell in a fixed abode agreed with the prior to whom she had made her oblation.

The Carmelite order had been founded in the twelfth century, in the Holy Land, when, in the wake of the Crusades, a group of Christian hermits settled on Mount Carmel, near the 'fountain of Elijah'. These men (and at that period the members of the order were all males) sought to live as contemplatives. When Moslem victories forced them to leave, they settled in Western Europe, establishing convents, but the aspiration towards the contemplative life remained.[31]

Until the fifteenth century there were no Carmelite nuns. Women could, nevertheless, be associated with the order in several ways, all without ceasing to be members of the laity. The details of such a connection prior to the fifteenth century are somewhat complex, but there were basically three possible levels of association: as a benefactress (or confraternity member), as an oblate (or *manumissa*[32]) and as a *conversa*. A benefactress supported the order financially, and in return received 'letters of affiliation', but she took no vows of any kind. An oblate (*manumissa*) took a vow of poverty, chastity and obedience, but no specific vows to the rule of the order. A *conversa* took solemn vows to the prior of the Carmelite house where she made her oblation, and became subject to the religious vow of *stabilitas*: residence in a fixed abode assigned to her by the prior.[33] In other words 'the degree of affiliation varied. *Conversæ* consecrated themselves to God through the three vows, like the friars themselves. Oblates (*manumissae*) also took at least one of the Vows. Confraternity members participated in the spiritual benefits of the Order and in exchange conferred some material benefice on the Order'.[34] *Conversæ* were usually unmarried women or widows, but they could be married. In May 1343, for example, in Florence, Salvino degli Armati and his wife Bartolomea simultaneously became oblates of the Carmelite order, he as a *converso*, she as a *conversa*.[35]

However, the 1460s – the time at which Eleanor formally associated herself with the Carmelites – marked a period of transition for the order. In October 1452 Pope Nicholas V (who, a year or so earlier, had received Eleanor's father during his visit to Rome) issued the bull *Cum nulla*, establishing the second and third orders of the Carmelites. The 'first order', of course, comprised the friars. The new 'second order' was for Carmelite nuns, while the 'third order' (members of which are called 'tertiaries') represented a formalised system of association for those lay people who wished to join the Carmelites without giving up their lay status.

The changes introduced by Pope Nicholas filtered their way across Europe gradually over the next fifty years or so. As a result, it is difficult to know precisely under what circumstances Eleanor formed her association with the Carmelites. What is beyond question, however, is that in the fifteenth century there were no Carmelite nuns in England, for the second order was not to reach this country before Henry VIII's break with Rome.[36] In fact, it appears that the second order spread somewhat slowly in Europe as a whole. Thus, while the Carmelite monastery of the Incarnation at Avila in Spain (where the future St Teresa would assume the habit of a Carmelite nun in 1536) had been founded as early as 1479, its foundation was initially 'as a hospice for pious ladies who wished to live as Carmelites'. It only formally became a monastery of the second order in 1515 (the year of St Teresa's birth).[37]

The implementation of the new rule for lay oblates may also have proceeded rather slowly. Thus, while it is to be presumed that in general terms Eleanor became a member of the third order as established by Nicholas V – and her apparent use of the scapular implies this – nevertheless, her association with the Carmelites may have retained features of the earlier system. It is possible, for example, that she started out as a benefactress, or confraternity member. But Dr Cosyn's characterisation of his friend and patroness as *Deo devota* clearly implies that she progressed beyond this level, and took vows of some kind. There are also indications that the rule of *stabilitas*, which had applied to Carmelite *conversae*, may have influenced her subsequent way of life, since she seems to have fixed her place of residence in the vicinity of Norwich, and probably at Kenninghall. Profession as a tertiary was and is open to married people. Eleanor's association with the Carmelites would, therefore, have been entirely compatible with the married state. Indeed, the fact that she chose this specific kind of religious life rather than opting to enter the monastery or convent of some other order could perhaps be seen as implicit evidence that she was not able to become a nun because she had a living husband.[38]

In its origin (and also as later reformed, in the sixteenth century, by St Teresa of Avila and St John of the Cross) the ethos of the Carmelite order comprises a contemplative and mystical element. It is difficult to know precisely to what extent this aspect of the order may have impinged upon Eleanor, but while the Middle Ages saw this element of the Carmelite way often subverted and submerged, it was never entirely lost to sight, and successive priors-general repeatedly attempted 'to restore something of its original spirit to the order'.[39]

Probably Eleanor's interest in the Carmelites arose initially as a response to their long-standing tradition of devotion to the Blessed Virgin. 'This promise of the special protection of Mary, together with the indulgences associated with the wearing of the scapular, would [probably] have outweighed any other motives for electing to become associated with [the Carmelites]'.[40] At the same time, however, contemplative Christianity undoubtedly flourished in late medieval England. 'Women saints and mystics proliferated in the thirteenth and fourteenth centuries … [and] on the whole [they] did not come from the lower orders of society'.[41]

Richard Rolle, Walter Hilton, the anonymous author of *The Cloud of Unknowing*, and Julian of Norwich all lived and wrote in England in the late fourteenth century. Their works of spiritual guidance may have been accessible to Eleanor. The author of *The Cloud*, who may well have been a friar (possibly even a Carmelite), gave the following advice to those seeking to follow the path of contemplation; words which Eleanor might have read:

> Go on, I beg you, with all speed. Look forward, not backward. See what you still lack, not what you have already; for that is the quickest way of getting and keeping humility. Your whole life must now be one of longing, if you are to achieve perfection. And this longing must be in the depths of your will, put there by God with your consent. But a word of warning: he is a jealous lover, and will brook no rival; he will not work in your will if he has not sole charge; he does not ask for help, he asks for you.[42]

Whether or not we can share, or even understand, such aspirations is of little importance. What matters is that at a certain point, probably in 1463, Eleanor Talbot committed herself to association with the Carmelite order. Her spiritual development may subsequently have led her in a contemplative direction, with the implicit call to renounce ambition and focus exclusively on her relationship with God. In the words of a modern Carmelite writer, such a vocation would have involved 'accepting her nothingness and making no fuss about it'.[43] Obviously anyone who chose to base their life upon such foundations will have taken no interest whatsoever in the thought of lengthy court proceedings aimed at establishing social status. 'Women mystics saw their way to the imitation of Christ through renunciation', and suffering was viewed as an integral part of the process.[44] Eleanor's total lack of interest in seeking recognition that she, rather than Elizabeth Woodville, was the real wife of the king, thus becomes entirely and totally comprehensible. Moreover, it is very difficult to imagine how a person with such aspirations could possibly have anything in common with an indolent, sensual and selfish hedonist like Edward IV.

The Woodville 'Marriage'

Eleanor's powerful uncle, Richard Neville, Earl of Warwick, had been a strong supporter of his cousin, the king, in his struggle to win and hold the crown. As a result he was generally seen (and saw himself) as wielding great power and influence. As the Yorkist hold on the kingdom was consolidated in 1464, Richard Neville thought to use his power to influence Edward IV in what was to be one of the most important decisions of the reign: the choice of a suitable bride to share the throne with him and perpetuate the dynasty.

Richard Neville may well have been aware that, for a time, in 1461, his niece, Eleanor Talbot, had attracted the king's attention, but it is clear that in 1464 at least, he knew nothing of the king's marriage with her. He likewise clearly knew nothing of the king's relationship with Elizabeth Woodville. What he will have seen (because it was, to a degree, public knowledge) was that the king's interest in Eleanor had waned by mid-1462, and that Elizabeth Wayte (Lucy) had become Edward's mistress. To Warwick, who had his eye on a French royal bride for Edward IV, the first piece of news may not have been unwelcome. As for the king's new attachment, while it reinforced the eclipse of Eleanor, it was clearly of no dynastic significance.

Thus, as far as Warwick knew, the king was free to marry, and in mid-September 1464, at a council in Reading, Warwick urged the king to agree to the dynastic alliance with France which he, Richard Neville, had been canvassing for some time.[1] To the astonishment not only of Warwick but also of everyone else, the king blithely announced that such an alliance was impossible because he was already married. Even more astonishing to those few people like Canon Stillington and the Duchess of Norfolk, who may have known the nature of his attachment to Eleanor, must have been the fact that the bride Edward now named was not Eleanor Talbot, but Elizabeth Woodville.

It is an interesting question why Edward IV, having entered into a secret contract with Elizabeth Woodville in May 1464, should then have decided to make the matter public in September. Pressure from the Earl of Warwick for the king to agree to marry Bona of Savoy hardly seems an adequate explanation. Later Warwick would press Edward to marry his sister, Margaret of York, in France rather than to the heir of Burgundy. On that occasion Edward apparently experienced no difficulty in simply saying no. One possible explanation for the king's behaviour is that Elizabeth Woodville found herself pregnant in September 1464. If so, however, she must have miscarried shortly afterwards, for Elizabeth of York, her first child by the king, was not born until 11 February 1466.

The king's announcement must most particularly have astonished and perplexed his keeper of the privy seal, Canon Robert Stillington, who had been present when the king had contracted himself to Eleanor.[2] If Canon Stillington now sought further information regarding the king's Woodville alliance then, as an expert in canon law, he cannot have been reassured by what he learned. The marriage to Elizabeth Woodville had been solemnised several months previously, on 1 May 1464. This meant that it post-dated by about three years the king's contract with Eleanor, and was therefore bigamous. Any children borne to the king by Elizabeth Woodville would thus be bastards.

As we have already seen, only if the second 'marriage' had been celebrated openly and in public would there have been anything to redeem it. Such circumstances would not indeed have made it a valid marriage, but because Elizabeth Woodville would then be presumed to have entered into her contract with Edward in good faith, her children could have been recognised as legitimate, and the church would have reserved its opprobrium for the king and Eleanor. As previously observed, Eleanor would have been held culpable on the grounds that she ought to have raised objections to the new 'marriage' at the wedding service, when the priest invited those present to voice any known obstacles to the proposed Woodville union.

However, it now became clear that the Woodville 'marriage' had not been solemnised in a public ceremony. It had, in fact, been a secret rite, celebrated clandestinely at Grafton Regis, with the bride's mother as a witness.[3] This meant that Eleanor, who had had no knowledge of what was going on, had also had no opportunity to protest, or stop the Woodville 'marriage' from taking place. She was thus an innocent party in the eyes of the church, while, under canon law, not only was the Woodville 'marriage' invalid, but also any children born of it would be illegitimate.[4] The fact that the Woodville marriage was subsequently publicly acknowledged by the king was completely irrelevant.[5]

What, if anything, Canon Stillington did about all this in the autumn of 1464, we do not know. Strictly speaking, he was not necessarily called upon to do anything at all at this stage. Nevertheless, it is probable that he would have seen it as his duty at least to warn Edward of the possible consequences for any future children that might be born as a result of his Woodville union. The fact that, as we have seen, the king determined, at about this time, to appoint Robert Stillington to the next vacant English bishopric (even in the face of initial difficulties with Rome) suggests that Edward was very conscious that Stillington possessed dangerous knowledge, and that he wished to placate him. In itself the episcopal nomination may suggest that the two men had discussed the situation. It can also be construed as evidence that Edward IV wished to encourage Stillington to keep quiet.

Of course, had Eleanor chosen to dispute the Woodville marriage in the ecclesiastical courts, she could have cited Stillington as a witness, and he would then have been obliged to give evidence under oath. Eleanor, however, did nothing. Possible reasons for her inaction have already been considered in Chapter 15 (above). Since Stillington himself was not a party to any dispute in respect of the king's marriage (and moreover since there was, in any case, no formal dispute) he too was at liberty to do nothing, and this is the course that he seems to have adopted at this stage. Indeed, it is difficult to see what else he could have done. He was, after all, confronted by Edward IV with a *fait accompli*.

Stillington's responsibilities in the matter only began to change when Elizabeth Woodville started producing children by the king – and most dramatically, when she gave birth to their first living son, in 1470. That, when it happened, raised issues which were not past, but future. It is likely that, from that date onwards, Stillington's conscience began to be seriously troubled. He could no longer evade the uncomfortable realisation that, if he outlived the king, he might one day be forced to speak out. Given their respective ages, however, he may as yet have taken refuge in the hope that, in all probability he would die before Edward IV.

As for the birth of Edward, Prince of Wales, while it must have sounded loud warning bells in Stillington's mind, it was not in itself a total disaster. Children, after all, often died young. However, the situation grew progressively more serious with the subsequent birth of two further sons to Edward IV and Elizabeth Woodville (Richard of Shrewsbury in 1473, and George in 1477). It is highly significant that it is precisely during the period 1473-1477 that we first find hints that Stillington may have mentioned the Talbot marriage to George, Duke of Clarence, formerly the heir presumptive to the throne, and the person most affected by the birth of Elizabeth Woodville's sons. We shall return to this point shortly.

Originally appointed keeper of the privy seal by Henry VI, Stillington had been retained in this post by Edward IV, who clearly trusted and liked him. Indeed, Edward stunningly demonstrated his faith in Stillington by entrusting him with the Talbot secret. He also gave him the post of chancellor. As for Stillington, he seems to have been (or become) a sincere supporter of the cause of the house of York, and must have viewed the prospect of renewed succession disputes – a danger clearly implicit in the dubious Woodville 'marriage' – with horror and alarm.

Although a priest, Stillington had bastard children of his own, from his student days in Oxford, so if the marriage question ever was discussed between himself and the king, he will have been able to address the issue with Edward frankly, man to man. As a result Edward may have learned from Stillington that he had nothing to fear so long as Eleanor held her tongue, since according to the normal procedure of the period it would have been for her, as the wronged party, to initiate any legal proceedings against the Woodville 'marriage' before the church courts.[6]

Edward IV had a strong streak of *laisser faire* in his make-up. As Eleanor's public silence lengthened, any anxieties and embarrassment which the king may initially have experienced will probably have been dispelled. It is even possible that Edward contacted her, and received an assurance of her lack of interest in the matter, because, as we have seen, there is circumstantial evidence that, while Eleanor lived, Edward took some account of her wishes. If he had not already done so, it may have been at about this time that, in some secrecy, Edward granted Eleanor property in Wiltshire.[7] It is also notable that his treatment of old Lord Sudeley changed very markedly the minute Eleanor had breathed her last. We shall explore the evidence for this in Chapter 18. As for Canon Stillington, we have already noted that Edward nominated him to the next vacant episcopal see in England. In view of Edward's subsequent reactions to any attempt to refer to the matter of the Talbot marriage, this was most probably the king's tactful way of indicating to his minister that everyone's best interests would be served by his silence.

For a number of years Bishop Stillington was to maintain that silence and go along with the *status quo*. Ultimately, however, he was to show by his actions that he remained troubled at heart by what the king had done, particularly insofar as it affected the succession. Thus he very probably raised the matter with Clarence in the 1470s. He certainly brought it to public notice after Edward IV's death in 1483. We shall see in Chapter 18 how far-reaching were the effects of his explosive revelations.

So long as Eleanor, in her Norfolk retreat, remained content to let matters rest, however, there was, for the moment, nothing more that Stillington or anyone else could do. No one, in 1464, seems to have said anything either to Eleanor's uncle, the Earl of Warwick, or to the person most affected by Edward's marital affairs, his brother, George, Duke of Clarence (who, failing heirs of the king's body, was heir presumptive to the throne). At this early stage, there was, after all, still the hope that the Woodville union might prove childless. Thus Warwick, together with Clarence, escorted Elizabeth Woodville to her enthronement at Reading Abbey on Michaelmas Day (29 September) 1464.[8]

The following year, on 26 May, the new queen was crowned at Westminster Abbey. Archbishop Bourchier placed the crown upon her head, and John, Duke of Norfolk, Earl Marshall of England, though not yet of age, presided over the ceremonial. If the Duchess of Norfolk, Eleanor's sister, Elizabeth, was present, she must have watched with mixed emotions her young husband and his uncle, the archbishop, presiding over the coronation of her sister's rival. However, she is not named among the guests, although both her husband and his grandmother, the senior dowager Duchess of Norfolk, are listed as having been present. It may be that Elizabeth stayed away, although her – and Eleanor's – nephew, Thomas, the young Viscount Lisle, certainly attended, for he was made a Knight of the Bath.[9] Eleanor's last surviving brother, Humphrey Talbot, was also knighted by Edward IV towards the end of 1464 or early in 1465. Furthermore, at about the same time, the king announced a retrospective grant to Eleanor's mother.[10] Possibly he felt the need to placate the Talbot family.

Death

The dowager Countess of Shrewsbury enjoyed Edward IV's generosity for less than two years, for she died on Sunday 14 June 1467, at the age of 63, and was buried in the Jesus Chapel of St Paul's Cathedral.[1] If she came to London for her mother's funeral, Eleanor may have met any number of important people on that occasion, for London was particularly crowded at that time due to the opening of Parliament, the presence in the capital of ambassadors from the Duke of Burgundy, the great tournament between Lord Scales and the Bastard of Burgundy at Smithfield, and the return of her uncle, the Earl of Warwick, from his embassy in France.

Warwick was, at this point, very angry with the king because in the matter of the negotiations for the marriage of Margaret of York the king was once again ignoring his advice. Also his brother, George, Archbishop of York, had just been dismissed as chancellor, a promised royal marriage for one of his nephews had been cancelled, and Edward IV was blocking the marriage of Warwick's daughter, Isabel, to the Duke of Clarence. Warwick was also at odds with Elizabeth Woodville's kindred, and in fact in incipient rebellion. Any hint to him at this point of the existence of a marriage between his niece and the king would have been potentially very dangerous for Edward.

However, Eleanor had kept silent for six years, and there is no reason to suppose that, even if she met her uncle at her mother's funeral, she spoke to him of her marriage to the king. The only hint that Warwick might have had some awareness of the Talbot marriage lies in his insistent promotion of his daughter Isabel's marriage to the Duke of Clarence, and he might well have adopted that policy in any event, since in 1467 Edward IV had, as yet, no son by Elizabeth Woodville, and Clarence therefore still had a good chance of one day being king.

Moreover, it is possible that Eleanor herself was unwell by this time, for she died just over a year after her mother, on 30 June 1468, at the comparatively early age of 32.[2] It is not known what caused her death. Buck merely remarks laconically that the king did not kill her with kindness,[3] a vague phraseology which permits varied interpretations. The circumstances surrounding the event were certainly somewhat unusual, although there is no proof of anything sinister.

On 4 June 1468 Eleanor made a deed of gift in favour of her sister Elizabeth.[4] The witnesses included her cousin by marriage, Sir William Catesby (whose son was later celebrated in rhyme as Richard III's 'Cat', and was ultimately hanged by Henry VII in the aftermath of the battle of Bosworth). Among other things, this deed proves Eleanor's active association with the Catesby family. In the deed Eleanor, describing herself as 'lately the wife of Thomas Boteler, knight, now deceased',[5] conveyed to her sister absolutely, and with immediate effect, the Warwickshire manor of Fenny Compton, and granted her also the reversion of all her Wiltshire property, which is specifically stated in the deed to be leased to John Cheney for life.

It has been observed that aristocratic women in the fifteenth century tended to develop networks centred on their female relations. 'These ties encouraged them to assist one another emotionally and materially throughout their lives and influenced the way in which widows distributed their property. Childless aristocratic widows often had particularly strong bonds with their sisters and nieces and chose them as major beneficiaries of their estates'.[6] The relationship between Eleanor and Elizabeth Talbot seems always to have been a close one. Elizabeth had protected and helped Eleanor, particularly since the death of her first husband. In return, what property Eleanor possessed, or the reversion thereof, now passed to Elizabeth.

As we have already seen, it may be that Eleanor wished and intended Elizabeth to use some or all of this property for religious endowments (as indeed the duchess ultimately did). It can hardly be coincidental that Eleanor's measures were put in place only weeks before she died. The deed was sealed on Saturday 4 June 1468, the eve of Whit Sunday. Less than four weeks later, on Thursday 30 June, Eleanor was no more.

The deed of gift is dated from Fenny Compton. Was Eleanor herself in Fenny Compton to issue it? As we have seen, her role as a Carmelite oblate may have involved a vow of *stabilitas*, which would have required her to live in a fixed abode within a reasonable distance of the priory; an abode which she would then not normally have left. Bearing this in mind, are we to contemplate a dying Eleanor (having presumably obtained a dispensation from Prior Richard Water of the Norwich Carmel) setting off on the not inconsiderable journey from Norfolk to Warwickshire and back, just to cede her property to her sister? It seems improbable. And what would have happened afterwards? Having deeded Fenny Compton away, Eleanor can hardly be supposed to have continued to reside there (if, indeed, she had ever done so). Her manor of Griff had been surrendered to Lord Sudeley by 1461 at the latest. Her property in Wiltshire was in the hands of a subtenant. The only property left to Eleanor where she might have resided for the last three weeks of her life was the manor of Burton Dassett, which she still held in dower.

However, there is evidence that Eleanor did not spend her last days at Burton Dassett. Nor can she have died anywhere in Warwickshire. In cases where the deceased had died in the county in which their inquisition postmortem was later held, the report to the chancery normally contained the phrase '… *obiit in comitatu predicto* ('… died in the aforesaid county'). This can be seen, for example, in the inquisition post mortem of Eleanor's mother-in-law, Elizabeth Norbury, Lady Sudeley.[7] Eleanor's Warwickshire inquisition does not contain this phrase, thus clearly implying that Eleanor died outside the county of Warwick.

It is far more likely that she resided at Kenninghall in Norfolk, and that during the summer of 1468, she never left East Hall. Eleanor's deed of gift is accompanied by letters of attorney.[8] It is therefore probable that neither she nor her sister was in Warwickshire on 4 June 1468, and that their respective attorneys and assigns acted for them. The Duchess of Norfolk was very busy with other matters at the beginning of June 1468. Exactly two weeks after the date of the deed of gift, she was in London. On Saturday 18 June the king's sister, Margaret of York, set out from the Royal Wardrobe on her wedding journey to the Low Countries. The princess's suite of attendants was headed by Elizabeth Talbot, Duchess of Norfolk, 'a very beautiful English lady',[9] who took with her a large train of her own.[10] The preparations for this wedding journey had been in progress since May.

It might be appropriate at this point to consider why Eleanor decided to give Fenny Compton to her sister during her own lifetime, and why she granted Elizabeth the reversion of all her Wiltshire properties at the same time. The answer to these questions is related to the medieval legal position of wives and widows in respect of the making of wills and testaments.

Wills and testaments in the fifteenth century were two quite different things. Wills disposed of real estate, testaments disposed of personal property. Fenny Compton and the Wiltshire estates represented the entirety of Eleanor's personal land holdings. The only other way in which she could have arranged for their transfer to her sister (or indeed, to anyone else) would have been by making a will.

In Eleanor's own eyes, however, this may not have been an option open to her. According to medieval law, a widow was free to make a will, but a wife could not do so without the permission of her husband. If Eleanor considered herself married to Edward IV, then she was not free to make a will, and the only way to ensure with absolute certainty that her lands passed to her sister was by a deed of gift executed in her own lifetime.

It is interesting, therefore, to discover that this is precisely the course which Eleanor took. It is significant that in the matter of the disposal of her estate, Eleanor chose to behave as a wife, rather than as a widow. Moreover, this conduct was entirely consistent with the choice that she had made earlier in respect of her religious commitment. On that occasion too, she had chosen an option which was open to a married woman.

She was, of course, still at liberty to make a testament, arranging for the disposal of her personal property after her death. And although no such document now appears to survive, it is certain that she made one, because her sister, Elizabeth, later described herself as the executrix of Eleanor's testament.

> The Lady Elizabeth, Duchess of Norfolk, sister of the said Eleanor and executrix of the testament of the said Eleanor ... has given to us the said master and fellows or scholars [of Corpus Christi College] two hundred and twenty marcs in good coined money, from the goods of the said Eleanor and Duchess Elizabeth for the upkeep, repair and renewal of the fabric of our houses, messuages and tenements, at the present time in decay.[11]

Eleanor's testament would have disposed of her personal jewellery, clothing, silverware and so on. Some of these valuables were apparently turned into money for the benefit of Corpus Christi College Cambridge.

It is highly likely that a further bequest favoured the Norwich Carmel, possibly with the intention of supporting Prior Water's ambitions to develop the priory's library, which had been built by his predecessor, Prior John Keninghale in 1450.[12] Improving the library of the Norwich Carmel was a project to which Agnes Paston (like Eleanor, a Carmelite tertiary)[13] later contributed 'a charger of silver in value x marke, and iij bollys of silver ... to th'entent that a certeyn coost shuld ben doon upon the liberarye of the Friers Carmelites aforesaid'.[14]

Curiously, Eleanor's death – which the king cannot but have greeted with some relief, and which she herself seems almost to have been prepared for – appears in others ways to have been unexpected. Her sister and executrix, the Duchess of Norfolk, was out of the country at the time, as were all Eleanor's other close living relatives.[15] As a result, the legal processes attendant upon her death were not, in fact, set in motion until two weeks later, when Elizabeth returned to England.

While it is entirely credible that Elizabeth Talbot would have found it difficult to refuse a royal command to accompany Margaret of York to Flanders, she seems to have participated very fully in the wedding celebrations, in a way which sits oddly with the notion that she knew her sister and closest friend to be dying. It is possible, therefore, that although Eleanor was known to be ill, she was not thought to be in imminent danger.

At all events, Elizabeth was not with her sister when she died. She had embarked with Margaret of York at Margate on Thursday 23 June, arriving at Sluis on Saturday 25. On Monday 27 June she was present at the exchange of promises between Charles and Margaret which transformed the English princess into the Duchess of Burgundy, and she was still in Sluis with the new duchess the last day of June, while at home in England, her sister lay dying. On Saturday 2 July she accompanied Margaret by water to Damme, where the formal marriage ceremony took place, and the following day she was in Margaret's train for her state entry to Bruge where she witnessed with the princess the pageantry of the tournament of the Golden Tree. Not until Wednesday 13 July, almost a fortnight after Eleanor's death, did Elizabeth and the other English guests finally take their leave of the ducal couple and begin their journey back to England, where the news of Eleanor's demise was awaiting the duchess.[16]

Eleanor almost certainly died at East Hall, the old manor house at Kenninghall which her sister held in dower. Writing in the sixteenth century, John Leland recalled the following tradition relating to the site of this house, which had by then been demolished by the Howard Dukes of Norfolk, to make way for a larger modern house not far away: 'There apperith at Keninghaule not far from the Duke of Northfolkes new place a grete mote, withyn the cumpace whereof there was sumtyme a fair place, and there the saying is that there lay a Quene or sum grete lady, and there dyed'.[17] No other explanation of Leland's story is known, and it is therefore likely that this is a reference to Eleanor.

In her lost testament Eleanor may have specifically requested burial at the Norwich Carmel. At all events, when Elizabeth returned to England that was where she had her sister's remains taken for interment. Widowed in her first marriage, deceived and then abandoned in her second, Eleanor had ultimately taken on the coverture of religion in place of that of a husband. This choice was reflected in the disposal of her remains. Sixty-six per cent of widows (even those who had remarried) chose to be buried with their first husbands.[18] Eleanor (or Elizabeth, on her behalf) chose otherwise. Like other Carmelite lay oblates and patrons of high rank she was buried in the choir of the Carmelite Priory Church in Norwich.[19]

This church stood a little to the north of the Cathedral, over the River Wensum across Whitefriars' Bridge and near the city wall in an area bounded by the river and Cowgate Street (now Whitefriars). The site is currently occupied by Jarrold's Printing. Almost nothing now remains of the friary above ground level. There is the archway of the great west door of the priory church (through which Eleanor's coffin must have passed), which has been rebuilt in the entrance of the magistrates' court, just across the river from its original site;[20] a so-called 'undercroft' which currently houses a printing museum, and a wall and entrance archway formerly leading to an anchorite's cell which adjoined the main friary. The 'undercroft' and the remains of the anchorite's cell are both still *in situ*. The anchorite's arch bears a modern plaque, commemorating Eleanor's burial at the priory.[21]

From time to time, during building work on the Whitefriars site, further fragments of the friary have come to light. What became of Eleanor's tomb is not known, and her body may still lie on the site, under the present printing works. Interestingly, however, a medieval female skeleton was discovered here during building work in 1958. It and what may have been its wooden coffin are now at Norwich Castle Museum. Remains of at least one other body, probably male, were also discovered at this time, together with fragments of painted masonry from a window and pottery shards, the latter dating from about the fourteenth century.

These remains were found in an area near the surviving wall and archway of the anchorite's cell, and well to the south of where the friary church is thought to have stood (although there is some doubt about the exact location of the church building). From the very meagre surviving accounts of the excavation it seems that the body now in Norwich Castle Museum was found with a coffin crushed and broken on top of it, lying in a sixteenth-century rubbish dump. This strongly suggests that the burial had been disturbed, and the evidence relating to the status of the dead person corroborates this, since an aristocratic lady (as this proved to be) is most likely to have been originally interred within the choir of the priory church.

There is little evidence that tombs were systematically despoiled at the time of the Dissolution. Moreover, it seems that substantial ruins of the Whitefriars Church in Norwich may have remained standing until the mid-seventeenth century at least. The west doorway (now re-erected in the Norwich Magistrates' Court) certainly remained *in situ* until the late sixteenth century, when it was dismantled by the then owners of the site, and incorporated (together with other portions of the priory) in a manor house which they were constructing. When Weever visited the Whitefriars, in the early seventeenth century, he was still able to find and record Eleanor's tomb. 'When Blomefield published his second volume in 1745, the Friars' Hall and kitchen below, the Chapel of the Holy Cross at the west end, and a part of the cloister were remaining'.[22] In fact the priory's Holy Cross Chapel was still standing, and in use for Baptist services, towards the end of the nineteenth century. Demolition in the area of the former choir must have taken place after Weever's visit, perhaps during the time of the Commonwealth. At that period desecration of a tomb would certainly have been a possibility.[23]

No detailed study had been made of the body from the Whitefriars until, at the request of the present writer, the Director of the Norfolk Museums Service agreed to an examination of the bones by a consultant osteologist, Mr. W.J. White. The aim of this examination was to seek to establish the age at death of the deceased person and other relevant information, in the hope of coming closer to being able to establish the identity of the remains.

Eleanor's was not the only female body interred in the Whitefriars' Church. Weever, who must have seen the surviving tombs himself, listed twenty aristocratic female interments, including Eleanor's. Extant wills indicate that several other interments of women (of lower social class) also took place in this church, but Weever makes no mention of these additional burials, and was probably unaware of them. The graves in question may always have been unmarked – or perhaps they had been marked by brasses, which could have been removed and sold as scrap metal before 1630.

The body at the Castle Museum was thought to be that of a laywoman who was a friend and benefactress of the friary, and who, for that reason, was given the privilege of burial within the friary precincts. This was a description which would certainly have fitted Eleanor Talbot. An examination of the remains took place on 29 August 1996. The resultant report, together with other evidence bearing on these remains and their identity, will be discussed in detail in Chapter 20.

18

Aftermath

It was probably about 17 July 1468 when Elizabeth, Duchess of Norfolk, arrived home in England, and the matter of Eleanor's death began to receive legal attention. On 18 July, more than two weeks after that death had occurred, the chancery at last dispatched a writ of *diem clausit extremum* to William Moton esquire, the royal escheator in Warwickshire, commanding that an inquisition post mortem be held to determine what property Eleanor had held in that county on the day of her death. In August, at the town of Henley-in-Arden, the inquisition took place, and in September a report was returned to the chancery.

The content of this report was somewhat strange and selective. Although it included mention of Griff (which Eleanor had surrendered to Lord Sudeley some years prior to her death) and gave full details of its disposal, there was no reference whatsoever to the manor of Fenny Compton, which Eleanor had transferred to Elizabeth only weeks before she died. In view of the sequel, it is legitimate to wonder whether this selectivity of reporting was not deliberate. We shall return to this point shortly.

Naturally Eleanor's Wiltshire property was not mentioned in the Henley enquiry, since it lay outside the competency of the Warwickshire escheator. The consequent omission of the Wiltshire holdings from William Moton's report is entirely natural. Nevertheless, one is left with the curious and unexplained fact that apparently no separate enquiry was ever made in respect of the Wiltshire tenures. An inquisition should certainly have been held, since Eleanor still held this property when she died, having granted her sister only the right of reversion. It is interesting to speculate as to why no inquisition post mortem was ever held in Wiltshire.

On the basis of William Moton's report, Edward IV was fully and publicly informed in respect of the Warwickshire manors of Griff and Burton Dassett. The king and his officials can scarcely have been hitherto unaware that Eleanor had held these manors (though the circumstances under which she had acquired them may have been imperfectly understood) but Edward had taken no action in respect of them during Eleanor's lifetime. However, now that Griff and Burton Dassett had reverted to Lord Sudeley, the king took instant exception to the fact that they had changed hands on more than one occasion without royal licence, and he used this as a pretext for their confiscation.[1]

It is immediately obvious that some hidden agenda must have lain behind both the official reporting, and the subsequent actions taken in respect of the Warwickshire manors. It is also obvious that this hidden agenda had Lord Sudeley as its target. If the manor of Fenny Compton (which Eleanor had held on the day of her death, but which had not reverted to Lord Sudeley) had also been included in Moton's analysis, precisely the same questions could and should have been raised regarding its transfers as were now raised by the king in respect of the other two manors. It therefore follows that the omission of Fenny Compton from the report of the inquisition post mortem must have been intentional, and officially sanctioned. That omission allowed the king to respond differently in the two cases of Fenny Compton on the one hand, and Griff and Burton Dassett on the other hand. Thus, unlike Griff and Burton Dassett, Fenny Compton was not repossessed by the crown, but was allowed to remain in the hands of the person to whom Eleanor had transferred it.

The same hidden agenda must also account for the inclusion of the manor of Griff in Moton's inquisition report. In point of fact its inclusion was completely unwarranted, since Eleanor did not hold Griff on the day of her death, having returned it to Lord Sudeley eight years previously.

One can hardly imagine that William Moton, on his own initiative, would have made such distinctions between the various properties. He must therefore have been acting on instructions received: instructions which must have originated with a person of very high rank. Since the surviving writ of *diem clausit extremum* which had been dispatched to him by the chancery was purely formulaic and contains no hidden messages, Moton must have received any additional instructions separately.

What possible purpose could there have been in all this? In the late summer of 1468 there was only one significant difference between Fenny Compton and the other two Warwickshire manors, namely that Fenny Compton was then held by Eleanor's sister; a person who was probably well aware of the nature of Eleanor's relationship with the king. Griff and Burton Dassett, on the other hand, should have reverted to Lord Sudeley, a man who may have been unaware of Eleanor's secret, and whom (as it now emerged) Edward IV wished to bring down.

As a result of the edited and selective nature of William Moton's report, Eleanor's gift of Fenny Compton to her sister was allowed to pass completely unchallenged. So too was her grant of the reversion of the Wiltshire properties (regarding which no enquiry was ever made). Furthermore any possibility of future queries in respect of Elizabeth's territorial acquisitions from Eleanor's estate was subsequently quietly smoothed over by the grant of a vaguely worded royal pardon to the Duchess of Norfolk (see below).

The case of Griff and Burton Dassett, however, was handled quite differently. Griff had, of course, been returned by Eleanor to Lord Sudeley in 1460, and Burton Dassett, which Eleanor had held only in dower, should also have returned to him upon her death. Instead, the king now confiscated both manors. This action was, perhaps, the first clear signal to Lord Sudeley that, with Eleanor's death, his circumstances had changed.

As we have seen, in 1462 (possibly influenced by Eleanor) Edward IV had granted Ralph Butler exemption from attending parliament and serving on royal commissions. He had also made him an annual donation of venison from the royal forest of Woodstock.[2] Although the subsequent sundering of the intimate connection between Edward and Eleanor seems to have resulted in the issue of commissions to Ralph in the usual manner (ignoring the 1462 grant of exemption), in a way this could be seen as a mark of trust. At all events, Lord Sudeley had served on such commissions in 1461, 1462, 1464, 1466 and February 1468, apparently enjoying, if not exactly Edward IV's favour, at least his acceptance.[3] Now, however, he was to find himself the victim of the king's rapacity.

Although Eleanor's Warwickshire inquisition post mortem had made no mention of Fenny Compton, the crown must certainly have been aware of her transfer of that property, together with the grant of the reversion of the Wiltshire estates. If the latter had indeed been given to Eleanor by the king, Edward must inevitably have discovered in what manner Eleanor had disposed of them, even without an inquisition *post mortem* in Wiltshire. At all events, just over five months after Eleanor's death, on 8 December 1468, the king granted a 'general pardon to Elizabeth, wife of the king's kinsman, John, Duke of Norfolk, of all offences committed by her before 7 December'.[4] While it is not explicitly stated that this pardon related to Elizabeth's acquisition of Fenny Compton and Eleanor's Wiltshire property without licence, it would certainly have covered that situation.

A similar pardon to Lord Sudeley followed on 17 December 1468, and on 6 February 1469 the king relented and allowed Ralph to repossess both Griff and Burton Dassett.[5] However, this small concession was ultimately purchased by Lord Sudeley at a very heavy price, for less than three weeks later he was induced to issue the following grant:

> Know all men present and to come that I, Ralph Boteler, Knight, Lord Sudeley, have given, granted and by this my present charter have confirmed to Richard, Earl Rivers, William, Earl of Pembroke, Antony Wydevile, Knight, Lord Scales, William Hastings, Knight, Lord Hastings, Thomas Bonyfaunt, Dean of the Chapel Royal, Thomas Vaughan, one of the Esquires of the King's body and Treasurer of the King's Chamber, and to Richard Fowler, the castle, domain and manor of Sudeley, with all its belongings, in the county of Gloucester, and also all lands, rents etc. in Sudeley, Toddington, Stanley, Greet, Gretton, Catesthorp and Newnton, and also the advowson of the church or chapel of Sudeley, to hold the same to them and their assignees.[6]

Superficially, the form of this grant is reminiscent of the standard formula for an 'enfeoffment to use'; a device by means of which a man would grant lands to a group of his friends in order to keep them out of the hands of his overlord and safeguard them for his heir.[7] But of course by 1469 Lord Sudeley had no direct heir, and it is apparent that, far from availing himself of what has been described as a 'legal fiction' to safeguard his property, he was in fact being constrained to surrender it. This is amply demonstrated by the sequel, for on 14 November of the same year Sudeley Castle was granted to the king's brother, Richard, Duke of Gloucester, who later exchanged it for the Castle of Richmond.

In the light of this, it is not, perhaps, surprising that in 1470, when Edward IV was forced to flee into exile and Henry VI briefly resumed the throne, Lord Sudeley's traditional Lancastrianism resurfaced. He had, after all, little cause to feel loyal to Edward IV. Thus Eleanor's former father-in-law is said to have carried the sword of state before the restored Henry VI, in the sad little procession that passed through London in 1470. This was probably Lord Sudeley's last significant public act (though he received commissions from the Lancastrian government, while it lasted).

It is said that when Edward IV regained the throne Ralph Butler was imprisoned. In 1473, two years after Edward IV's return, he died at the venerable age of 80. The *post mortem* documentation relating to his estate shows that his once mighty holdings had dwindled very considerably. Only the counties of Warwickshire and Worcestershire were required to hold inquisitions, following his demise. Of his ancestral holdings in Gloucestershire, nothing, apparently, remained to him.[8]

At some point between 1468 and 1474 Eleanor's former manor of Fenny Compton was conveyed by John and Elizabeth, Duke and Duchess of Norfolk, to John Wenlock, Richard Southwell and Robert Bernard. The original documentation no longer survives, but this transfer of the manor is known from later references. The first of these men, from a family long-established in the service of the Talbots,[9] had become an annuitant of the Duke of Norfolk by the 1470s.[10] Southwell and Bernard were well-known members of the Mowbray affinity. Indeed, Southwell was the steward of Kenninghall, at least, in 1473–76, and he may have served Eleanor, for he had probably immediately succeeded Robert Arnold in this post, though the precise date of his appointment is not known.[11] As for Robert Bernard, in company with Eleanor's and Elizabeth's brother, Sir Humphrey Talbot, he had received the crimson Mowbray livery from the Duke of Norfolk's cousin, Sir John Howard, on 25 May 1465. He was also a Mowbray annuitant.[12]

In 1470, while Edward IV was in exile in the Low Countries, Elizabeth Woodville, having borne several daughters, at last gave birth to a son by the king. This event, generally perceived as a cause for rejoicing, may have provoked a rather different response in one quarter. After ten years of silence, the Bishop of Bath and Wells may now have started wondering whether he had done the right thing, and what on earth he was to do next. For he, at least, will have been conscious at once that the new-born 'prince' was illegitimate, and could not succeed to the throne. The person who was now being wronged was not the dead Eleanor Talbot, but the king's brother, the Duke of Clarence, and since Clarence had extensive land holdings in the West Country, he was, in a sense a neighbour of the bishop (who, if he visited his diocese but rarely,[13] certainly lived at the episcopal manor house in Hampshire).[14] It may well be that Robert Stillington decided at some point between 1471 and 1477 (and most probably between 1473 and 1477) to take his information to the Duke of Clarence.[15]

While it remains uncertain whether or not Eleanor's uncle, the late Earl of Warwick had ever been aware of the nature of his niece's relationship with the king, there is excellent reason for believing that his protégé and son-in-law, the Duke of Clarence, had knowledge of it, though probably not until the mid-1470s. Such awareness on Clarence's part would explain both his conduct and his eventual execution. It seems, therefore, that something must have happened in the mid-1470s to bring the matter of the Talbot marriage to Clarence's attention. Since the only living person known for certain to have possessed this dangerous knowledge (apart from the king himself) seems to have been Bishop Stillington, the latter must be considered the most likely source for Clarence's information, and in fact Stillington was subsequently imprisoned for a short time 'on account of some dubious action on his part connecting him with the treason of George, Duke of Clarence'.[16]

There were other possible sources of information, however. Clarence was a close friend of the Duke and Duchess of Norfolk. It is very probable that the duchess had some knowledge of her sister's marriage to the king, and possible that she had shared this dangerous secret with her husband. The Duke of Norfolk could perhaps have passed it on to Clarence. There is no record of Edward IV taking any reprisals against John Mowbray, but then of course, the latter had died, suddenly and very unexpectedly, early on the morning of Wednesday 17 January 1476.

It is interesting, incidentally, that Elizabeth Talbot seems to have shown little enthusiasm for Edward IV's subsequent plans to marry her infant daughter, Anne, to Richard of Shrewsbury, his second son by Elizabeth Woodville. There is no extant statement from the dowager duchess herself upon this point. However, her friends the Pastons voiced anxiety at the prospect of the marriage. Moreover, the duchess was subjected to pressure from the king to surrender 'a great part' of her jointure, and she subsequently took steps to try to safeguard the interests of the Mowbray co-heirs, Lords Berkeley and Howard, when the marriage became a *fait accompli*. Elizabeth Talbot's participation in her daughter's splendid wedding festivities was minimal.[17]

For fifteen years or so there had been no sign that the Duke of Clarence had any knowledge of the Talbot marriage, but in about 1476–77 he not only appears to have acquired such knowledge, but he also, very unwisely, allowed that fact to become apparent. As a result, Elizabeth Woodville took fright. Mancini records that she came to fear both that her own marriage was invalid, and that her son would never succeed to the throne unless Clarence was removed.[18]

Clarence's execution on Wednesday 18 February 1478 closely coincided with the arrest and imprisonment of Bishop Stillington. The bishop, who had probably still been at liberty on 19 January (when he was appointed to a commission of the peace for Southampton)[19] was reported to be held in the Tower by Friday 6 March. The evidence for this derives from a letter written on that date by Elizabeth Stonor, who states that Stillington had been imprisoned since her correspondant departed. The precise date on which Stillington entered the Tower is not recorded, but Gairdner estimates his imprisonment to have dated from between 13 and 20 February, and given the date of Elizabeth Stonor's letter, he can hardly have been imprisoned later than about 27 February.[20]

It is difficult to avoid the conclusion that not only Clarence but also Elizabeth Woodville had found out about the Talbot marriage, and that the king, for his part, had drawn the obvious (though possibly erroneous) conclusion that Clarence's informant had been Stillington. The bishop's imprisonment does not absolutely prove his complicity, and it could simply be that Edward was alarmed, and decided that Stillington would be safer out of the way for a time. Alternatively, Edward may have considered it wise to give the bishop a firm and dramatic warning.

Apparently Stillington remained in the Tower until about the end of the second week of April. On Tuesday 14 April 1478 he was appointed to a commission of the peace for Berkshire, which implies (but does not guarantee) that he was by then once again at liberty.[21] Commynes states that he had only been released upon payment of a fine.[22] Stillington was not formally granted a pardon until Saturday 20 June 1478. This pardon was accompanied by a 'declaration that Robert, Bishop of Bath and Wells, has been faithful to the king and done nothing contrary to his oath of fealty, as he has shown before the king and certain Lords'.[23]

The accusations which were brought by the king against his brother, the Duke of Clarence, are set out in the act of attainder against him, and while this act – rarely published – is quoted in full in Appendix 1, it will be helpful to consider a summary of the indictment here, together with a brief commentary.

Summary of the act of attainder against George, Duke of Clarence, 16 January 1478[24]

First, the king recalls that in the past he has perforce defended himself against many treasons, although he has also shown mercy. Now, however, a new treason has lately come to light: a plot against himself and the queen, and against their eldest son and heir, and all their children; a plot which threatens the public weal. This new plot is particularly heinous because it has been perpetrated by the king's own brother, George, Duke of Clarence.

The king recalls how he had nurtured and cared for Clarence as a brother should; had richly endowed him, and had forgiven his many past offences, to the extent of putting them quite out of mind. Despite this, Clarence's malice has grown. He has now plotted the 'disherityng of the Kyng and his Issue', seeking to subvert the king's subjects from their true obedience. Specifically:

- Clarence has publicly questioned the lawful condemnation of his servant, Thomas Burdett
- He has accused the king of involvement with the Black Arts
- He has conspired to gain the crown for himself and his heirs
- He has claimed that the king is a bastard
- He has taken oaths of loyalty to himself 'noon exception reserved'[25]
- He has claimed that the king planned to destroy him
- Secretly and without the king's knowledge he has kept and shown people his agreement with Margaret of Anjou, naming him as Lancastrian heir to the throne in default of heirs of the body of Henry VI
- He has plotted with the abbot of Tewkesbury and others to send his son and heir to Flanders or Ireland, keeping a substitute child in his place
- He has prepared an armed insurrection and planned to seize the throne by force.

For his part, the king would wish to forgive Clarence once again, but the Duke has shown himself incorrigible and has threatened the kingdom with violence. The king's solemn oath binds him to preserve himself, his royal issue, the church and the public weal. He therefore commands Parliament to convict and attaint Clarence of high treason. The Duke and his heirs are to forfeit the ducal rank, together with all their property.

Specific elements of the wording of this act of attainder are certainly of interest. Naturally, in the case of those accused of high treason, it was routinely asserted that they had plotted against the king. It was, however, by no means routine to claim that they had also plotted against the queen, the heir to the throne and the royal children.[26] The underlying implication is very clear and specific: Clarence had intended to completely alter the order of succession to the throne, sweeping aside Elizabeth Woodville and all her offspring.

The reference to the Lancastrian succession agreement with Margaret of Anjou appears to imply that it was a *Lancastrian* claim to the throne which Clarence had intended to assert. The creation of this impression is certainly not an accident. It was undoubtedly deliberate and intentional on the part of the king. Equally clearly, however, the Lancastrian succession agreement is a red herring, for if it represented the whole substance of Clarence's imputed claim, there would have been no need to mention Clarence's alleged assertion that Edward IV was a bastard. This is surely an amazing story for the king himself to publicise in Parliament, even if he was only seeking to discount it (and in point of fact he says very little against the allegation, beyond describing it as 'unnatural'). Clearly Edward was trying to substantiate his case that Clarence had sought the throne. Logic suggests, however, that he would only have published such a dangerous allegation against himself in a situation where the only possible alternative would have been even worse. And surely the only worse alternative that one can imagine would have been for Edward to have been forced to publicise what had hitherto been very successfully concealed, namely the allegation that his marriage to the queen was bigamous, and all his children by her, illegitimate.

Although we cannot be certain that Stillington spoke of the Talbot marriage to Clarence, there is no doubt whatever that in 1483 he revealed this information to Richard, Duke of Gloucester and to the royal council. This revelation is a key element of the events of the summer of 1483. Stillington's allegations in respect of the Talbot marriage may or may not have been true. His revelation may have been voluntary and spontaneous, or it may have been made under the influence or compulsion of others. But whatever the circumstances surrounding the event, it cannot reasonably be questioned that in June 1483 the bishop made a statement to the council to the effect that Edward IV had already been married to Eleanor Talbot when he contracted his Woodville 'marriage' of May 1464; that he, Stillington, had been present on the occasion of the Talbot marriage; and that in consequence of this earlier contract all the children of the Woodville 'marriage' were *ipso facto* illegitimate and excluded from the succession.

Once stated publicly, in this way, such a revelation could have only one possible consequence – which was quite clearly the intention. The only possible question for debate is whether that intention was Stillington's (arising out of his conscience) or the Duke of Gloucester's (arising out of worldy ambition). Even in the latter case, however, as Gairdner very clearly saw, and specifically stated,[27] the fact that Richard or his adherents may have found the account of the Talbot marriage convenient for their purposes would in no way demonstrate that it was a fabrication.

The marriage of Edward IV and Eleanor Talbot was now accorded the two elements of validation which it had previously lacked: publicity and formal acknowledgement (by the Act of Parliament of 1484). There can be very few (if any) other fifteenth-century marriages which have been accorded such impressive legal confirmation as to be authenticated by an Act of Parliament, yet the *titulus regius* of 1484 is quite explicit and absolutely unequivocal: 'King Edward was and stoode marryed and trouth plight to oone Dame Elianor Butteler, daughter of the old Earl of Shrewesbury'.

Stillington's testimony evidently convinced the royal council, as it did the group of parliamentary representatives gathered in the capital in June 1483. Acknowledging that Edward IV's bigamy disinherited his Woodville children, they petitioned Richard, Duke of Gloucester, to ascend the throne by virtue of the fact that he was the next legitimate male heir. Not one single member of the royal family raised a voice in protest. The dowager Duchess of York, together with the Duchess of Suffolk and all her family, closed ranks in support of the new king. Likewise in the Low Countries, '*Madame la Grande*' (who, as the sequel would show when Henry VII took the throne, was very well able to give practical expression to any disapproval she might feel at the course of events in England) said and did nothing. Even the demoted queen, Elizabeth Woodville, found not a word to say. She was an intelligent woman and, as Mancini has already made clear, was only too well aware of the consequences which must inevitably follow for her children if the validity of her marriage to the king was called into question.[28]

The brief reign of Richard III came and went. Eleanor's sister, Elizabeth Talbot, attended his coronation, was well treated by Richard, and apparently enjoyed a good relationship with him.[29] Other members of Eleanor's extended family also served Richard, apparently without any qualms, and her Catesby connections supported the new king until his defeat by Henry Tudor at the battle of Bosworth in August 1485.[30]

Once Richard was gone, the new Tudor monarch showed through his actions that he had some interesting priorities. Among his first orders as king were the execution of William Catesby and the imprisonment of Bishop Stillington.[31] Early in his first Parliament, Henry VII also enacted his own laconic act of *titulus regius*, which said, in effect, that he was king because he was king.[32] He also arranged for a bizarre and absolutely unique procedure: the repeal, unquoted, of the *titulus regius* of 1484. When acts of parliament were revoked it was usual at least to precis the original text in the act of repeal.[33] Henry, however, neatly avoided this by quoting only the first, innocuous, thirteen words of Richard's act. He also made unique provision for all copies of the 1484 act to be destroyed 'upon Peine of ymprisonment', explaining with a refreshing burst of honesty that his purpose was 'that all thinges said and remembered in the said Bill and Acte maie be for ever out of remembraunce and allso forgot'.

The complete destruction of Richard's act was of vital importance to Henry because under its terms his intended bride, Elizabeth of York (whom he now sought to pass off as the Yorkist heiress) was a bastard. However, the most logical procedure for Henry would clearly have been to disprove in Parliament this key contention of Richard's act. The fact that instead of doing so, Henry VII chose to suppress the act entirely, strongly suggests that the case against the Woodville marriage set out in Richard's *titulus regius* was, in fact, unassailable.

In England, just as Henry wanted, Eleanor and the Talbot marriage were gradually forgotten. In case anyone happened to remember that Edward IV's children had been set aside as illegitimate, that allegation was actually allowed to stand in the public memory, but with the useful substitution of the name of Elizabeth Wayte (Lucy) for that of Eleanor Talbot. In this carefully tailored new form, the story became unimportant, because it could be (and was) laughed-off as ridiculous. For a while, at least, Elizabeth Woodville was publicly reinstated as queen dowager, and even Yorkists (who, after the death of Richard III, focussed their attentions first on surviving sons – or possible sons – of Edward IV and Elizabeth Woodville, and later on the sons of Edward's sister, Elizabeth, Duchess of Suffolk) found no useful reason for calling to mind that earlier marriage of Edward IV's, which had achieved nothing but to wreck the hopes of the house of York.

But Eleanor was not everywhere forgotten. She was remembered with affection at Corpus Christi College, Cambridge, as 'our benefactress and intimate friend'. Probably she was likewise remembered at the Norwich Carmel, though the priory records do not survive. Folklore at Kenninghall in Norfolk also remembered, albeit anonymously, the great lady who had lived and died at East Hall. In similar anonymity, Eleanor was remembered abroad: by Philippe de Commynes, who, in the 1490s, included mention of her royal marriage in his memoirs, and by foreign diplomats, who found the Talbot marriage and the consequent illegitimacy of Henry VII's queen a very useful weapon against the house of Tudor well into the sixteenth century.[34]

Most particularly, Eleanor was remembered by her sister, the Duchess of Norfolk, who, in 1496, confirmed and augmented Eleanor's endowment at Corpus Christi College. One thing which emerges very clearly from Elizabeth Talbot's Corpus Christi indentures is the closeness of the relationship between the Talbot sisters. In one sense, this is more surprising than might at first sight appear, because Eleanor and Elizabeth cannot have spent much of their childhood together. The particular affection and regard in which Elizabeth seems to have held her, argues that Eleanor must have made a strong impact on her little sister during the latter's infancy.

It may also be the *titulus regius* of Richard III, and its subsequent repeal and destruction by Henry VII, which accounts for the extraordinary detail regarding Eleanor's identity and pedigree which is supplied in Elizabeth Talbot's first surviving Corpus Christi College indenture.[35] The names of Eleanor's parents, her first husband and her father-in-law are specified very precisely, with some redundant repetition, although this information is not at all relevant to the ostensible purpose of the document, and actually makes the text rather difficult to follow. Even one of Eleanor's grandparents – Richard Beauchamp, Earl of Warwick – is named, establishing her descent from the house of Warwick, and since he is the only grandparent to be mentioned, it seems that the Warwick family connection was considered to be particularly important.

At first sight it might be thought that the listing of family names was merely to ensure that their souls were prayed for, but a careful examination of the names mentioned in the indenture undermines this explanation. Thus, although Richard Beauchamp's name is included, he was not one of the relatives whose commemoration at Corpus Christi College was to be perpetuated by this indenture. Conversely the name of Eleanor's mother-in-law, Elizabeth Norbury, Lady Sudeley, who was to be commemorated, is actually omitted from the text and she is referred to only as Sir Thomas Butler's mother.

In fact, the real reason for describing Eleanor's family connections in such detail in the indentures seems to have been in order to establish very clearly who Eleanor was, in a context where her name had been brought briefly into the limelight and had then been deliberately obscured and even confused with the name of Elizabeth Wayte; a context, nevertheless, in which some people still remembered that King Edward IV was said to have once been involved with a relative of the Earl of Warwick. One is left with the impression that the Duchess of Norfolk, in addition to wishing to extend Eleanor's endowment in order to create a second scholarship, and to include prayers for herself and other members of the family, also had a desire to leave some record, however obliquely worded, of facts about her sister which could not easily be voiced in 1495 and which she knew were being deliberately confused and concealed elsewhere.

Elizabeth's indentures show that Eleanor had endowed a scholarship for a fellow of the college. This endowment the duchess confirmed, donating the sum of 220 marks to the college (to be paid partly from the inheritance which she had received from her sister). It was stipulated that Elizabeth was now to nominate a new holder of this fellowship (which, as we saw earlier, had probably fallen vacant about seven years earlier, in October 1487, when Thomas Cosyn had been promoted to the office of master of the college). Subsequently the fellows would be free to elect successors. The priest-fellow selected would be paid eight marks a year by the college, and would be known as the Talbot sisters' priest. He would offer daily mass for the repose of their souls. This daily mass would not be a requiem mass, but the equivalent of a chantry mass, that is to say the ordinary mass of the day, offered for the intention of the repose of the souls of Eleanor and her family, and celebrated without special solemnity.[36]

In addition the duchess added a new studentship. This student's stipend was set at the lower sum of 40s a year, and if and when the student graduated as a master of arts he would lose the emolument which would then pass to another student. It is clear that the holder of this studentship need not be a priest, for he is not required to celebrate mass, but only to give a daily reading, which he must end with the standard formula for prayers for the dead, on behalf of Eleanor, Elizabeth and all the faithful departed.

In addition to the two scholarships with their attendant obligations, the college itself undertook to keep in perpetuity five solemn annual anniversary commemorations. The principal anniversary, consisting of the celebration of vespers and matins of the dead and requiem mass for Eleanor and her family every year on 13 and 14 June, marked the actual anniversary of the death of Margaret, Countess of Shrewsbury. The second commemoration, on 17 July, marked the death of the Earl of Shrewsbury. This was planned to be slightly lower key, repeating the celebration of matins of the dead and requiem mass, but omitting vespers on the vigil of the anniversary.

Furthermore, all the priests of the college undertook to pray for the repose of the souls of Eleanor and her family annually on the feasts of St John the Baptist and St Michael the Archangel, and also at Christmas, saying matins of the dead and requiem mass again for them on those days. Finally, taking account, perhaps, of the fact that Eleanor's original endowment may have lapsed for a few years, the college undertook to ensure that it would never be forgotten again, wherefore it was stipulated that the duchess' indenture would be read aloud at the installation of each successive holder of the Talbot sisters' fellowship.

The Duchess of Norfolk's re-establishment of Eleanor's endowment endeavoured to be foolproof, and to ensure that her sister would never be forgotten. Of course, it has, to some extent, failed in its purpose. The present holder of this fellowship no longer celebrates the stipulated requiem masses and hours of the office of the dead for the repose of Eleanor's soul. The anniversaries are no longer kept, nor is Elizabeth's agreement regularly read aloud as specified. However, as she intended, the survival of the Duchess of Norfolk's indentures has ensured the preservation of very clear details relating to Eleanor's identity. At Corpus Christi College, Cambridge, Eleanor Talbot is, to this day, not forgotten.

Eleanor and the Historians

Eleanor Talbot's story does not end with her death, nor with Henry VII's rewriting of history. However, anyone in quest of earlier books about Eleanor will search in vain, for there are none. In reviewing Eleanor's historiography over the last 500 years it is therefore necessary to seek out snippets, which are generally to be found in studies focussed on such better-documented fifteenth-century figures as Edward IV or Richard III. Since, for writers on Richard III, Eleanor constitutes part of the controversy which surrounds that sovereign, what the author has to say about Eleanor tends to depend largely upon what attitude he or she wishes to take in respect of Richard.

There are many published works which mention Eleanor briefly. There are even more books which might have been expected to do so, but which opt instead to follow the Tudor line and leave Eleanor out. Only the most important can be considered in this necessarily brief overview. Writers such as Mancini, the parliamentary clerks of 1484, the continuator of the *Crowland Chronicle* and Commynes have already been considered, and will not be re-examined here. Although his reference to Edward IV's involvement with a member of the Earl of Warwick's family has also already been noted, we shall begin with Polydore Vergil, who published his *English History* in 1534.

In studying Eleanor's historiography the omissions of writers are potentially as interesting as their statements. Thus the fact that Polydore Vergil makes no mention whatsoever of Eleanor is highly significant. From the contemporary letters of Eustace Chapuys (see below, Appendix 1) we know that the issue of Edward IV's marriage to Eleanor was actively being discussed in Europe in the very year in which Vergil's history was published. Vergil's decision not to mention this question can therefore only be a matter of deliberate choice on the part of himself, his sources, or his patron. His account of the Woodville marriage is nevertheless interesting. Having described Warwick's embassy to France, seeking a marriage for his king with Bona of Savoy, Vergil explains that 'King Edwardes mynde alteryd uppon the soddayn, and he tooke to wyfe Elyzabeth, dowghter to Richerd earle Ryvers ... which mariage because the woman was of meane caulyng he kept secret'. When this marriage was revealed, the nobility 'found muche fault with him ... and imputyd the same to his dishonor, as the thing wherunto he was led by blynde affection, and not by reule of reason'.[1] Vergil's picture of a king who was well-known to be very much at the mercy of his own libido and a queen whose tenure was in question is not without relevance in the present context.

Vergil's account of the accession of Richard III also contains material which requires consideration. He relates in some detail how the Duke of Gloucester,

> being blinde with covetousnes of raigning ... had secret conference with one Raphe Sha, a divyne of great reputation ... to whom he utteryd, that his fathers inherytance ought to descend to him by right, as the eldest of all the soones which Richard his father Duke of York had begotten of Cecyly his wyfe: for as much as yt was manyfest ynowghe ... that Edward who had before raignyd, was a bastard, ... praying the said Sha to instruct the people therof in a sermon at Powles Crosse.[2]

Having thus represented Richard's claim to the throne as being based on the illegitimacy of *Edward IV*, Vergil continues: 'ther ys a common report that King Edwards chyldren wer in that sermon caulyd basterdes, and not King Edward, *which is voyd of all truthe*'.[3] Fabyan's *Chronicle* of 1516 had certainly quoted the sermon as arguing 'that the childyr of King Edward were not rightfull enherytours unto the crowne'.[4] But unfortunately for Vergil's denial of this statement, we now know beyond any question, from the text of the *titulus regius* of 1484, that Richard III's claim to the throne was indeed based upon the illegitimacy of Edward IV's *children*. Either Vergil was misinformed, or he is deliberately setting out to mislead us.

Like Vergil, Sir Thomas More makes no mention whatsoever of Eleanor Talbot in his *History of King Richard III*, various versions of which were published from 1543 to 1557.[5] However, More does not completely eschew the allegation that Edward IV's relationship with Elizabeth Woodville was bigamous. He chooses to address this issue, but in such a way as to make it appear ridiculous. According to More's English text, when she heard of his relationship with Elizabeth Woodville, Edward IV's mother begged him 'to refrain you from her mariage, sith it is an unsitting thing, and a veri blemish, and highe disparagement to the sacred magesty of a prince … to be defouled with bigamy in his first mariage'.[6] This sounds paradoxical, but presumably Cecily Neville's imputed reference is to the fact that *Elizabeth Woodville* had been married previously. Edward's reply is even more curious, for More puts into his mouth the sentence: 'as for the bigamy … I understand it is forbidden a prieste, but I never wiste it yet that it was forbidden a prince'.[7] His intended reference is to the rule which prohibited marriage with a widow to clerks in minor orders (for of course, priests of the western church were meant to be celibate).[8]

According to More's narrative, the Duchess of York,

> nothyng appeased … devised to disturbe this mariage, and rather to help that he shold mary one dame Elizabeth Lucy, whom ye king had also not long before gotten with child. Wherefore the kinges mother obiected openly against his mariage, as it were in discharge of her conscience, that the kinge was sure [i.e. committed] to dame Elizabeth Lucy, and [was] her husband before god.[9]

The fact that 'Lucy' was Elizabeth Wayte's *married* surname, and that she must therefore have been ineligible as a royal bride is ignored.

The substitution of the name of Elizabeth Wayte (Lucy) for that of Eleanor Talbot constitutes a fascinating *tour de force* of manipulation on two levels. First, More's chronology is very nearly accurate, since Elizabeth Wayte was probably already the king's mistress at a time when he was still peripherally involved with Eleanor Talbot, and certainly before he became infatuated with Elizabeth Woodville. This fact lends More's account a veneer of verisimilitude. Second, the issue of a prior attachment is thereby explicitly addressed, but in a very clever way, because More is able to explain that 'when she [Elizabeth Wayte] was solempnely sworne to say the trouth, she confessed that they were never ensured [committed]',[10] thus apparently undermining the entire story.

It is hard to avoid the conclusion that More (or his informant) is deliberately muddying the waters just sufficiently to thoroughly confuse anybody who happened to have retained some memory of the real bigamy allegation of 1483–84. One is reminded of Henry VII's more blatant attempt to obscure the true course of events by his repeal and destruction of Richard III's *titulus regius*.

Needless to say, apart from More's account, we have no surviving evidence that Cecily Neville intervened in the matter of her son's marriage in 1464 (although she may have done so), nor that Elizabeth Wayte (Lucy) was ever quizzed on the subject. If Elizabeth was questioned, it must have been before the death of Edward IV, since she died before 1482 (and probably as early as 1467).[11] Edward Halle's version of More's history as published by Grafton in 1550, contains the additional statement that a sermon, preached by Dr Ralph Shaw at Paul's Cross in 1483, called Elizabeth Wayte (Lucy) 'the very wife of King Edward'.[12]

Early in the seventeenth century two significant developments took place. One was the publication of the text of Richard III's *titulus regius*.[13] The second was the appearance, in 1631, of Weever's *Funeral Monuments*, which fortuitously recorded (before all trace of it was lost) the existence of Eleanor's tomb in the ruins of the church of the former Carmelite Priory in Norwich. But for this fact, we should have no notion where Eleanor was buried. It is unlikely that Norwich would have been thought of, since her family background and her tenure of manors would have tended to focus attention on quite different geographical areas.

Buck's *History of King Richard the Third*, published in 1619, had a good deal to say on the subject of Eleanor Talbot. Indeed, it was the first historical study to mention her at all, since her name, cast to oblivion by the deliberate policy of Henry VII, had previously been generally unknown, at least in a royal context. Buck was aware of the principal documentation relating to Eleanor: the Act of Parliament of 1484, the *Crowland Chronicle* and the *Mémoires* of Commynes. His introduction of Eleanor comes in a quotation from the *Crowland Chronicle*, reciting the tenor of the Act of Parliament of 1484. Buck's quotation is interesting, however, since his text differs slightly from our standard text of the chronicle (see below, Hanham). Consider, for example, Buck's phrase:

filii regis Edwardi erant bastardi, supponendo illum præcontraxisse matrimonium cum quadam domina Alienora Boteler antequam reginam Elizabetham duxisset in uxorem.[14]

The children of King Edward were bastards, on the pretext that he had previously contracted a marriage with a certain Lady Eleanor Boteler before he espoused Queen Elizabeth.

This contains the word *matrimonium* (marriage), which is absent from the standard Crowland text. Whether Buck made a mistake, or had access to a slightly different version of the chronicle, which is now lost, cannot be resolved.

Later, Buck goes back in time to offer further explanation of who Eleanor was. He relates that King Edward 'had many mistresses or *amasia*s', of whom 'the most famous were Catherine de Claringdon, Elizabeth Wayte (alias Lucy), Joanne Shore, [and] the foresaid Lady Eleanor Talbot'.[15] Buck is the first writer to use the word 'mistress' to describe Eleanor's relationship with the king, for no fifteenth-century source does so. Some later authors have gleefully seized upon this word, but we must be very careful and tread warily. In the early seventeenth century 'mistress' described the object of a man's affection; not necessarily his illicit sexual partner. This can be seen from literature of the period, such as Marvel's sonnet 'To his coy mistress'. Indeed, Buck himself makes this point explicitly by his addition of the synonym *amasia*, a late Latin term meaning 'sweetheart'. Elsewhere we discover that Buck employs the word 'concubine' when he wishes to refer explicitly to an illicit sexual relationship.[16] However, he never applies the word 'concubine' to Eleanor. In the present passage he is therefore telling us that Eleanor was the object of Edward's love. He is not suggesting that she was the king's sexual partner outside of marriage.

We may note that Buck was generally well-informed, and may possibly have had access to some sources which are no longer extant. He tells us, for example, that when Edward left Eleanor, 'her heart was so full of grief that she was ready to burst, and that she could no longer conceal it. She revealed her marriage to a lady who was her sister, or, as some say, her mother, the Countess of Shrewsbury, or to both'.[17] The subsequent conduct of the Duchess of Norfolk makes it entirely credible that she was aware of her sister's relationship with Edward IV. However, no contemporary text now surviving explicitly involves Elizabeth Talbot at this stage. Buck also knew enough about Elizabeth Lucy to be able to supply her maiden name. Likewise he has correctly identified, and uses, Eleanor's maiden name (which is not supplied in either the *titulus regius* or the *Crowland Chronicle*). Moreover, he was able to name Catherine de Claringdon in connection with the king, though she is not identified in any other surviving source. However, even Buck was apparently unable to penetrate the late sixteenth-century disguise of 'Joanne Shore': a point upon which we may very briefly digress.

The name of the latter has generally been given as *Jane* Shore. In fact, however, the first name *Jane* is pure invention. *Jane Shore*'s real name was Elizabeth Lambert, though she was first married to William Shore. After her seduction by Edward IV, she petitioned the Bishop of London for an annulment of this marriage on grounds of non-consummation. Her case was referred to the pope in 1476, and the Shore marriage was duly annulled. Despite this, and her subsequent marriage to Thomas Lynom, contemporaries continued to call her 'Mistress Shore'. As a result, by the sixteenth century her real first name seems to have been completely forgotten, and in 1609, when Beaumont and Fletcher produced their play, *Knight of the Burning Pestle*, they could find no record of it, so they then invented *Jane Shore* to give the character a name on stage.

To return to Buck, he does make some mistakes in respect of Eleanor. He wrongly identifies her mother as Lady Catherine Stafford, and tells us that when the king abandoned her, Eleanor's predicament was communicated to her father, which is impossible, for the earl was long dead.[18] Buck was familiar with the text of Philippe de Commynes, and quotes the latter's version of how Stillington married Edward and Eleanor.[19] However, he also makes use of Polydore Vergil and, extrapolating from his knowledge of the fact that elsewhere the name of Elizabeth Wayte (Lucy) had been substituted for that of Eleanor, he gives Vergil's account of the intervention of the Duchess of York in 1464, but substituting Eleanor as the 'former love and wife' to whom Cecily Neville begs her son to return.[20]

During the eighteenth century two further important contributions were made to Eleanor's historiography. The first of these is rather distinctive, being Masters' history of Corpus Christi College Cambridge, published in 1753. Robert Masters notes Eleanor as a benefactress of the college, but he was unable, even at that date, to find any extant evidence of her involvement dating from her own lifetime.[21] Masters was well aware of Eleanor's identity. He states that she was the sister of Elizabeth Talbot, Duchess of Norfolk, the wife of the late Sir Thomas Botelar (son and heir of Ralph, Lord of Sudeley), and the daughter of John Talbot, first Earl of Shrewsbury by his second wife, Margaret Beauchamp. He also cites the Act of Parliament of 1484 naming Eleanor as Edward IV's wife.[22] Given that Masters was able to publish all this information in the mid-eighteenth century it is somewhat astonishing that some later writers apparently remained in ignorance of these basic facts. However, most historians were unaware of Eleanor's connection with Corpus Christi College, and therefore failed to consult Masters and his sources.

Horace Walpole, writing in 1768, explicitly noted the conflict between the accounts of George Buck and Thomas More in respect of the bigamy allegation levelled against Edward IV, concluding: 'I am unwillingly obliged to charge that great man [More] with *wilful falshood*'.[23] Walpole had a good grasp of his material. He was aware that Elizabeth Wayte (Lucy)'s family originated in Southampton (though he misconstrues her maiden name as 'Wyat'). He also knew that 'Edward's precontract or marriage, urged to invalidate his match with the Lady Grey, was with the Lady Eleanor Talbot, widow of the Lord Butler of Sudeley [*sic*], and sister of the Earl of Shrewsbury, one of the greatest peers in the kingdom'.[24] His statements are generally accurate, though he repeats Buck's error of identifying Eleanor's mother as Catherine Stafford.

Walpole was also familiar with, and cited, the evidence of the *Crowland Chronicle*, the text of the *titulus regius* of 1484, and the account of Philippe de Commynes. Having quoted the Act of Parliament, he enquires 'could Sir Thomas More be ignorant of this fact? Or, if ignorant, where is his competence as an historian?'[25] Nor does Walpole forbear from casting acidulated aspersions upon 'the art used by Sir Thomas More (when he could not deny a pre-contract) in endeavouring to shift that objection on Elizabeth Lucy, a married woman, contrary to the specific words of the act of parliament'.[26]

Writing in the first half of the nineteenth century, Caroline Halsted largely based her assessment of Eleanor and the surrounding issues upon Buck and Commynes. Consequently she added very little in the way of new material. That little, however, is important, despite the fact that Halsted consigned it to a footnote. She informs us that 'the Lady Eleanor did not long survive the king's infidelity: retiring into a monastery, she devoted herself to religion, and dying on 30th of July, 1466, was buried in the Carmelites' church at Norwich. She was a great benefactress to Corpus Christi College in Cambridge, as she was likewise to the University'.[27]

Halsted was, of course, mistaken regarding the date of Eleanor's death, and she misinterpreted Eleanor's choice of religious life. However, with the exception of the college historian, Masters, Halsted was the first writer to mention Eleanor's association with Corpus Christi, Cambridge. She was also the first to intimate that Eleanor retired into a religious life of some kind; was associated with the Whitefriars, and was buried at the Norwich Carmel. She cited Weever as her source, and doubtless for Eleanor's Carmelite connections and her burial, this was correct. However, Weever does not mention Corpus Christi College, so it seems that Halsted must also have seen Masters' history of the college, although she does not say so.

In his study of Richard III, published initially in 1878, James Gairdner both reported and analysed in some detail the allegation of the Act of Parliament of 1484 that Edward IV was married to Eleanor Talbot prior to his Woodville marriage. Observing that 'the evidence of Edward IV's precontract with Lady Eleanor Butler rested on the single testimony of Robert Stillington',[28] Gairdner went on to examine the account given by Buck (above), regretting that 'we cannot tell the precise evidence from which [he] derived his information'.[29]

Unlike some other historians, however, Gairdner approached the entire question in a spirit of academic enquiry and investigation:

The imprisonment of Bishop Stillington is mentioned by Commines, and is, moreover, confirmed by the Stonor Family Letters, from which we know that it took place in the year 1478. But the words of Commines scarcely indicate that his imprisonment had anything to do with the secret of the pre-contract; indeed they might rather be taken to imply that, in the opinion of the author, the pre-contract story was a falsehood maliciously invented by the bishop to revenge his imprisonment as soon as he could do it with safety. On this view of the case, we may assume that Stillington was, like many other people, an enemy of the Woodvilles, and attributed his misfortune to them. Yet it must be remarked that, by the same authority, his antipathy to them dated from a much earlier period than that of his imprisonment, for Commines says that he smothered his revenge for nearly twenty years, which would imply that he took offence at the very time when the Woodvilles originally rose into influence by Edward's marriage. If so, there is nothing improbable in the assumption that he was from the first disliked by the queen and her relations as the depository of a dangerous secret.[30]

Gairdner's careful and balanced analysis is very much to be commended. As we have already seen, he concluded that, while the account of the Talbot marriage had been generally discounted by historians, there were, in fact, insufficient grounds to justify this.

Noteworthy in view of the apparent ignorance of some later writers on the subject, is the fact that in 1878 Gairdner had absolutely no doubt as to Eleanor's parentage and family connections. Also he seems to have been the first to perceive the potential link between the imprisonment of Stillington by Edward IV, and the Clarence attainder. He cited the primary evidence of the Stonor letters to underline the fact that the dates of these two events closely coincided. Like Walpole, Gairdner also noted the discrepancies between the *titulus regius* of 1484 and the later account of Thomas More, in which 'a courtesan of obscure birth is made to take the place of an earl's daughter' as Edward IV's marriage partner.[31] He concluded that More's account was a misrepresentation, asserting with impeccable logic that 'the care afterwards taken to suppress and to pervert [Richard III's Act of Parliament] ... is perhaps rather an evidence of the truth of the story' of Edward IV's marriage as therein reported.[32]

Sir Clements Markham, in his defence of Richard III, published in 1906, had little to add on the subject of Eleanor, though he gave a fairly full account, including details of Eleanor's birth family and marriage family, and her burial at the Norwich Carmel.[33] He assumed (probably incorrectly) that she also died in Norwich, and he failed to note her association with Corpus Christi College, Cambridge.

However, he made a real attempt to supply new information about Robert Stillington and observed that Henry VII 'kept him in close and solitary imprisonment in Windsor Castle until his death in June 1491'.[34] Markham was right in thinking that it is helpful to know as much as possible about Stillington. However, when he deduced from Henry VII's life-imprisonment of the bishop, and from his repeal of Richard III's *titulus regius* that 'the conclusion is inevitable that the previous contract of Edward IV with Lady Eleanor Butler was a fact', this was clearly an oversimplification.[35] Henry VII was bound to hound Stillington, and repeal Richard's Act of Parliament, simply to defend his wife's legitimacy. He would presumably have acted in this way whether or not the alleged Talbot marriage was a fact.

Cora Scofield, writing about Edward IV seventeen years later, was much more circumspect, both in respect of the Talbot marriage and in respect of Stillington. 'How much truth, if any, there was in the story of Edward's seduction, by means of a promise of marriage, of Lady Eleanor Butler … it is impossible to say',[36] and 'why Stillington was imprisoned so soon after Clarence's execution is as much a matter of doubt as the immediate cause of Clarence's punishment'.[37]

However, Scofield herself by no means always avoided speculation. According to her, 'the story of Edward's precontract … was not told to Gloucester until after Edward's death when Stillington, *who never forgave Edward for sending him to the Tower*, related it to the Duke – *probably invented it for him* – in order to furnish him with grounds for declaring Edward's children illegitimate'.[38] This passage contains two rather large assumptions, one of which – Stillington's supposed rancour against Edward IV – is simply stated as though it were a fact, while the other – Stillington's invention of the Talbot marriage – is glossed as 'probable'. Both of these assumptions can certainly be questioned.

In his 1955 biography of Richard III, Paul Murray Kendall has been accused of theorising beyond his data in certain instances. In respect of Eleanor, however, he strenuously sought to contribute new information. He suggested that Eleanor was the daughter of Lord Shrewsbury's second marriage (a fact which has now been amply verified), and proposed that Eleanor was a few years older than Edward IV. Kendall misinterpreted the evidence of the patent rolls regarding the confiscation of Eleanor's manors by the king (an event which has now been shown to post-date Eleanor's demise). However, he picked up Gairdner's observation of a possible connection between the arrest of Stillington and the death of Clarence. This he amplified with new source material relating to the accusation levelled against Stillington in 1478. He followed Markham in noting that Stillington was subsequently hounded by Henry VII.[39] Finally, in a detailed footnote, Kendall supplied a complete summary of the surviving evidence in respect of Eleanor Talbot, as known at that date.[40]

In his study of Edward IV, Charles Ross did not mention Eleanor at all.[41] This is, perhaps, curious, since he doubts neither her existence, nor her involvement with the king. We know this because in his study of

Richard III, when describing Edward IV's confiscation of Sudeley Castle, he unhesitatingly categorises Eleanor as Edward's 'former mistress'.[42] Later he cites the *Crowland Chronicle* in respect of the claim that Edward was married to Eleanor before his marriage to Elizabeth Woodville,[43] a claim which he equally unhesitatingly dismisses as a 'hugely tendentious piece of propaganda'.[44]

In view of the fact that at least two fifteenth-century sources exist which report the claim that Eleanor was Edward's *wife*,[45] while there is not a single fifteenth-century source in existence which names her as his *mistress*, Ross's preference for this latter, unsubstantiated label, and his rejection of the marriage claim seems at best unscientific. His dismissal of the marriage claim is redolent with unsupported assertions and red herrings: Parliament, he informs us, had no jurisdiction in moral matters, and the validity of a marriage did not fall within its area of competence. This is disingenuous. The Parliament of 1484 was adjudicating neither morals nor the marriage question, but the right of succession to the throne. Likewise, the fact (emphasised by Ross) that Edward V and Richard of Shrewsbury were born after Eleanor's death is utterly irrelevant to the question of their legitimacy.

Unqualified but unsubstantiated judgements in respect of Eleanor's alleged marriage with the king are not uncommon. One very clear example of this phenomenon is Dr Alison Hanham's statement that the continuator of the *Crowland Chronicle* 'makes it clear that the petition referring to Edward's alleged marriage with Eleanor Butler was fraudulent'.[46] Of course the Crowland continuator does no such thing. He simply makes clear *his opinion* that it was fraudulent. This opinion is only what one would expect, given the chronicler's clear political stance.

As for Hanham's assessment of Buck's published quotations from the *Crowland Chronicle* (which, as we have seen, differ somewhat from the extant standard text, and include specific use of the word *matrimonium* with reference to Edward IV and Eleanor), her firm conclusion that 'Buck's alterations ... were designed to support his thesis in support of Richard' seems mischievous, in the light of her acknowledgement that the extant evidence is incomplete and renders the drawing of firm conclusions difficult.[47]

It is also interesting to find here an example of the historical double standards which so extensively bedevil attempts to study subjects which bear upon Richard III. For even if it could be demonstrated beyond question that Buck had falsified his text in order to favour Richard's case, it is difficult to understand why that should be considered any more reprehensible than Henry VII's deliberate attempts to rewrite history, for example by means of his repeal and attempted destruction of the Act of Parliament of 1484.

Sean Cunningham's recent study of Richard III picks up a much earlier theme of Vergil's, suggesting that 'Richard's claim to the throne as the only true heir of his father Richard, Duke of York, was publicly proclaimed during a sermon by Ralph Shaw at St Paul's Cross. This alleged firstly that Edward IV was conceived in adultery and that therefore he and all his children were bastards'.[48] Unsurprisingly, Cunningham cites no source for this assertion. It can, indeed, only be based on hearsay, since the text of Shaw's sermon is not extant. We have already noted that Vergil's account is selective, probably deliberately partisan, and not simply to be accepted at face value. Cunningham seeks to reconcile it with the evidence of the *titulus regius* of 1484 by stating that 'this was later changed to a declaration that Edward's marriage of 1464 was invalid because of an existing pre-contract to the Earl of Shrewsbury's daughter'. His phraseology carefully avoids the use of the word 'marriage' in respect of Eleanor, though his unequivocal acceptance of her pedigree is encouraging. However, there is, in point of fact, no evidence that the claim advanced on Richard's behalf was ever changed. Thus Cunningham's statement is merely an opinion, based on selective use of the available evidence.

In conclusion, one may note that those historians who have accepted the potential significance of Eleanor Talbot's role in fifteenth-century history have (perhaps not surprisingly) made a much greater contribution to our knowledge of her than those who, from the outset, have chosen to dismiss or blue-pencil her. Since it is now an undeniable fact that she was named in relationship to Edward IV, it is surely desirable to seek to elucidate the part she played in events. This objective is not best achieved by pretending that she, or her relationship with the king, did not exist.

20

Eleanor's Body

We left Eleanor Talbot's body reposing in a tomb within the priory church of the Norwich Carmel, where it was laid to rest by her sister in the summer of 1468. What subsequently became of Eleanor's tomb, and the physical remains which it contained? Of course, English burials in the churches of religious orders found themselves at a something of a disadvantage in the sixteenth century, when Henry VIII's Dissolution of the Monasteries robbed them of their home. Lurid tales have been recounted of such bodies being cast out of their tombs and mistreated as a result of the Dissolution.[1]

Such stories seem to be mere sensationalism. They all appear to be later inventions, and they are given the lie by the fact that modern excavations on the sites of religious houses generally find intact burials preserved under the ground, even though their tomb superstructures may have vanished. Eleanor's resting place was apparently still identifiable amongst the ruins of the Carmelite priory when Weever passed that way in the early seventeenth century, eighty years or more after the Dissolution. It is therefore reasonable to suppose that her body remained in its original burial place for at least 100 years following the Dissolution, and probably remained at the Whitefriars until recent times. Indeed, it could still be there.

In 1958, however, a rescue excavation took place on the former Carmelite priory site in Norwich, ahead of further development by Jarrolds Printers (to whom this property now belongs). Unfortunately this excavation was never properly published by the archaeologists, and the only surviving contemporary accounts of it seem to be a newspaper report in the *Eastern Daily*

Press, and two short reports in Jarrolds' own in-house magazine.[2] Moreover, the formal site notes and plans of the excavation appear to be no longer extant. Nevertheless, after much searching, the present author was able to find the original private notebooks of the excavator in the Record Office in Norwich. These include sketches and plans, but no dimensions.

The excavation was located towards the southern boundary of the priory precinct, near the River Wensum and Whitefriars Bridge. A little to the east of the surviving arch of an anchorite's cell the excavators found what appeared to be a rubbish dump, filling a pit. In a level which contained broken pottery of the seventeenth century, two human skeletons were found. One of these (it is not recorded which) had a medieval oak coffin upside down on top of it. Fragments of medieval stonework were also found. The implication would appear to be that the bodies had been thrown into a rubbish dump at about the middle of the seventeenth century (around the time of the Civil War). The find location was clearly not the original place of burial, so the bodies had presumably originally been buried elsewhere on the priory site. One of the bodies was judged to be male and the other female, but no detailed study was undertaken.

The skeleton which was adjudged to be female, identified as *Carmelite Friary Inhumation II* (or CFII), was placed on exhibition at St Peter Hungate church Museum in Norwich, lying in the restored wooden coffin (which may or may not originally have belonged to it). The coffin and bones were displayed upon a much later wooden bier which had no connection with either of them. There the skeleton remained until 1996, when it was removed from exhibition and taken into storage at the Castle Museum in Norwich. Attempts on the part of the author to locate the other (possibly male) remains, and the associated finds of stonework have so far been unsuccessful. These seem to have vanished. In 1996 the Director of the Norfolk Museums Service kindly agreed to an examination of CFII by Mr W.J. White (now curator of the Centre for Human Bioarchaeology, Museum of London).

Following his examination, Mr White reported his findings to the Norfolk Museums Service (30 September 1996) as follows:

The bones of the lower leg were damaged therefore the maximum length of the femur was used in the formula for the estimation of height during life.[3] This person would have stood 169 cm (5'6") tall ... The skull was sufficiently preserved for the conventional measurements to be made. The calculated *cranial index* was 81.2, *ie* within the brachycephalic or 'short-headed' range.[4] ... The skeleton examined was of a sturdily-built woman aged between 25 and 35, who, appears to have enjoyed generally good health from at least late childhood until her early death and who almost certainly had never experienced childbirth... The above data, including non-parous state and age 25-35 are not inconsistent with what is known of Lady Eleanor Butler [*sic*] ... The Norwich skeleton did share one trait with John Talbot, namely brachycephaly, his cranial index being calculated as 92.0. However, this trait was shared with the majority of the population of medieval England.

An additional comparison might be made between the height of CFII and that of the first Earl of Shrewsbury, for the earl was 5ft 8.5in (174.5 cm) tall,[5] based upon Egerton's measurement of his femur as 18.5in in length.[6]

Mr White also noted that there were indications, particularly from the state of the teeth (which suggested a refined diet containing sugar) that the individual was a member of the nobility. In this case the dental evidence might further suggest that the age at death was towards the upper limit of the range established. In 1996, when Mr White wrote his report, it was still considered possible to assess whether (and how many times) a woman had borne children, based upon an examination of the pelvic bones, but sadly such assessments are now considered unreliable.[7]

In addition to Eleanor Talbot, Weever, whose account was published in 1631, listed eighteen other females and twenty-two males as having been interred in the church of the Carmelite Friary, Norwich, excluding the Carmelite religious themselves, whom he lists separately, and only one of whom was female: an anchoress. The list of female burials (to which the Carmelite anchoress has been added) is as follows:

1. Lady La ... Argentein
2. Lady Eleanor Butler [Talbot]
3. Lady Alice Boyland
4. Lady Katherine, wife of Sir Bartholomew Somerton, Kt.
5. Lady Alice, wife of Sir Will. Crongthorp
6. Lady Joan, wife of Sir Thomas Morley
7. Marg. Pulham
8. Lady Elizabeth Hetersete

9. Lady Katherin, wife of Sir Nich. Borne

10. Joan, wife of John Fastolph

11. Alice, wife of Thomas Crunthorp

12. Lady Alice Everard, died 1321

13. Lady Alice With, died 1561

14. Lady Elizabeth, third wife of Sir Thomas Gerbrigge (who died 1430), formerly wife of Sir John Berry and daughter of Robert Wachesham, died 1402.

15. Lady Alice, wife of Sir Edmund Berry (who died 1433) and daughter of Thomas Gerbrigge

16 Elizabeth, first wife of William Calthorp and daughter of Sir Reignold, Lord Hastings, Waysford and Ruthin, died 1437

17. Cecily, child of William Calthorp

18. Lady Margery, wife of Sir John Paston and daughter of Thomas Brews, died 1495

19. Lady Margaret, wife of Sir Thomas Pigott, died 1489

20. Emma (Stapleton) Carmelite anchoress, died 2 December 1422.

Weever was writing nearly 100 years after the Dissolution, and the source for his list is not known but the eastern end of the Carmelite church is thought to have been still standing (in ruins) in the mid-seventeenth century. Indeed, although the main church building had been demolished by the eighteenth century, part of the Holy Cross chapel was still intact, and in use as a Baptist chapel, as late as 1883.[8] Thus Weever himself may well have seen the tombs he lists. At all events their existence would appear to have been within living memory in 1631. Where his list can be checked by reference to other source material it proves to be accurate.[9]

In addition to Weever's list, wills indicate that six further female burials also took place at the Carmelite church, as follows:

21. Christian Savage, widow of Peter Savage of Norwich, died 1440

22. Margaret Furbisher, widow, died 1466

23. Christian Boxworth, widow, died circa 1500

24. Elizabeth, widow of Will. Aslake, died 1502/3

25. Margaret Beaumond, died 1523

26. … Hevyngham, mother of John Hevyngham, parson of Kesgrave, died circa 1500.[10]

Probably, however, all of these can be eliminated as candidates for identification with CFII on the grounds of their social status This would leave a total of twenty possible candidates who might possibly be CFII.

For the female interments listed by Weever, the following additional information has been discovered:

1. Lady La ... Argentein: first name Laura; sister of Robert de Vere, Earl of Oxford; wife of Sir Reginald Argentein, and probably the mother of his son, John. She was the daughter of Hugh de Vere, Earl of Oxford and his wife, Hawise de Quincy, who were married in about 1223. Laura was born at Hedingham Castle, *c.*1230, and died in 1292 in her early sixties.[11] Her age at death shows that she cannot be CFII.

2. Lady Eleanor is the subject of this book.

3. Lady Alice Boyland: wife of Roger de Boyland. who died before 1256. Their son, Richard de Boyland, was a successful lawyer and was appointed to the bench in 1279. He was still living in 1298. Lady Alice must have died after 1256 (when the Norwich Carmel was founded), but her date of death is unknown.[12]

4. Katherine Somerton's husband, Sir Bartholomew Somerton, was related by marriage to the Pastons, and possibly also to Friar John Somerton (*fl.* 1479) who may have been a Carmelite though he is not listed as such by Weever. Bartholomew had at least two children, Thomas and Constantia, but the name of their mother is not stated.[13]

5. Lady Alice Crongthorp is identified by Weever as the wife of Sir William Crongthorp. Two individuals of this name are known, in connection with the manor of Crownthorpe, near Wymondham: Sir William Crongthorp II (*fl. c.*1346) and his father (*fl. c.*1280–1320). Both had at least one son called William, but the name of the mother is in neither case recorded. Sir William Crongthorp I was almost certainly Alice's husband, however, as Weever lists among the Carmelite Friars also buried at the friary in Norwich, a Friar William Crongthorp, who had been a knight before he became a friar, and who had died on 12 April 1332. This suggests that his wife had predeceased him and he buried her at the friary, perhaps in about 1330, before himself entering the Carmelite order. Moreover, William II is known to have had a wife called Katherine.[14]

6. Joan Morley's husband, Thomas, ultimately had a higher rank than Weever allows him, for in 1379 he became the fourth Baron Morley. Joan, however,

probably died shortly before this, since her husband remarried in about 1380. Joan's age at death is not recorded. However, her husband was born in about 1354, and she is unlikely to have been older than he was, so she was almost certainly under 25 at the time of her death. She is therefore unlikely to be CFII. Joan had at least one son, Robert.[15]

7. Marg Pulham is perhaps to be identified with the unnamed first or second wife of Sir Thomas Pulham of Stradbroke, Suffolk, (who died 1532), who left 10s. to the Norwich Carmelites in his will. She was possibly also the mother of his daughter, Margery. The family may have been related to the Carmelite Friar, Robert Pulham, who Weever also lists as being buried at the White Friars.[16]

8. Elizabeth Hetersete can be identified with Elizabeth, wife of Sir John Hethersett, by whom she had a son, William. Sir John died *c.* 1355, but Elizabeth survived him and remarried. She probably died in about 1376. Since she must have been at least 16 when her first husband died (or she could not have borne him a son) she seems almost certain to have been more than 35 years old at the time of her death, and is therefore unlikely to be CFII.[17]

9. Katherine Borne is perhaps to be identified with the unnamed mother of Elizabeth Borne, wife of John Harling.[18]

10. Joan Fastolph cannot, at present, be identified and no further details about her are available.

11. Alice Crunthorp, wife of Thomas Crunthorp, is fairly certainly the unnamed wife of Thomas Crungethorpe (died *c.* 1400). It is not known whether this couple had children.[19]

12. Alice Everard was the wife of Sir Thomas Everard, who was alive as early as the reign of Henry III. She may not have been his first wife, and must have been considerably younger than her husband, but even so, she would have been an old lady by the time of her death in 1321. She is known to have had at least one son, Thomas.[20] Her age at death means she cannot have been CFII.

13. Lady Alice Withe is said by Weever to have been buried at the Norwich Carmel in 1561. This is certainly an error for 1361. No burials could have taken place at the priory after the Dissolution. Blomefield gives Lady Alice as the wife of Sir Oliver Wythe, who was also buried at the Norwich Carmel, as were other members of his family. Oliver and Alice are thought to have been the parents of Sir John Wyth (died 1387).[21] Alice was therefore probably too old at death to be CFII.

14. Elizabeth Gerbrigge was the mother of No. 5. Alice Berry. She was probably about forty-seven when she died. Thus she cannot be CFII.

15. Alice Berry was the mother of Agnes, wife of Judge William Paston. She died at about the age of 50.[22] Thus she cannot be CFII.

16. Elizabeth Calthorp was the wife of Sir William Calthorp II. Although Weever describes her father as Lord Hastings, this title was, in fact, disputed, but Reynold did hold the title Lord Grey, which Weever omits. Elizabeth was about thirty at the time of her death, and had at least three children, John, Anne and William.[23] Based on her age at death she could be CFII.

17. Cecily probably died about 1390. She was probably the daughter of William Calthorp I (*c.* 1360–1420) by his first wife, Eleanor Mawtby. Weever states that she was a child at the time of her death.[24] She therefore could not be CFII.

18. Margery Paston is well known from published editions of the Paston family papers. She was aged about 35 at the time of her death, in 1495, and had had at least six children: Christopher, Sir William, Dorothy, Elizabeth, Philippa and Philip.[25] On the basis of her age at death, however, she could be CFII.

19. Margaret Piggott may be the Margaret who was wife to Jeffrey Pigot, *fl. c.*1457/8. No other details are known.[26]

20. Emma, the Carmelite anchoress, was the daughter of Sir Miles Stapleton. Unfortunately more than one individual is known to have borne the name Miles in different generations of the Stapleton family, and it is not clear which one was Emma's father, which makes it difficult to estimate her age at death. One would expect her to have been childless, since she does not seem to have been married before she became an anchoress. Living, as she did, a life of asceticism, it may be considered doubtful whether, if she died in her early thirties, she would by then have consumed sufficient sugar to display the incipient caries found in CFII, or whether she would have been buried in an oak coffin. She cannot, however, be ruled out of consideration.

By excluding numbers 1, 6, 8, 12, 13, 14, 15 and 17 from Weever's list, the evidence of age at death reduces the list of candidates for identification with CFll from twenty to twelve. Clearly, this is insufficient for a positive identification of the remains. As Mr W.J. White indicated in his report to the Norfolk Museums Service, this could perhaps be achieved by mito-chondrial DNA analysis, which would, however, require the identification of a control sequence of DNA from a female-line relative of Eleanor. No such sequence has as yet been identified. Carbon dating and strontium 90 analysis of the enamel of the teeth to determine geographical origin might also be helpful. Nevertheless, the skeleton preserved in Norwich certainly could be that of Eleanor Talbot. There are two further kinds of evidence which might conceivably strengthen the evidence for the possible identification of the CFII remains with Eleanor. These concern 'the Talbot fingers' and the congenital absence of certain teeth in fifteenth-century members of the Talbot family.[27]

The anomaly known as 'the Talbot fingers' is more properly called symphalangism. It is popularly known as 'stiff fingers'. It is the condition of 'hereditary absence of one or more proximal interphalangeal joints',[28] that is to say that the knuckle joints nearest the palm, which in a normal hand allow the fingers to bend, are fused in cases of symphalangism, so that normal movement is not possible, hence the term 'stiff fingers'. This condition reportedly exists in some members of the Talbot family at the present day, and is traceable in that family back to at least the eighteenth century. The further claim had been advanced that the condition had also been present in the skeleton of the first Earl of Shrewsbury (died 1453), who was Eleanor's father. If this claim were well founded, the question would have arisen whether Eleanor might not also have suffered from this congenital condition, in which case one might have expected evidence of it in the Norwich skeleton, CFII.

In the event, however, symphalangism proved not to be helpful in identifying CFII. When the Norwich skeleton was ejected from its tomb, probably in the mid-seventeenth century, it seems likely that its coffin was overturned. One report of the discovery of CFII, in 1958, speaks of a coffin being found crushed on top of one of the sets of bones.[29] Probably as a result of such treatment, the skeleton, while substantially intact, is lacking some small bones, including most of the bones of the fingers and toes, where the evidence of symphalangism, if it existed, would have been found. More importantly, however, the contention that symphalangism existed in the Talbot family as long ago as the fifteenth century has been questioned. The transmission of such a congenital abnormality through fourteen generations of a family would be unusual. There is, in fact, nothing in the medical report which was drawn up in the last century when the remains of the first Earl of Shrewsbury were examined, which would substantiate the claim that his bones showed any evidence of this anomaly,[30] and the most recent re-examination of the case of John Talbot concluded that 'adequate proof ... is lacking'.[31]

Of greater interest is the phenomenon of congenitally missing teeth, because the existence of this anomaly can certainly be substantiated in at least one close relative of Eleanor Talbot. Lady Anne Mowbray, Duchess of York and Norfolk, who died in 1481, a little short of her ninth birthday, was Eleanor's niece, the daughter of her younger sister, Elizabeth Talbot, Duchess of Norfolk. Anne's body was examined in 1965, and a report on her teeth was published in the *British Dental Journal*.[32] This report established, among other things, that Anne exhibited:

> congenital absence of upper and lower permanent second molars on the left. There is no sign of these tooth germs or of any relevant disturbance of the bone structure, so that it is clear that the teeth could never have been present. There is no indication of third molars and it is rather probable that these also would have been lacking.[33]

Rushton was of the opinion that the congenital absence of these particular teeth was a very unusual anomaly. He also stated that congenital absence of teeth is usually an hereditary trait although not necessarily having the same expression in different members of a family.[34] One would therefore expect that Anne Mowbray must have shared the trait of congenitally absent teeth with some, although not necessarily with all, of her relatives in one of her family lines. On the basis of her case alone, however, it would be impossible to guess whether the congenital abnormality was inherited from her father's Mowbray ancestors, from her mother's Talbot ancestors or from one of her many other lines of descent. If similar dental anomalies were present in the case of CFII, it would suggest that CFII could be one of Anne's close relatives (and therefore probably Eleanor Talbot) and it would lend support to the proposition that Anne inherited the trait from her Talbot ancestors.

In fact CFII does show some dental peculiarities, including the absence of the left upper second premolar. A dental X-ray examination was conducted by Christine Meadway, BDS, in July 1998. As a result of this examination she offered the following report:

> Report on the radiograph of the skull from the Carmelite Priory, Norwich (CF2 148.958)

The radiograph was taken using KV6O MA4

Damage to the skull is shown in ⌐543⌐ region

The teeth present are:

8 7 6 3	3 4 6 7 8
8 7 6 5 4 3 2	2 3 4 5 6 7 8

Caries is present in ⌐5⌐ . There is evidence of extensive occlusal decay in ⌐7⌐ which may have involved the pulp.

⌐5⌐ is absent. The trabecullar pattern in this region is normal and well defined, although the bone crest is at a lower level than would be expected. ⌐6⌐ shows a normal degree of inclination. The space between ⌐4⌐ and ⌐6⌐ is less than would accommodate either a deciduous molar or a permanent premolar.

All occlusal surfaces show a marked degree of attrition.

The interproximal bone pattern is normal showing little evidence of pocketing and peridontal bone loss, although there is flattening of interproximal bone consistent with the amount of attrition.

All the 8s are fully erupted. ⌐8⌐ is in close proximity to the inferior dental canal.

Conclusions

- The radiograph is that of an adult, probably in the fourth decade.
- Dental health is fair to good, although there is some evidence of decay. The decay in ⌐7⌐ may well have caused some discomfort and would almost certainly have progressed to abscess formation.
- The area in the upper left quadrant with a missing tooth is of some interest. The absence of a permanent premolar, the flattening of the interdental bone margins, the lack of tilting of the first permanent molar and the width of the interdental space all suggest that a deciduous molar was retained into adult life and then subsequently shed. The most common causes of retained deciduous molars are an impacted permanent successor or its congenital absence. Here there is no impacted tooth so the most likely explanation for the radiological appearance is the congenital absence of ⌐5⌐.
- It is possible that the marked attrition of the teeth is due to bruxism but this wear pattern is commonly noted in individuals with a largely unrefined diet.

It thus emerges that CFII probably congenitally lacked her upper left premolar (no. 5). Although the congenital absence of this particular tooth is less rare than the pattern of congenital absence of the left molars which Anne Mowbray exhibits, under the circumstances (place of discovery, age at death, evidence of social status) this dental evidence does tend to reinforce the possibility that the Norwich remains may well be those of Eleanor Talbot, Anne Mowbray's aunt.

It would assist in establishing for certain from which line of her ancestry Anne Mowbray inherited her congenitally missing teeth if the remains of her parents could be examined. Unfortunately neither of these bodies has come to light. Although the remains of Elizabeth Talbot, Duchess of Norfolk, must have been lying quite close to those of her daughter at the site of the Convent of the Poor Clares ('the Minories') at Aldgate, they were apparently not noticed, or at any rate, not identified, when Anne's body was found in 1965. As for the body of John Mowbray, fourth Duke of Norfolk, that must be presumed to lie still where it was buried, between two of the now ruined piers on the south side of the choir of Thetford Priory. Although the superstructure of his tomb has vanished, its base can be distinguished, but the contents of this tomb have not been investigated.

In the absence of information regarding the dentition of either of her parents, Rushton, with some reservations, and other writers, with the appearance of greater enthusiasm and certainty, assumed that Anne Mowbray did not inherit her congenitally absent molars from the Talbots. Comparisons have been made between her dentition and those of two persons of uncertain gender whose remains were found at the Tower of London in 1674. Although these remains were eventually reburied, on the orders of King Charles II, at Westminster Abbey as those of the 'Princes in the Tower', in actual fact their identity is by no means certain so they will be referred to here as *Tower of London 1* and *2* respectively (hereinafter TL1 and TL2, TL1 being the remains of the older of the two individuals).

Like Anne Mowbray, TL1 showed congenital absence of teeth. In this case the missing teeth were the upper second premolars on both sides (the left one of which is also absent in CFII) and the lower wisdom teeth on both sides. By comparison with the very unusual dental anomalies of Lady Anne Mowbray, the absence of these particular teeth is considered a not uncommon phenomenon. Indeed, the present writer also exhibits the congenital absence of both lower wisdom teeth. In addition it has been suggested that

TL2 also showed the congenital absence of a tooth, but in the opinion of Rushton 'this cannot be considered proved beyond doubt since the tooth could have been lost early'.[35] In the case of TL2 the tooth in question was the lower right deciduous last molar, the absence of which is considered to be quite a common phenomenon. Nevertheless, on the basis of the congenitally missing teeth of TL1 and the possibly congenitally missing tooth of TL2, it has been claimed that TL1 and TL2 must be related to each other and to Anne Mowbray, and hence that TL1 is Edward V and TL2 is Richard, Duke of York.[36]

Anne Mowbray was related to her husband, Richard Duke of York, and to his brother, in a number of lines of descent. They shared common ancestors in Edward I and Edward III, but these were relatively remote relationships. Their really close relationship, the one to which Pope Sixtus IV referred when, at the request of Edward IV, he granted a dispensation for Anne to marry Richard,[37] was their common Neville descent: Anne's great grandmother, Catherine Neville, dowager Duchess of Norfolk, and Richard's grandmother, Cecily Neville, Duchess of York were sisters. If those who have claimed that Anne Mowbray's congenitally missing teeth prove that she was related to TL1 and 2, (and that therefore these were Edward V and Richard, Duke of York), are correct, Anne's dental anomaly must almost certainly have descended to her *via* her Neville ancestry.

Yet, curiously, further evidence does exist that the absence of teeth was, in fact, a Talbot trait. It is recorded that when Anne's grandfather, John Talbot, first Earl of Shrewsbury, was killed at the battle of Castillon, it was by his missing left molar that his disfigured body was identified. According to the contemporary account of Mathieu d'Escouchy, the earl's herald was asked to identify his master's body. He at once felt inside the mouth, and when he found a place on the left side where there was a molar missing, the herald declared that the body was certainly that of Lord Shrewsbury.[38]

Whether this molar was missing congenitally, or had simply been lost through age or accident, we cannot tell. The surviving account tends to suggest that latter interpretation, but this may have been merely an assumption on the part of the chronicler, who may never have heard of congenitally absent teeth. Nevertheless, it is certainly a very interesting coincidence that the tooth in question was a left molar. Unfortunately when Lord Shrewsbury's remains were examined in 1874, the point was not addressed. A photograph taken at the time shows few teeth remaining in the skull, but this may be misleading, for the earl's remains had been several times disturbed since their first burial in France.

It is a pity that this point cannot be more clearly elucidated, for if Anne Mowbray did inherit her missing teeth from her grandfather, the first Earl of Shrewsbury, then those same missing teeth cannot very well be cited as evidence that TL1 and TL2 are Edward V and his brother, since the relationship of these latter to the Earl of Shrewsbury was extremely remote. In fact their latest common ancestor was King Edward I, from whom the earl was descended on both his father's and his mother's side in the fifth and sixth generation respectively.

Meanwhile, however, we have interesting evidence that certain members of the Talbot family who lived in the fifteenth century exhibited the congenital absence of some back teeth. Taken in association with the evidence of age, diet and lifestyle of the skeleton from Norwich, not to mention its find location, this fact does tend to suggest that the female bones now stored in a cardboard box at Norwich Castle, may indeed be those of Eleanor Talbot. It is an intriguing thought that those bare bones could be the last mortal remains of the beautiful and high-born lady who so captured the attention of Edward IV that the young king, ensnared by his own passions, was led to commit a fatal error which would ultimately topple the royal house of York.

Summary of Key Events

1421(?)	Birth of Thomas Butler, son and heir of Lord Sudeley.
Summer 1435	Lord Talbot visits England. Eleanor's conception.
Spring 1436	Eleanor Talbot is born, probably at Blakemere, Shropshire.
Late Feb. 1442	Eleanor sees her father for the first time.
20 May 1442	Lord Talbot created Earl of Shrewsbury. Eleanor thus becomes 'Lady Eleanor'.
End of May 1442	The Earl of Shrewsbury returns to France.
Winter 1442/3	Eleanor's sister, Elizabeth, born.
Summer 1443	Lord Shrewsbury visits England; marriage of Eleanor's eldest full brother, John Talbot III; murder of her half-brother, Sir Christopher Talbot.
26 July 1444	Eleanor's brother, John Talbot III, created Lord Lisle.
Spring 1445	Eleanor's mother goes to France to escort Margaret of Anjou to England for her marriage with Henry VI.
1448	Birth of Eleanor's nephew and eventual heir, Thomas Talbot of Lisle.
1449	Eleanor marries Thomas Butler and enters Lord Sudeley's household at Sudeley Castle.
1450	Elizabeth Talbot marries John Mowbray, Lord Warenne, son and heir of the Duke of Norfolk. Kenninghall is purchased from the Earl of Arundel for Elizabeth as part of her jointure.

1451	Lord Shrewsbury returns to England for the first time since 1443.
March 1452	Consummation of Eleanor's marriage, following her sixteenth birthday.
1 Sept. 1452	Lord Shrewsbury makes his will at Portsmouth. The will includes an injunction to his executors to take action, if necessary, against Lord Sudeley, in respect of Eleanor's jointure. He then returns to France with Lord Lisle.
10 May 1453	Lord Sudeley grants Thomas and Eleanor the manors of Burton Dassett, Griff and Fenny Compton. They establish their own household.
17 July 1453	The Earl of Shrewsbury and Lord Lisle killed at the battle of Castillon.
22 May 1455	First Battle of St Albans. Lord Sudeley wounded.
1455–56	Thomas Butler knighted.
May 1456	Lord Sudeley concludes an agreement with St Alban's Abbey, naming his son as *Sir* Thomas Butler.
Oct. 1458	Death of Eleanor's eldest surviving brother, Sir Louis Talbot of Gresford.
23 Sept. 1459	Battle of Blore Heath.
Dec. 1459	Sir Thomas Butler dies.
Jan. 1460	Eleanor returns Griff to Lord Sudeley. He grants her Fenny Compton absolutely. She continues to hold Burton Dassett in dower.
10 July 1460	Eleanor's half-brother, John Talbot II, second Earl of Shrewsbury, is killed at the battle of Northampton.
Dec. 1460	Battle of Wakefield. Death of the Duke of York.
2/3 Feb. 1461	Battle of Mortimer's Cross.
17 Feb. 1461	Second Battle of St Albans.
3 March 1461	Edward IV proclaimed king in London.
29 March 1461	Battle of Towton. Edward IV returns south *via* Norfolk.
Spring 1461	Eleanor meets Edward IV, perhaps in Norwich. Secret marriage in the presence of Canon Stillington.
24 July 1461	Edward IV brokers a settlement of the dispute between Margaret, Countess of Shrewsbury and her step-grandson, the third Earl of Shrewsbury, recognising Margaret's tenure of the manor of Painswick (Glouc).

Autumn 1461	Edward IV seduces Elizabeth Wayte (Lucy).
1 Nov. 1461	Edward IV awards an annual salary of £365 to Canon Stillington.
6 Nov. 1461	Elizabeth Talbot becomes Duchess of Norfolk.
26 Feb. 1462	Edward IV (possibly at Eleanor's behest) grants an exemption to Lord Sudeley.
	Possibly at about this time Edward IV grants Eleanor property in Wiltshire.
30 May 1462	Edward IV (possibly at Eleanor's behest) grants venison from Woodstock Park to Lord Sudeley.
1462	Elizabeth Wayte (Lucy) bears Edward IV a daughter, Elizabeth (later Lady Lumley), whom the king recognises. Eleanor endows a new fellowship at Corpus Christi College Cambridge, to which Thomas Cosyn MA is appointed.
20 Oct. 1462	By letters patent, Edward IV grants Elizabeth Talbot control of her jointure (including Kenninghall).
Oct. 1462	Edward IV's exemption grant to Lord Sudeley is effectively revoked.
March 1463	Eleanor becomes a Carmelite tertiary.
1 May 1464	Edward IV secretly, and bigamously, marries Elizabeth Woodville.
July 1464	Death of Eleanor's sister-in-law, Joan, dowager Viscountess Lisle. Margaret, dowager Countess of Shrewsbury becomes guardian of the three Lisle children.
Sept. 1464	Edward IV's Woodville 'marriage' made public.
1464	Eleanor's brother, Humphrey Talbot, knighted.
January 1465	Edward IV seeks to appoint Stillington to the first bishopric to fall vacant (Bath and Wells). The pope, however, proposes an alternative candidate.
25 Oct. 1465	Edward IV grants a retrospective pension to Margaret, dowager Countess of Shrewsbury.
30 Oct. 1465	Papal licence finally granted for Stillington's episcopal appointment.
14 June 1467	Margaret, dowager Countess of Shrewsbury, dies (probably in London). Eleanor, Elizabeth and Humphrey assume joint guardianship of the Lisle children.

4 June 1468	Eleanor cedes Fenny Compton to Elizabeth and grants her the reversion of her estates in Wiltshire.
18 June 1468	Elizabeth Talbot, accompanied by her brother, Humphrey, and the Lisle children, leaves London for Flanders as chief lady-in-waiting to Margaret of York on her wedding journey.
30 June 1468	Death of Eleanor Talbot.
13 July 1468	Elizabeth Talbot leaves Flanders to return to England.
18 July 1468	Writ of *diem clausit extremum* to the escheator of Warwickshire, following Eleanor's death.
Late July 1468	Eleanor buried in the choir of the Carmelite Priory Church, Norwich.
16 August 1468	Eleanor's inquisition *post mortem* held at Henley-in-Arden.
7 Sept. 1468	Copy of Eleanor's Warwickshire inquisition delivered to the chancery.
Feb. 1469	Edward IV compels Lord Sudeley to surrender Sudeley Castle.
1470	Restoration of Henry VI. Lord Sudeley carries the sword of state before Henry through the streets of London. Birth of Edward, first son of Edward IV and Elizabeth Woodville, at Westminster.
1471	Restoration of Edward IV. Lord Sudeley imprisoned.
1473	Birth of Richard of Shrewsbury, second son of Edward IV and Elizabeth Woodville. Death of Lord Sudeley.
17 Jan. 1476	Sudden and unexpected death of Eleanor's brother-in-law, John Mowbray, Duke of Norfolk (friend of the Duke of Clarence).
1477	Birth of George, third son of Edward IV and Elizabeth Woodville. Elizabeth Woodville becomes doubtful about the validity of her marriage and perceives the Duke of Clarence as a threat to her children. Clarence is arrested. Edward IV seeks Elizabeth Talbot's daughter, Lady Anne Mowbray, as a bride for his second son, Richard of Shrewsbury, Duke of York.
15 Jan. 1478	Eleanor's niece, Anne Mowbray, marries Richard, Duke of York.
18 Feb. 1478	Clarence is executed.

28(?) Feb. 1478	Bishop Stillington is briefly imprisoned for some unstated action which connected him with the treason of George, Duke of Clarence.
9 Apr. 1483	Death of Edward IV.
June 1483	Bishop Stillington tells the royal council that Edward IV was married to Eleanor Talbot. Richard III proclaimed king. Elizabeth Talbot attends his coronation.
Jan. 1484	The Act of Parliament known as *titulus regius* formally acknowledges Edward IV's marriage to Eleanor Talbot.
22 Aug. 1485	Richard III killed at Bosworth.
23 Aug. 1485	Henry VII orders the arrest of Bishop Stillington, who is kept in prison for the rest of his life.
25 Aug. 1485	Henry VII executes William Catesby, a relative by marriage of Eleanor Talbot.
Sept. (?) 1485	Henry VII repeals the *titulus regius* of 1484, and orders all copies of it to be destroyed.
Oct. 1487	Dr Thomas Cosyn elected master of Corpus Christi College. Eleanor's fellowship at the college lapses because no new fellow is appointed.
June 1491	Bishop Stillington dies in prison at Windsor.
1492	Death of Eleanor's last surviving brother, Sir Humphrey Talbot, on pilgrimage to the Holy Land.
1495	Elizabeth Talbot re-establishes and extends Eleanor's endowment at Corpus Christi College.
Oct. 1506	Death of Elizabeth Talbot, dowager Duchess of Norfolk.
*c.*1525	Writing his posthumously published *Richard III*, Thomas More substitutes Elizabeth Wayte (Lucy)'s name for that of Eleanor Talbot as the person named in the bigamy allegation against Edward IV.
1533–34	Letters from Eustace Chapuys, ambassador from the Emperor Charles V to Henry VIII, state that Henry's only real claim to the English throne (through his mother, Elizabeth of York) is invalid because of Edward IV's bigamy, and the consequent bastardy of his children by Elizabeth Woodville.
1534	Polydore Vergil's *History of England*, written for Henry VII, avoids any mention of Eleanor Talbot.

1611	Speed first publishes the text of the *titulus regius* of 1484.
1619	Buck's *Richard III* contains the first published account of Eleanor and her relationship with Edward IV.
1631	Weever first publishes details of Eleanor's burial in Norwich.
1753	Masters first publishes details of Eleanor's association with Corpus Christi College, Cambridge, and correctly identifies her family connections.
1844	Halsted first suggests that Eleanor retired into some kind of religious life.
1878	Gairdner states that there are insufficient grounds for dismissing Edward IV's alleged Talbot marriage.
1955	Kendal draws attention to the references to Eleanor in the Patent rolls, and to her inquisition post mortem.
2006	The present author first publishes the Warwickshire archive material relating to Eleanor.

Appendix 1

Documentary Evidence – Summary

All sources are listed. Five documents are reproduced in full. Extracts of nine others are included.

1 September 1452: Will of John Talbot, first Earl of Shrewsbury.[1]
And as to the Ml li. [£1000] that ys paide for my dowghter, Elianore['s], mariage, in case the covenantes be not performed on the Lord of Sudeley's part, that then myn executours suee for the repayment of the summe aforesaide ayenst the seide Lorde Sudeley.

10 May 1453: Deed of gift of Lord Sudeley to Thomas Butler and Lady Eleanor Talbot.[2]

10 May 1453: Letter of attorney of Thomas Butler and Lady Eleanor Talbot.[3]

15 January 1460: Quitclaim of Lord Sudeley to Lady Eleanor.[4]

2 August, *c.*1463–68?: Letter from Dr John Botwright, master of Corpus Christi College Cambridge, possibly to Sir John Howard.[5]

Right honorabil Syr and our most tender frend, I and all my hool felachip recomende us as hertili as it can be thought unto your most feythful love and diligent favour. Rescityng, that above your magnificous present and affermed promise unto us doon bi your jantilman Cotton[6] (but late[7] bi for thys tyme), yet your jantil hert cowde not so be content, but for to send now estesounys agayn another more special massager of my graciouse Ladye service, and your referendary, to wryte un your assured wysdom every parcelle of costs that schuld atteyne to only on of your botraces,[8] to be made up in all goodly hast possibil, and the nomber of the same, upon your gracious almes.

Unto the first article we answher thus, after the wisest mason, maister of the werkes, wyth many worthie men, howbeit he may not attende in his propir persone, whos sentens thorowed we wryte to your providence in parcell. As for the secunde article, qwhat nomber is pure necessarie within our courtyerd, so thei may appear altogeder, at the next comyng of myn and our most bountous lady, for to make a perfaite work, we arn aboute the grounde of X [*ten*]. And for as moch as we may not be prescisly, for depnesse of the grounde,[9] ascertayned of the unntermost costs, goode Maister Thomas Cosyn schall, with help of our bourseres, alwey acertayn your great providence from tyme to tyme ase the case requireth.

And Syr, at the reverence of God, and our pouer contemplacion, late[10] our gracious lady, by this simple bille, and by your circumspecte enformacion, understand clerly, that bisydes all other almesses doon by her greet astat, her noblesse is ensuerd of VII [*seven*] perpetuell chaplayns for evermore of hir owen, and to have hir *placeat*, hir commandement, that knowyth the Kyng of kyngs, the qwhych have her Hyghnesse and your blessed persone in his conservacye.

Write at Cambrig, the seconde day of August.

Your daily oratoures, the Maister and Felaws of Corpus
Christi and Blessed Mary College in Cambrig.

4 June 1468: Deed of gift of Eleanor Talbot to her sister, Elizabeth, Duchess of Norfolk.[11]

4 June 1468: Letter of attorney of Eleanor Talbot.[12]

4 June 1468: Letter of attorney of Elizabeth, Duchess of Norfolk.[13]

18 July 1468: Writ of *diem clausit extremum.*[14]

7 September 1468: Inquisition post mortem.[15] [Translation]

It was delivered to the Chancery on the 7th day of September in the 8th year of the reign of Edward IV by the hands of Simon Adams.

Inquisition held at Henley in Arden in the county of Warwick on Tuesday, the morrow of the Assumption of the Blessed Mary in the eighth year of the reign of King Edward the fourth after the Conquest [Tuesday 16 August 1468] before William Motone esquire, escheator of the Lord king in the aforesaid county, by virtue of a writ of the same Lord king addressed to the same escheator, and this inquisition took place by the sworn oath of Thomas Waryng, John Duston, Richard Boteler, William Fulford, John Haloughton, Thomas Veysy, John Deyster, Laurence Blith, Henry Smyth, William Tyscote, William Hane, Thomas Blith. Who say upon their oath that Ralph Butler, knight, Lord of Sudeley, who is yet living, was formerly seised of the manors of Greve and Great Dorset with their appurtenances in the aforesaid county in his demesne as of fee, and being thus seised thereof in the time of the Lord Henry, lately in fact and not of right king of England, the sixth after the Conquest, that is in the twenty-eighth year of his reign [1449/50] he gave them to Thomas Butler, knight, son of the same Ralph, and to Eleanor, late wife to the same Thomas, both named in the said writ, and to the heirs of the body of this same Thomas legitimately begotten, to hold of the chief Lords of that fief by the services that belong in perpetuity to the aforesaid manors. By virtue of which gift the aforesaid Thomas and Eleanor were seised of the said manors with their appurtenances, that is the same Thomas in his demesne as of fee tail, and the aforesaid Eleanor freely. Afterwards the aforesaid Thomas, while this was the case, died seised thereof without an heir issued of his body, and after his death the aforesaid Eleanor held the same manors with [their] appurtenances and was seised thereof freely for the term of the life of the same Eleanor by right of reversion, and she subsequently died thus seised of the aforesaid manor of Great Dorset with its appurtenances by reversion, which thence, following the death of Eleanor herself, pertains to the above mentioned Ralph and to his heirs. And furthermore the said jurors say upon their oath that the aforesaid Lady Eleanor, before her death, in the time of the aforesaid late (as previously mentioned) king, to wit in the thirty-ninth year of his reign [1460/1], surrendered all her property rights, which she had of and in the aforesaid manor of Greve with its appurtenances, to the aforesaid Ralph, to hold as he had done formerly. To which surrender the same

Ralph agreed, and he was then seised of the same manor of Greve with its appurtenances at the time of the aforesaid surrender, and from that time he has remained seised thereof in his demesne as of fee. And thus the aforesaid jurors say that the aforesaid Eleanor had nothing in the same manor of Greve at the time of her death.

And moreover the aforesaid jurors say upon their oath that in the aforesaid manor of Greve [there] is a certain site which is worth annually over and above reprises 3s 4d. There are also in the same manor 200 acres of land which are worth annually over and above reprises £7; 8 acres of meadow which are worth annually over and above reprises 10s; 200 acres of grazing which are worth annually over and above reprises £6; 100 acres of woodland which are worth annually over and above reprises 6s 8d; 28s 2d of rents of villein tenants and £4 11s of rents of customary tenants, paid annually at the feasts of Easter and of St. Michael the Archangel following, in equal portions.

And in the aforesaid manor of Great Dorset is a certain site which is worth annually over and above reprises 6s 8d. And that there are in the same manor 125 [?] acres of arable land which are worth annually over and above reprises 101s 6d; 62 acres of meadow which are worth annually over and above reprises 62s; 17 acres of grazing which are worth annually over and above reprises 8s 6d together with a rabbit warren which is worth annually over and above reprises 60s; one windmill which is worth annually over and above reprises 27s 8d And also there are in the same place eight pounds of rents of villein tenants paid annually at the terms of Easter and Michaelmas, in equal portions, and ten pounds of rents of customary tenants paid annually at the aforesaid feasts in equal portions.

And the above-mentioned jurors say that the aforesaid manors are held in chief from the Lord king for the service of one knight's fee. And that the aforesaid Eleanor held nothing else, neither lands nor holdings, in demesne or in service, of the Lord king nor of anyone else, in the aforesaid county on the day when she died. The which Eleanor died the last day of June last aforesaid.

And that Thomas Talbot, knight, Lord Lisle, is her closest heir (being evidently the son of John Talbot, Lord Lisle, brother of the aforesaid Eleanor) and he is of the age of twenty years, and of full age.

In witness whereof the said escheator and the said jurors have in turn affixed their seals to this indented inquisition. Given on the above mentioned day and in the above mentioned year and place.

16 January 1478: Act of Attainder against George, Duke of Clarence.[16]

The Kyng, oure Sovereigne Lorde, hath called to his remembraunce the manyfold grete conspiracies, malicious and heynous tresons that hertofore hath be compassed by dyverse persones his unnaturall subgetts, rebelles and traytoures, wherby commocions and insurrections have been made within this his royaulme, for entent and purpose to have destroyed his moost roiall persone, and with that to have subverted the state, wele publique and politic of all his said royaulme (ne had so been, that by th'elp of Almyghty God, with the grete laboures and diligences and uttermost explette of his persone by chevalrye and werr, he had mightly and graciously repressed the same). Wherthrogh grete nowmbre of the said his rebelles and traytours he hath at dyvers tymes punysshed, as well by swerd as other punysshments, in exemple to others to have been ware of suche attempting hereafter. And yet as a benigne and a gracious prince moeved unto pitie, after his grete victories sent hym by God, not oonly he hath spared the multitudes in theire feldes and assembles overcomen, but thaym and certeyn other, the grete movers, sturters and executours of suche haynous tresons, at the reverence of God, he hath taken to his mercy and clerly pardoned, as may not be unknowen to all the worlde.

This notwithstondyng, it is comen nowe of late to his knowlage, howe that agaynst his mooste royall persone, and agaynst the persones of the blessed princesse oure alther soveraigne and liege lady the Quene, of my Lorde the Prince theire son and heire, and of all the other of thaire moost noble issue, and also against the grete parte of the noble of this lande, the good rule, politike and wele publique of the same, hath been conspired, compassed and purposed a moch higher, moch more malicious, more unnaturall and lothely treason than atte eny tyme hertoforn hath been compassed, purposed and conspired, from the Kyng's first reigne hiderto. Which treason is, and must be called, so moche and more henyous, unnaturell and lothely, for that not oonly it hath proceded of the moost extreme purpensed malice (incomparably excedyng eny other that hath been aforn) but also for that it hath been contryved, imagined and conspired, by the persone that of all erthely creatures, beside the dutie of ligeaunce, by nature, by benefette, by gratitude, and by yeftes and grauntes of goodes and possessions, hath been moost bounden and behalden to have dradde, loved, honoured, and evere thanked the kyng more largely, than evere was eny other bounden or behalden. Whom to name, it gretely aggruggeth the hert of oure said sovereigne Lorde, sauf oonly that he is of necessite compelled, for the suertie, wele and tranquillite of hym and all this royaulme, which were full neer the poynt of perdicion, ne were the help and grace of Almyghty God.

He sheweth you therefore, that all this hath been entended by his brother, George, the Duke of Clarence. Wherein it is to be remembered that the Kynge's Highnesse, of tendre youthe unto now of late, hath evere loved and cherysshed hym as tenderly and as kynderly and eny creature myght his naturell brother, as well it may be declared, by that that he beyng right yonge, not borne to have eny lifelode, butt oonly of the Kynge's grace he yave hym soo large porcion of possessions that noo memorie is of, or seldom hath been seem, that eny kyng of Englande hertoforn within his royaulme yave soo largely to eny his brothers. And not oonly that, butt above that, he furnyssed hym plenteously of all manere stuff that to a right grete prynce myght well suffice, so that aftre the kynge's, his lifelode and richesse notably exceded any other within his lande at thatt tyme.

And yet the kyng, not herewith content, butt beyng ryght desirous to make hym of myght and puissance excedyng others, caused the greate parte of all the nobles of this lande to be assured unto hym next His Highnesse, trustyng that not oonly by the bond of nature, butt also by the bondes of soo grete benefitt, he shulde be more obeissaunt to all the kyng's good pleasures and commaundments, and to all that myght be to the politik wele of his lande.

All this notwithstondyng, it is to remember the large grace and foryevnesse that he yave hym uppon, and for that at dyverse tyme sith he gretely offended the kyng, as in jupartyng the kyng's royall estate, persone and life, in straite warde, puttyng hym thereby from all his libertie, aftre procuryng grete commocions. And sith the voydaunce oute of his royaulme, assistyng yevyng to his enemies mortall, the usurpers, laboryng also by Parlement to exclude hym and all his from te regalie, and enabling hymself to the same. And by dyverse weyes otherwyse attemptyng; which all the kyng (by nature and love moeved) utterly foryave, entendyng to have putte all in perpetuell oblivion.

The said duke, nathelesse for all this, noo love encreasyng, but growyng daily in more and more malice, hath not left to consedre and conspire newe treasons, more haynous and lothely than ever aforn: how that the said Duke falsly and traitrously entended, and puposed fermely, the extreme distruction and disherityng of the kyng and his issue, and to subverte all the polityk rule of this royaulme, by myght to be goten as well outewarde as inwarde. Which false purpose the rather to brynge aboute, he cast and compassed the moyans to enduce the kynge's naturell subgettes to withdrawe theire herts, loves and affections from the kyng, theire naturell sovereigne Lorde, by many subtill, contryved weyes, as in causyng dyverse his servauntes (suche as he coude imagyne moste apte to sowe sedicion and agrugge amonge the people) to goo into diverse parties of this royaulme, and to laboure to enforme the people largely in every place where they shulde come, that Thomas Burdett, his servaunte (which was lawefully and truly atteynted of treason) was wrongefully putte to deth. To some his servauntes of suche like disposicion he yave large money, veneson, therewith to assemble the kynge's subgects to feste theym and chere theym, and by theire policies and resonyng, enduce hem to beleve that the said Burdett was wrongfully executed, and so to putte it in noyse and herts of the people.

He saide and laboured also to be noysed by such his servauntes apte for that werk, that the kyng, oure sovereigne Lorde, wroght by nygromancye, and used crafte to poyson his subgettes, suche as hym pleased, to th'entent to desclaundre the kyng in the moost haynous wyse he couth in the sight and conceipt of his subgettes. And thefore to encorage theym to hate, despice and aggrugge theire herts agaynst hym, thynkyng that he ne lived ne dealid with his subgettes as a Christien Prynce.

And over this, the said Duke beyng in full purpose to exalte hymself and his heires to the regallye and corone of Englande (and clerely in opinion to putte aside from the same for ever the said corone from the kyng and his heirez, uppon oon the falsest and moost unnaturall coloured pretense that man myght imagyne) falsely and untruely noysed, published and saide, that the kyng oure sovereigne Lorde was a bastard, and not begottone to reigne uppon us. And to contynue and procede ferther in this his moost malicious and traytorous purpose, after this lothely, false and sedicious langage shewed and declared amonge the people, he enduced dyverse of the kynge's naturall subgetts to be sworne uppon the blessed Sacrament to be true to hym and his heires, noon exception reserved of theire liegeaunce. And after the same othe soo made, he shewed to many other, and to certayn persones, that suche othe had made, that the kyng had taken his lifelode from hym and his men, and disheryed theym, and he wolde utterly endevoire hym to gete hem theire enheritaunce as he wolde doo for his owen.

He shewed also that the kyng entended to consume hym in like wyse as a candell consumeth in brennyng, wherof he wolde in brief tyme quyte hym. And overe this, the said Duke continuyng ín his false purpose, opteyned and gate an exemplification undre the grete seall of Herry the sexte (late in dede and not in right kyng of this lande) wherin were conteyned alle suche appoyntements as late was made betwene the said Duke and Margaret, callyng herself quene of this lande, and other, amonges whiche it was conteyned that if the said Herry, and Edward, his first begoton son, died withoute issue male of theire bodye, that the seid Duke and his heires shulde be kyng of this lande. Which exemplificacion the said Duke hath kepyd with hymself secrete (not doyng the kyng to have eny knowlegge therof) therby to have abused the kynge's true subgetts for the rather execucion of his said false purpose.

And also, the same Duke purposyng to accomplisse his said false and untrue entent, and to inquiete and trouble the kynge, oure said sovereigne Lorde, his leige people and this his royaulme, nowe of late willed and desired the Abbot of Tweybury, Mayster John Tapton, clerk, and Roger Harewell esquier, to cause a straunge childe to have be putte and kept in likelinesse of his sonne and heire, and that they shulde have conveyed and sent his said sonne and heire into Ireland, or into Flaundres, oute of this lande, whereby he myght have goten hym assistaunce and favoure agaynst oure said sovereigne Lorde. And for the execucion of the same, sent oon John Taylour, his servaunte, to have had delyveraunce of his said sonne and heire, for to have conveyed hym (the whiche Mayster John Tapton and Roger Harewell denyed the delyveraunce of the said childe, and soo by Goddes grace his said false and untrue entent was lette and undoon).

Over all this, the said Duke, compassyng subtelly and trayterously to brynge this his trayterous purpose to the more redy execucion by all meanes possible, and for to putte these said treasons fynally to pleyn execucion, falsely and trayterously he commaunded and caused dyverse of his servauntes to goo unto sundry parties of this royaulme to commove and stirre the kynge's naturall subgetts (and in grete nowmbre) to be redy in harnays within an houre warnyng, to attend uppon hym and to take his parte to levy werre agaynst the kynge's moost royall persone, and hym and his heirez utterly to destroye, and therby the corone and royall dignite of this royaulme to obteigne, have, possede and enjoye to hym and to his heirez for evere, contrarie to all nature, ryght and duetie of his ligeaunce.

The kyng, remembryng over that to side the neernesse of blode, howe be nature he myght be kynde to his brother; the tendre love also, whiche of youthe he bare unto hym, couthe have founden in his hert (uppon due submission) to have yet foryeven hym estsones, ne were furst that his said brother (by his former dedes, and nowe by this conspiracye), sheweth hymself to be incorrigible, and in noo wyse reducible to that (by bonde of nature, and of the grete benefices aforn reherced) he were moost soveraynly beholden of all creaturez; secondly, ne were the grete juparty of effusion of Christien blode which most likkely shulde therof ensue; and thridenly and principally, the bond of his conscience, wherby (and by solempne othe) he is bounden anenst God, uppon the peryll of everlastyng dampnacion, to provyde and defende, first the suertie of hymself and his moste royall issue, secondly, the tranquilite of Godde's Churche within this, his royaulme, and after that, the wele publique, peas and tranquilite of all his Lordez, noblemen, comens and others of every degree and condicion; whiche all shulde necessarily stande in extreme jupartie yf justice and due punyshement of soo lothely offencez shulde be pardoned (in pernicious example to all mysdoers, theves, traytours, rebelles and all other suche as lightly wolde therby bee encoraged and enbolded to spare noo manner of wikkednesse).

Wherfore thof all [*sic*]¹⁷ the kynge's Highnesse be right sory to determyne hymself to the contrarie, yet consideryng that justice is a vertue excellently pleasyng Almyghty God, wherby reaulmes stande, kynges and pryncez reign and governe, all goode rule, polyce and publique wele is mayteigned. And that this vertue standeth not oonly in retribucion and rewarde for goode dedes, butt also in correccion and punysshement of evil doers, after the qualitees of theire mysdoyngs. For whiche premissez and causez the kyng, by the avyse and assent of his Lordes speretuell and temporell, and by the commons, in this present parliament assembled, and by the auctorite of the same, ordeyneth, enacteth and establith that the said George, Duke of Clarence, be convicte and atteyntit of heigh treason commyttet and doon agaynst the kynge's moost royall persone; and that the same Duke, by the said auctorite, forfett from hym and his heyres for ever the honoure, estate, dignite and name of Duke. And also that the same Duke, by the said auctorite, forfett from hym and his heyres for ever, all castelles, honoures, maners, landes, tenements, rents, advousons, hereditaments and possessions that the same Duke nowe hath by eny of the kynge's lettrez patents to his owen use, or that any other persone nowe hath to the use of the same Duke by eny of the kynge's letterez patents, or that passed to hym fro the kyng by the same. And that all lettrez patents made by the kyng to the said Duke bee from henseforthe utterly voyde and of noon effecte.

And that it be also ordeigned by the same auctorite that noo castelles, honoures, maners, landez, tenementz, rents, advousons, hereditaments or possessions that the same Duke nowe hath joyntly with other, or sole to hymself, to the use of eny other persone, be forfett, nor conteyned by or in this present acte; but that by the said auctoritee, every other persone to whose use the said Duke is sole seised in enycastelles, honours, maners, landez, tenements, rents, advousons, hereditaments and possessions, otherwyse than by the kyng's lettres patents, have power and auctorite by this present acte lawefully to entre into theym, and theym to have and holde after the entent and trust that the said Duke nowe hath theryn.

And also where the same Duke is joyntly seased with any other persone in any castells, maners, landez, tenementz, rents, hereditaments or possessions to the use of eny other persone, otherwyse than by the kyng's lettrez patents: that by the said auctorite, the said joynt feffez stonde and be feoffez to the same use and entent as they nowe arre and be. And that suche right, interest and title as the same Duke nowe hath with theym in the same premyssez, by the said auctorite be in his cofeffez to the same entent as the Duke nowe ys: savyng to every of the kynge's liege people (other than the said Duke and his heyrez), and all other persone and persones that clayme or have eny tytell of interest in eny of the premyssez by the same Duke, suche right, tytle and interest as they owe or shulde have in eny of the premyssez, as if this acte had never been made.

A cest Bille les Comunez sont assentuz.

Le Roy le voet.

26 June 1483: Petition to Richard, Duke of Gloucester, as quoted in the Act of Parliament of January 1484 (*titulus regius*).[18] [Extract]

Over this, amonges other thinges, more specially we consider howe that the tyme of the raigne of Kyng Edward IV, late-decessed, – after the ungracious, pretensed marriage (as all England hath cause so say) made betwixt the said King Edward and Elizabeth (sometyme wife to Sir John Grey, Knight), late nameing herself (and many years heretofore) 'Queene of England', – the ordre of all politeque rule was perverted, the laws of God and of Gode's church, and also the lawes of nature, and of Englond, and also the laudable customes and liberties of the same (wherein every Englishman is inheritor) broken, subverted and contempned, against all reason and justice, so that this land was ruled by self-will and pleasure, feare and drede (all manner of equitie and lawes layd apart and despised), whereof ensued many inconvenients and mischiefs (as murders, estortions and oppressions: namely of poor and impotent people) soo that no man was sure of his lif, land ne lyvelode, ne of his wif, doughter ne servaunt; every good maiden and woman standing in drede to be ravished and defouled. And besides this, what discords, inward battailes, effusion of Christian men's blode (and namely, by the destruction of the noble blode of this londe) was had and comitted within the same, it is evident and notarie through all this reaume (unto the grete sorrowe and heavynesse of all true Englishmen).

And here also we considre howe the said pretensed marriage betwixt the above-named King Edward and Elizabeth Grey was made of grete presumption, without the knowyng or assent of the Lordes of this lond, and alsoe by sorcerie and wichecrafte committed by the said Elizabeth and her moder, Jaquett, Duchess of Bedford (as the common opinion of the people and the publique voice and fame is through all this land; and hereafter – if, and as, the case shall require – shall bee proved suffyciently, in tyme and place convenient).

And here also we considre how that the said pretensed marriage was made privatly and secretly, without edition of banns, in a private chamber, a profane place, and not openly, in the face of church, aftre the lawe of Godds churche, but contrarie thereunto, and the laudable custome of the churche of England. And howe also that at the tyme of contract of the same pretensed marriage (and bifore, and longe tyme after) the said King Edward was, and stoode, marryed, and trouth-plyght, to oone Dame Elianore Butteler (doughter of the old Earl of Shrewesbury)[19] with whom the saide King Edward had made a precontracte of matrimonie longe tyme bifore he made the said pretensed mariage with the said Elizabeth Grey in manner and fourme aforesaide.

Which premises being true (as in veray trouth they been true), it appeareth and followeth evidently that the said King Edward (duryng his lyfe) and the said Elizabeth lived togather sinfully and dampnably in adultery, against the lawe of God and his church. And therefore noe marvaile that (the souverain Lord and head of this londe being of such ungodly disposicion and provokyng the ire and indignation of oure Lorde God) such haynous mischiefs and inconvenients as is above remembered were used and committed in the reame amongst the subjects.

Also it appeareth evidently, and followeth, that all th'issue and children of the said king beene bastards,[20] and unable to inherite or to clayme anything by inheritance, by the lawe and custome of England.

November 1483: *Domenico Mancini: de occupatione regni Anglie.*[21] [Translated extracts]

The queen [Elizabeth Woodville] then remembered the insults to her family and the calumnies with which she was reproached, namely that according to established usage she was not the legitimate wife of the king. Thus she concluded that her offspring by the king would never come to the throne unless the Duke of Clarence were removed.

He [Richard] argued that it would be unjust to crown this lad [Edward V], who was illegitimate, because his father King Edward [IV] on marrying Elizabeth was legally contracted to another wife to whom the Duke [*sic* = earl] of Warwick had joined him.

November 1485: First Parliament of Henry VII: repeal of *Titlus regius* of Richard III.[22]

Where afore this tyme, Richard, late Duke of Gloucester, and after in dede and not of right King of England, called Richard the III[d], caused a false and seditious Bille of false and malicious ymaginaciones, ayenst all good and true disposicion to be put unto hyme, the beginning of which bill is thus:

'Please it your noble Grace to understand the consideracions, Elleccion and Peticion underwritte' &c.

Which Bill, after that, with all the continue of the same, by auctoritee of Parliament, holden the first yeere of the usurped Reigne of the said late King Richard the III[d], was ratified, enrolled, approved and authorised; as in the same more plainly appereth. The King, atte the special instance, desire and prayer of the Lordes Spirituell and Temporell and Commons in this present Parlement assembled, will it be ordeined, stablished and enacted, by the advys of the said Lordes Spirituell and Temporell and the Comunes in this present Parlement assembled, and by auctoritee of the same, that the said Bille, Acte and Ratificaion, and all the circumstances and dependants of the same Bill and Act, for the fals and seditious ymaginacions and untrouths thereof, be void, adnulled, repelled, irrite, and of noe force ne effecte. And that it be ordeined by the said auctorite that the said Bill be cancelled, destrued, and that the said Acte, Record and enrollinge shall be taken and avoided out of the Roll and Records of the said Parliament of the said late King, and brente, and utterly destroyed. And over this, be it ordeined by the same auctoritee, that every persoune having anie Coppie or Remembraunces of the said Bill or Acte, bring unto the Chaunceller of England for the tyme being, the same Coppiesand Remembraunces, or utterlie destrue theym, afore the Fest of Easter next comen, upon Peine of Ymprisonment, and making fyne and ransome to the Kinge atte his will. So that all thinges said and remembered in the said Bill and Acte thereof maie be for ever out of remembraunce and allso forgott'.[23]

? **30 April 1486:** *Crowland Abbey Chronicle.*[24] [Translated extract]

Richard the protector claimed for himself the government of the kingdom with the name and title of king. ... It was put forward, by means of a supplication contained in a certain parchment roll, that King Edward's sons were bastards, by submitting that he had been precontracted to a certain Lady Eleanor Boteler before he married Queen Elizabeth and, further, that the blood of his other brother, George, Duke of Clarence, had been attainted, so that, at the time, no certain and uncorrupt blood of the lineage of Richard, Duke of York, was to be found except in the person of the said Richard, Duke of Gloucester.

c. **1490:** Philippe de Commynes: *Memoirs.*[25] [Translated extracts]

In the end, with the assistance of the Bishop of Bath, who had previously been King Edward's Chancellor before being dismissed and imprisoned (although he still received his money), on his release the Duke carried out the deed which you shall hear described in a moment. This bishop revealed to the Duke of Gloucester that King Edward, being very enamoured of a certain English lady, promised to marry her, provided that he could sleep with her first, and she consented. The bishop said that he had married them when only he and they were present. He was a courtier so he did not disclose this fact but helped to keep the lady quiet and things remained like this for a while. Later King Edward fell in love again and married the daughter of an English knight, Lord Rivers. She was a widow with two sons.

[Richard] had the two daughters of Edward [IV] degraded and declared illegitimate on the grounds furnished by the Bishop of Bath in England. The bishop had previously enjoyed great credit with King Edward, who had then dismissed him and imprisoned him before ransoming him for a sum of money. The bishop said that King Edward had promised to marry an English lady (whom he named) because he was in love with her, in order to get his own way with her, and that he had made this promise in the bishop's presence. And having done so he slept with her; and he made the promise only to deceive her.

20 March 1496[26]: Indenture of Elizabeth, Duchess of Norfolk.[27] [Translation]

To all Christ's faithful people to whom the present Indented letter shall come, Thomas Cosyn, master or warden of the college or house of Corpus Christi and of the Blessed Mary, commonly called the College of St Benedict of Cambridge, and the fellows or scholars of the same college or house [give] eternal greetings in the Lord.

We the aforementioned master and fellows or scholars, in our chapter house assembled, with one accord after much previous discussion, namely on the twentieth day of the month of March in the year of the Lord one thousand four hundred and ninety five, taking into consideration the fervent love and unfailing devotion which, out of reverence for the body of our Lord Jesus Christ, and for the most blessed Mary, his mother, and the special mindfulness, maintaining and increase of the faith of Jesus Christ, the renowned and devout Eleanor Butler,[28] deceased, once the wife of Sir Thomas Butler (son and heir of Ralph Butler, Lord of Sudeley) and the daughter of John, late Earl of Shrewsbury and of Margaret, wife of the said earl (eldest daughter and one of the heirs of Richard Beauchamp, late Earl of Warwick) and once the wife of Sir Thomas Butler (son and heir of Ralph Butler, once Lord of Sudeley) our benefactress and close friend, demonstrably bore most sincerely towards us, zealous for the faith of Christ; and because the Lady Elizabeth, Duchess of Norfolk, sister of the said Eleanor and executrix of the testament of the said Eleanor, also wishing well towards us the said master and fellows or scholars, and graciously bearing in mind our favour, has given to us the said master and fellows or scholars two hundred and twenty marcs in good coined money, from the goods of the said Eleanor and Duchess Elizabeth for the upkeep, repair and renewal of the fabric of our houses, messuages and tenements, at the present time in decay, which belong or pertain to us within the said town of Cambridge or elsewhere, – taking all the aforesaid into consideration, we, the said master and fellows or scholars grant, promise and for ourselves and for our successors confirm by this our present written deed to the said Elizabeth, Duchess of Norfolk, that we must choose and establish a well-disposed priest, capable of study, having graduated in arts, as a fellow of the said college at the nomination of the said duchess; and after his first nomination aforesaid, the nomination and choice are to belong to the said master and fellows or scholars of the said college on all future occasions. He is to be capable of studying sacred theology or in another field according to the direction of the master and fellows for the defence and increase of the faith of Jesus Christ. And he will say mass every day unless he is prevented by a good and worthy cause, praying and calling upon God for the souls of the said Thomas Butler and of Eleanor, [and] of Ralph Butler, father of the said Thomas, and for the good estate and the health of body and soul of the said duchess during her lifetime and for the soul of the said duchess when she shall depart from this light, and for the souls of John, Earl of Shrewsbury, and of Margaret his wife, and of all those for whom they were bound [to pray]. And that the said priest when elected a fellow of this house college or house shall say every day a litany with the intercession following, just as other fellows of the said college are bound to do for all the aforesaid souls.

And further we the said master [and] fellows or scholars grant and promise that we and our successors shall give to the said chosen fellow his stipend, wages and salary, namely eight marcs to be paid to him each year and taken with all other annual payments, emoluments and customary payments in manner and form just as the other fellows or scholars of the said college are accustomed to take.

And further we wish and grant that the said chosen fellow will be named and called the priest of the said Eleanor Butler and of the said Duchess of Norfolk.

And further we grant and promise truly that as often as and whenever it shall happen that the place of the said chosen fellow becomes vacant by death, promotion, surrender, resignation or by any other means, that then we the said master and fellows or scholars must proceed to a new selection within the one or two months next following the said vacancy, and we must select and install another graduate priest in the aforesaid manner as a fellow and into the said place, so that he may do and observe all the foregoing which pertain to him, to the best of his power, in manner and form as is aforesaid.

And we the said master and fellows or scholars and their successors shall do and observe all the foregoing which pertains to us in manner and form aforesaid on all future occasions. And moreover having considered the manifold gifts and benefits given to and conferred upon us by the said Eleanor and Duchess Elizabeth, we grant for ourselves and for our successors that we must select one scholar learned in grammar who must study in arts in the same way. And we the said master and fellows or scholars and our successors promise and grant to give to the same scholar forty shillings each year for his maintenance. And that this scholar, by the direction of us [the master] for the time being, or in his absence a deputy, shall read a Bible reading or another reading before our Dean or his deputy, the fellows of the said college being in hearing. And that this scholar, at the end of his reading thus read, shall say in Latin: 'May the souls of Eleanor Butler and of Elizabeth, Duchess of Norfolk' (when the duchess has departed from this light) 'and the souls of all the faithful departed rest in peace'.[29] And as often as and whenever it shall happen that the place of this scholar shall be vacant in any way, or the said scholar shall become a master of arts, that then we the said master and fellows or scholars must proceed within the one or two months next following to the selection of another scholar in the manner and form as said before, and thus from one to another when the occasion may require as is said before, on all future occasions.

Moreover, beyond the foregoing, by the unanimous agreement and likewise consent of us all, we wish and grant by this present deed that each and every one of the priests of our said college in saying and celebrating all their masses for evermore will pray for the souls of the said Eleanor and the said duchess (when she has departed from this light) and for the souls for whom he is bound [to pray], just as for the other founders and benefactors of the said college.

Likewise we each and every one of us by universal consent, grant and promise by this present deed that the anniversary day of the said Thomas Butler and of Eleanor, his wife, of Margaret, the mother of the said Eleanor, and of John, Duke of Norfolk and of the aforesaid Elizabeth, his wife, will be observed on the second day after the feast of St Barnabas the Apostle [i.e. 13 June],[30] by the said chosen fellow every year with funeral rites and a Requiem mass being said for the said souls for ever. And also we promise and grant that the anniversary day of John, Earl of Shrewsbury, and of John, Lord Lisle (son of the said John) and of Ralph Butler, Lord of Sudeley, and of his wife, and of the parents of the said Thomas Butler, will be observed by the said chosen fellow every year on the feast of St Kenelm [17 July],[31] with the funeral rites of the nine readings[32] and a Requiem mass to be said for the said soul for ever.

And moreover we wish and grant that any said fellow chosen in the aforesaid form, will forever say on three other terms of each year, namely at the term of St John the Baptist [24 June], at the term of St. Michael the Archangel [29 September] and at the term of the Nativity of the Lord [25 December], once at each aforesaid term, the funeral rites of the nine readings and a Requiem mass for all the above-mentioned souls, and for those for whom they are bound [to do so], and for the souls of all the faithful departed.

Moreover, having considered the manifold gifts given to us by the said Eleanor and duchess, we grant for ourselves and our successors that as often and whenever it shall happen that the said chosen fellow and priest preaches the word of God, at the end of his discourses he shall commend [to God] the souls of the said Eleanor and duchess (when she departs from this light) and the souls of all those for whom they are bound.

Therefore so that this our grant, agreement and arrangement may be commended to a more perfect remembrance for all time to come, we grant and promise that we and each one of us and our successors in full receipt and payment of the said two hundred and twenty marcs will keep our word given by a solemn oath that we shall observe faithfully and for ever each and every one of the foregoing arrangements set out in this grant, arrangement and agreement as far as concerns our individual or several persons without trickery, fraud or bad faith.

And further we grant and promise that each one who shall chance to be chosen as master or fellow or scholar of the said college in the future shall give his word by a solemn oath before he is admitted or instituted into the said college that he will stringently observe all the foregoing expressed in the said grant, arrangement or agreement.

And to observe each and every one of these arrangements very stringently, all fraud or trickery cast aside, we bind ourselves in our pure consciences before God and his angels and [we bind] our successors in their pure consciences forever as they will answer before God and his angels. And lest by the lapse of time (may it not happen) all the foregoing be consigned to oblivion, we wish and grant that this present indenture may be read forever clearly and openly in front of the said priest or fellow at his admission.

In witness of which the seals of the said Duchess Elizabeth and of the said college have been placed upon the present indentures the day and year aforesaid.

18 July 1496: Second indenture of Elizabeth, Duchess of Norfolk.[33]

c.1517: Polydore Vergil, *English History*.[34] [Extracts]

E[dward] 4 is supposed to deflowre some woman in the E[arl] of Warwickes house.

… Yt caryeth soome colour of truthe, which commonly is reportyd, that king Edward showld have assayed to do soome unhonest act in the earles[35] howse; for as much as the king was a man who wold readyly cast an eye uppon yowng ladyes, and loove them inordinately.

16 December 1533: Letter from Eustace Chapuys, Imperial ambassador in England, to the Holy Roman Emperor Charles V.[36] [Extract]

You cannot imagine the grief of all the people at this abominable government. They are so transported with indignation at what passes, that they complain that your Majesty takes no steps in it, and I am told by many respectable people that they would be glad to see a fleet come hither in your name … [for] they say you have a better title than the present King, who only claims by his mother, who was declared by sentence of the Bishop of Bath [Stillington] a bastard, because Edward [IV] had espoused another wife before the mother of Elizabeth of York.

3 November 1534: Letter from Eustace Chapuys, Imperial ambassador in England, to the Holy Roman Emperor Charles V.[37] [Extract]

Richard III declared by definitive sentence of the Bishop of Bath that the daughters of king Edward, of whom the king's mother was the eldest, were bastards, by reason of a precontract made by Edward with another lady before he married their mother.

Sixteenth century: John Leland, *Itinerary*.[38] [Extract]

There apperith at Keninghaule not far from the Duke of Northfolkes new place a grete mote, withyn the cumpace whereof there was sumtyme a fair place, and there the saying is that there lay a Quene or sum grete lady, and there dyed.

Appendix 2

Eleanor in Fiction

The greater part of this study has been concerned with the attempt to resurrect and clarify the lost story of Eleanor Talbot. As an adjunct to this work it may be useful, finally, to consider Eleanor and her reputation as these have been presented in fiction. The appeal of fiction is widespread, so that probably many more people have encountered Eleanor's name in a novel, than have done so in a serious historical study – the more so given that serious historical studies have, until now, generally expended very little time and effort on Eleanor. However, Eleanor's fictional appearances have also contained some important errors.

Eleanor's first recorded manifestation in fiction was a rare appearance upon the stage. John Crowne's *The Misery of Civil War* had clear contemporary relevance when it appeared in 1680. However, coming as it did towards the end of the century which had seen the publication of the *titulus regius* of 1484, Weever's *Funeral Monuments* and Buck's study of Richard III, it availed itself of the opportunity for the introduction of a novel character: Lady Elianor Butler, 'a young lady of great quality, that was one of King Edward's mistresses'.[1] Despite his use of the word 'mistress', Crowne's portrayal of Elianor is equivocal. At the battle of Wakefield she tells Edward IV that she is 'his wife in hopes and promises', and earlier in the play she reminds the king of the oaths he has sworn to her.[2] Dramatically, Elianor is present at the play's Woodville marriage, during which she voices her feelings to both Edward and Elizabeth Woodville. Elianor finally dies at Edward's hands at the battle of Barnet, warning the king that his injurious treatment of her will prove his undoing. The inclusion of the character of Elianor in *The Misery of Civil War* must have done much to make Eleanor Talbot's long-obscured name more widely known, and may have contributed to her subsequent appearance in Whig pamphlets, where her name and claim to be the rightful wife of Edward IV were eagerly pressed into service to bolster the much more doubtful cause of Lucy Walter and her son by Charles II, James Scott, Duke of Monmouth.[3]

There are numerous historical novels which deal with the Yorkist period, and it would hardly be possible to mention all of them. Those included here are therefore either particularly well known, or have something interesting to say about Eleanor. Among their positive contributions to Eleanor's reputation, one must unhesitatingly catalogue the fact that novelists have almost universally been much more willing than historians to credit the notion of a marriage between Eleanor and Edward IV. As Josephine Tey remarked, 'Edward seems to have made a habit of secret marriages. …It must have been difficult for him … when he came up against unassailable virtue. There was nothing for it but marriage'.[4] On the negative side, however, historical novelists have perhaps confused the picture in other respects. Of course, one must remember that novelists are, by definition, writing works of imagination, not of history. They therefore have a perfect right to adapt Eleanor's story to fit their wider narrative intentions. While their distortions are certainly no worse that those perpetrated by some serious historians,[5] it is possible that novelists have been more influential than historians in colouring the popular perception of Eleanor.

Rosemary Hawley Jarman, while asserting Edward's marriage to Eleanor, makes the king declare the fact of this earlier marriage to Elizabeth Woodville when the latter is trying to seduce Edward into marriage with herself:

'I would wed with you tomorrow, save that … I am married already'. He said dully. … 'I was crazy to marry her. She was chaste, like you, Bessy, and would have me no other way. It has been a secret for three years. She has no royal blood, but – her name is Eleanor Butler, daughter of Talbot. … Lancastrian, the whole family. Nell was so saintly, so good. Sudeley, curse him, was trying to cheat her out of her estates. She was widowed, she came suing to me for restoration. And we were wed. … Only my lady mother knows. Well – she and a very few more. Bishop Stillington, he bound us together'.[6]

It is, in fact, very unlikely that Elizabeth Woodville knew of the Talbot marriage at the time of her own contract with the king. Had she known, she was certainly intelligent enough to have realised that a secret marriage in her own case would not serve, and that a very public ceremony was essential.

Jarman's account contains other historical inaccuracies: the fact that at the time of this imagined conversation between Edward and Elizabeth Woodville, Stillington was not yet a bishop; the implication that Lord Sudeley was trying to cheat Eleanor out of her jointure; the asseveration that Eleanor had no royal blood. On the other hand it is conceivable that the dowager Duchess of York did indeed have some knowledge of the Talbot marriage as Jarman suggests. As we have seen, this is implied (albeit with inevitable distortions) by Sir Thomas More.[7]

Like historians, novelists have generally presented Eleanor under the surname Butler. This is regrettable. The more so since almost all novelists are then inconsistent, and refer to Elizabeth Woodville by her maiden name. (Since both ladies were widows, they should be treated alike in this respect – as they were in reality by Richard III – and either both should be referred to by their maiden names, or both by their married names.) An interesting, early and laudable exception is Lord Lytton, who presents the following conversation between Richard, Duke of Gloucester and Lord Montagu in 1468:

'Thou knowest well that the king was betrothed before to the Lady Eleanor Talbot; that such betrothal, not set aside by the pope, renders his marriage with Elizabeth against law; that his children may (would to Heaven it were not so!) be set aside as bastards, when Edward's life no longer shields them from the sharp eyes of men.'

'Ah!' said Montagu, thoughtfully; 'and in that case, George of Clarence would wear the crown, and his children reign in England'.

'Our Lord forfend', said Richard, 'that I should say that Warwick thought of this when he deemed George worthy of the hand of Isabel'.[8]

It is noteworthy that Lytton believes the Talbot marriage to have been known and talked about while Eleanor was yet living. Also that he not only draws the obvious conclusion in respect of the potential advantage to the Duke of Clarence, but goes on to imply Warwick's possible awareness of the situation. On the other hand, Richard of Gloucester, who was, in reality, only 16 years old at the time of this imagined conversation, seems, perhaps, rather excessively perspicacious for one so comparatively young!

Unfortunately, Lord Lytton's story ends with the death of the Earl of Warwick, so that we have no opportunity to see fully how he would have handled the Talbot marriage in respect of the events of 1478 and 1483. He provides a foretaste, however, when he refers to Elizabeth Woodville's children in 1483 'subjected to the stain of illegitimacy, and herself recognised as the harlot'.[9] Lytton, incidentally, is robust in his handling of Elizabeth Woodville, painting throughout a clear, if unflattering portrait of 'the grey cat'. He is particularly insistent on the inferiority of her birth – which, given his own rank and period, is interesting – calling her 'scarce of good gentleman's blood' and even 'mud-descended', while her father and brothers were 'knaves' sons' and 'little squires', so that Lord Dorset is invited to recall 'the day when, if a Nevile mounted in haste, he bade the first Woodville he saw hold the stirrup'.[10]

Josephine Tey, while acknowledging Eleanor to be the Earl of Shrewsbury's daughter,[11] simply calls her 'Lady Eleanor Butler' and does not say whether Butler was her maiden or her married name. Sharon Penman, while employing the surname Butler, makes some attempt to grasp this nettle in her narrative. She sets a scene at Windsor Castle, in September 1477, in which Edward IV and Elizabeth Woodville confront one another over what is to be done with the Duke of Clarence. In the course of this, Edward reveals to Elizabeth that his marriage to her was bigamous, explaining that he was already married to 'Eleanor Butler. Shrewsbury's daughter'. Elizabeth Woodville is stunned, but eventually responds: 'Butler's not the family name of Shrewsbury ... She was married, then?'[12] leading Edward to explain about Eleanor's marriage to Thomas Butler. In this version, Eleanor's maiden name is never supplied, but presumably Penman was aware that it was Talbot – though it has to be said that she commits the unforgivable sin of consistently referring to Edward IV's mistress, Elizabeth Lambert, as 'Jane Shore'![13]

Among the most interesting contributions to the picture of the fictional Eleanor is that of Sandra Wilson. While, like most of her fellow novelists, she consistently refers to Eleanor under the surname Butler, Wilson has a very clear awareness of Eleanor's family connections, and presents her throughout as the niece of Anne Beauchamp, Countess of Warwick (and hence the niece by marriage of the 'Kingmaker'). Wilson is also aware that Robert Stillington was not a bishop at the time of Edward's meeting with Eleanor.[14]

However, she makes some errors in her chronology. When Eleanor first appears in her story, on 10 October 1460, she is described as being 22 years old.[15] At that date she had in fact passed the age of 24 and was well on the way to her 25th birthday. Wilson goes on to describe Eleanor's 'thick black hair', and says that 'Nan could see in her niece the ghost of her long-dead half-sister, Margaret'.[16] While Wilson is very probably correct in respect of Eleanor's hair colouring, Eleanor is more likely to have inherited this from her father than from her mother, and of course, in 1460, far from being long-dead, Margaret, Countess of Shrewsbury still had almost seven years of life remaining to her.

Perhaps the most common error perpetuated by the novelists is the fallacy that Eleanor retired to a convent and became a nun. In *We Speak No Treason*, Rosemary Hawley Jarman neatly managed to avoid this error by skating rapidly over Eleanor's association with the Carmelites. Bishop Stillington simply states that Eleanor is 'dead these fifteen years … in the house of Carmelites at Norwich'.[17] However, since, in this version, Stillington's information is conveyed to Lord Howard (who, in reality, probably knew more about Eleanor's last years than the bishop) the narrative is historically flawed in another respect. Later, in *The King's Grey Mare*, Jarman is much more specific. Edward IV refers to the nuns of Norwich, stating that 'Eleanor is in a convent there', and again, later, 'Eleanor is with the nuns'.[18]

Tey, for her part, firmly locates Eleanor in a convent.[19] Penman, too, makes this mistake,[20] and Majorie Bowen, Rhoda Edwards and Jean Plaidy likewise fall into the trap.[21] In a scene of Bowen's which is undated, but which appears to be set in 1469,[22] the Duke of Clarence takes his brother of Gloucester to meet a dying nun who knew Eleanor in Norwich. The implication that they lived in the same nunnery is clear. Later, in 1483, Bishop Stillington reveals Eleanor's royal marriage to the council. The following exchange ensues:

'Why did not the Lady Eleanor speak?' asked Buckingham.

'Sir, she was a woman perplexed, humiliated and betrayed,' replied the bishop. 'She went into a convent in Norwich, and there died, silent, in the year 1466.'[23]

In this passage, Bowen not only misplaces Eleanor in a convent, but also anticipates her demise by two years!

Bowen's chronological errors involve other characters in addition to Eleanor. In her 1469(?) scene, Clarence at first implies that Stillington is in hiding.[24] Almost immediately afterwards, however, Bowen states that '[Richard] could make nothing of the mystery of the imprisonment of Dr Stillington'.[25] These accounts are mutually incompatible. Moreover, both are wrong. Stillington was not in hiding in 1469, nor was he imprisoned until the end of February 1478, when Edward IV consigned him to the Tower, following the execution of Clarence.

In her 1478 episode, Jarman once again skirts around the issue. Neither Stillington nor Eleanor is mentioned in connection with the execution of her Duke of Clarence. All we hear is 'Elizabeth [Woodville]'s soft voice from the shadows … "My children are not safe while Clarence lives"'.[26] Bowen involves Stillington with Clarence much more directly than does Penman. The latter produces an interesting idea, which might even be true, when she describes Dr Stillington as a long-term member of the Talbot affinity.[27] Her thought recalls the Talbot sisters' real historical patronage of Dr Thomas Cosyn. Penman's Stillington is a terrified and tortured figure, who only finally reveals the truth to Clarence in the Tower, when the Duke is about to die, in the mistaken belief that he already knows all about it. Her evocation of Stillington, summoned to court by the king in the autumn of 1477, is highly dramatic:

Elizabeth [Woodville] had never understood why Edward had named Stillington as his Chancellor. A mild-mannered, self-effacing man in his fifties, he had neither the intellect nor the ambition for a position of such power, and Elizabeth hadn't been the only one to wonder why Edward had chosen to honour Stillington so lavishly. He'd exercised his authority unobtrusively and, when his health began to suffer, seemed almost relieved to resign the Chancellorship and retire to his native Yorkshire. Elizabeth had not seen him in more than two years and she was shocked now at sight of the haggard, ageing man being ushered into Edward's private chambers. Was he as ill as that? But then he glanced back over his shoulder and her breath stopped. What she saw on his face was sheer terror, the look of a condemned prisoner about to mount the steps of the gallows.[28]

Edwards, whose story starts late, chronologically, has no 1478 scene as such, but she deals with the Clarence episode retrospectively. When Stillingon makes his revelation to Richard and Anne (in this case, in private), he explains that his long silence has been due to hounding by Elizabeth Woodville, moreover 'I was not the only one she hounded. Your Grace's own brother, the Duke of Clarence …'.[29] Richard is distraught at this news.

> You mean my brother George died for that? I never knew why, that last time, he was not forgiven, as he had been before. The Queen – the pretended Queen – killed him, for fear it might be discovered that she was nothing but a whore. She made one of my brothers kill the other because he'd begotten the heir to the throne of England in adultery, and was terrified of being found out.[30]

This is fine dramatic stuff, but perhaps rather overstates the case. By no stretch of the imagination is it justifiable to call Elizabeth Woodville a whore. Indeed, had she been, the whole problem would have melted away. Edwards also seems keen to shift all responsibility in the matter from the shoulders of Edward IV, which, after all, is where it truly belongs.

Edwards introduces a novel element, however, in the form of an oath of silence, which Stillington was forced to swear before Edward would release him from the Tower. Other authors also introduce imaginative elements into the story. Plaidy unfortunately shares with Penman the major crime of having a character in her story called *Jane Shore*, (in Plaidy's case, actually the leading character), however, she shares the talent for unusual but plausible detail. Both Plaidy and Edwards date Eleanor's meeting with Edward to the period before the latter ascended the throne. Although historically this is almost certainly incorrect, it is a novel twist. Moreover, Plaidy's Eleanor was almost as ambitious as Elizabeth Woodville in demanding marriage, and Eleanor's family knew all about it, although when the king 'refused to recognise the marriage, they had been wise enough to keep silent'. Here, Plaidy is picking up and running with a thread from Buck's account, and like Buck she mentions 'a child who had died'.[31]

Wilson varies Eleanor's story by introducing her to Edward while Sir Thomas Butler is still living, and before Edward becomes king. Unfortunately we now know that Sir Thomas Butler was dead before 1460, so he cannot possibly have played the dramatic role in the battle of Wakefield which Wilson would like to assign to him.[32] Apart from that it is feasible that Edward and Eleanor's relationship predated Edward's accession to the throne, although on balance they seem more likely to have met after Edward became king.

Another novel twist is supplied by Lytton. He was aware of the allegations preserved for us by Commynes andVergil that Edward IV besmirched the honour of a 'lady ofWarwick's house', but had no idea, apparently that Eleanor Talbot might fit this description. Consequently he applied the references to Anne Neville, causing an inebriated Edward IV to attempt the seduction of his future sister-in-law.[33] In Lytton's account, this attempted seduction was the reason why Anne had then to be hidden away for her own protection. This ill-advised move on the king's part is then used to partly account for his desertion by the Earl ofWarwick. Of course, in reality, Anne's concealment is normally dated rather later, after her father's death.

What is omitted by novelists can be as significant as what is included. Lytton is by no means alone in his ignorance of Eleanor's wider family connections. With the (partial) exception ofWilson, no novelist seems to have realised that Eleanor was the Duchess of Norfolk's sister, Anne Mowbray's aunt, and Queen Anne Neville's cousin. Eleanor's patronage of Corpus Christi College, Cambridge also passes unremarked, there is little interest in her religious convictions, and there is generally no indication as to where (let alone upon what) Eleanor lived after the death ofThomas Butler.There are even more extraordinary omissions. Penman, for example, has Anne Neville present in 1483 when Bishop Stillington (brought to Crosby Place by Buckingham) finally reveals the Edward/Eleanor marriage to the Duke of Gloucester.[34] Possibly it is Anne Neville's discomfort at having just been caught, by Buckingham and the bishop, *in flagrante delicto* with her own husband, which keeps her silent, but she certainly gives no indication that she recognises Eleanor's name, nor does she appear to realise that Stillington is talking about her cousin. Earlier in her narrative, Penman makes the obvious chronological link between the marriage of Anne Mowbray and the execution of the Duke of Clarence. She fails, however, to point out the fact that Anne Mowbray is Eleanor's niece.

Penman brings Eleanor into her story at a late stage.The first hint occurs only on page 555. By this time Eleanor is already dead, of course, so we never meet her in the flesh.This is a common novelists' approach. Interestingly, however, Penman does allow her readers just a glimpse of Eleanor, through the eyes of the king.

He closed his eyes, only to have a woman's face form against his lids. A gravely beautiful face, lovely and remote. A fair Madonna, he'd once called her and she'd been shocked, chided him for blaspheming. But it fitted her – all too well. Was that why he'd had to have her – because she'd seemed beyond reach, unattainable?[35]

Plaidy, on the other hand, has an entirely unmemorable Eleanor. Edward can scarcely recall what she looked like.[36] However, Penman has every right to evoke a lovely Eleanor. There is no necessity for novelists to compromise on Eleanor's beauty, given that she succeeded in attracting the king. Eleanor's religious faith is also subtly encapsulated in Penman's brief description. What she intended by her use of the word 'fair' is open to interpretation, given that the adjective has more than one meaning, and if she was referring to Eleanor's colouring, she was probably on the wrong track, for other members of the Talbot family were certainly dark. It is probable however, that Penman was merely seeking a synonym for 'beautiful'.

We see, then, that a range of novelists has handled the Eleanor story. Most of them seem to have enjoyed it, for even without invention the tale of Stillington's revelation to the council in the summer of 1483 is, after all, dramatic. Apparently without exception they have believed in Eleanor as Edward IV's wife. They have done the story – and Eleanor herself – justice, and while they may have made mistakes, fiction writers generally seem to have grasped basic facts which have been ignored by some serious historians.

Appendix 3

What makes a Lady?

The title 'Lady' has several distinct meanings, and its various uses are not always well understood, in these egalitarian times. The application of this title is naturally contingent upon the existence of an aristocracy. In a fifteenth-century context the word 'lady' is actually an anachronism, and Eleanor's contemporaries would have been more likely to give the title in its French form, *dame*. However, since surnames such as Butler are also (here and elsewhere) generally rendered in their equally anachronistic modern spellings, we need not scruple over the term 'lady'. Four categories of women can be identified to whom this title was and is applied.[1] We shall see that Eleanor Talbot was a 'lady' on two counts.

The daughter of a senior English peer (earl, marquis or duke) has the courtesy title 'Lady' [+ her Christian name]. She holds this title automatically and for life. She retains it even if she marries an untitled husband. This rank is often held from birth, as it certainly was in the case of Eleanor's younger sister, Elizabeth, Duchess of Norfolk. Eleanor herself was perhaps not, strictly speaking, *porphyrogenita*, since her father did not attain his English and Irish earldoms until she had already passed her sixth birthday (though he was already Count of Clermont at the time of Eleanor's birth). But certainly from the moment her father became an earl, Eleanor was *Lady Eleanor* for life.

The wife of an English knight or baronet has the title 'Lady' [+ her husband's surname]. This is a rank quite distinct from (and inferior to) that of a senior peer's daughter. Nevertheless, when Thomas Butler was knighted, in about 1455, Lady Eleanor also acquired this title of ladyship, thereby becoming Lady Butler.

There is also a third kind of ladyship, where the rank pertains to the wife of a peer. In such a case it is used in the form 'Lady' [plus husband's title]. Had Sir Thomas Butler not predeceased his father, Eleanor would also, in due course, have become a lady of this third category, with the style Lady Sudeley. In the event, the premature death of Sir Thomas precluded her acquisition of this additional title.

A fourth use of this title, which still today retains the French form, *dame*, is as applied to female professed religious, particularly, in the modern world, to nuns of the Benedictine order. This religious use of the title seems to have been more widespread in the fifteenth century. However, since Eleanor was never a nun of any order, the title is unlikely to have been bestowed upon her for religious reasons, particularly since there were ample secular grounds for its application in her case.

Notes

Introduction

1. C. El Mahdy, *Tutankhamen: the Life and Death of a Boy King*, London 1999, p. 79, 81.
2. '*Le nez de Cléopâtre: s'il eût été plus court, toute la face de la terre aurait changé*'. ('If Cleopatra's nose had been shorter, the whole face of the earth would have been different'.) L. Brunschvicg, ed., Blaise Pascal, *Pensées*, (fifth edition, 1909), vol. 2, p. 162.
3. E. Duffy, *The Stripping of the Altars*, London 1992.

Chapter 1

1. Probably. One of John Talbot's daughters died young. Her mother's identity is uncertain.
2. Bannes had served Talbot in France on and off since 1436. In 1401–2 the Talbot livery colour was green. B. Ross, *Accounts of the Stewards of the Talbot Household at Blakemere, 1392–1425*, Keele 2003, pp. 44–45. *EA*, p. 146, asserts that John Talbot's livery colour in the 1450s was magenta. No evidence for this is cited, but Talbot may have changed his livery colour on his elevation to the earldom of Shrewsbury, as John Howard apparently did on becoming Duke of Norfolk (see Ashdown-Hill, Phd. Thesis, 2008).
3. G.H.F. Vane, 'The Will of John Talbot, First Earl of Shrewsbury'. *TSAS*, 3rd series, vol. 4, 1904, pp. 371–378, and J. Ashdown-Hill, 'The Wills of John Talbot, first Earl of Shrewsbury, and of his sons, Lord Lisle and Sir Louis Talbot', *TSAHS* (forthcoming).
4. For John Talbot's career, see A.J. Pollard, *John Talbot and the War in France, 1427–1453*, London 1983; *DNB*, vol. 55, London 1898, and *EA* (which, however, contains some errors).
5. John Talbot was probably born in the same year as Henry V (1387).
6. He had been supporting John of Gaunt's claim to the throne of Castile.
7. *EA*, p. 23, implies that John Talbot's betrothal to Maud Neville antedated his mother's marriage to her father, but cites no authority for this chronology.
8. *EA*, p. 45.
9. The precise sequence of Talbot's children by Maud Neville is unclear. Some writers would have John as the eldest son, and born c.1413.

10. Brown sauce.
11. i.e. minced.
12. Whiting.
13. See below, note 24. Lesche is always a kind of custard. Lesche lumbarde, was usually flavoured with cinamon and pepper. One recipe includes red wine.
14. 'Meat' in this context means 'dish', not necessarily animal flesh.
15. See below, note 24.
16. Minced chicken or fish in a sauce of almond milk and sugar, thickened with rice flour. On this occasion fish was presumably served (see below, note 24).
17. Roach.
18. Cranes. It is odd to find game birds on a Lenten menu, but perhaps, since they lived in marshy areas, cranes counted as 'fish'.
19. Another kind of custard.
20. Flemish pastry.
21. Stewed.
22. Crayfish sprinkled with vinegar and pepper.
23. Yet another custard.
24. J. Gairdner, ed., *The Historical Collections of a Citizen of London*, London 1876, p. 141. Katherine's coronation took place during Lent of 1421, so this is lenten fare, hence the large variety of fish and seafood on offer. 'Baked mete in paste' was not meat but a kind of quiche. 'Lesche lumbarde' was a sweetmeat which ressembled halva: M. Black, *The Medieval Cookbook*, London 1992, pp. 123–124. 'Powdered' whelks and trout were perhaps prepared with 'powders' (herbs and spices) rather than actually ground into small fragments. 'Subtleties' were edible sculptures made of sugar and/or marzipan, and the 'creyme' was made, probably, with ground rice.
25. Joan Talbot is something of a mystery. No reference to her seems to predate her very late marriage to Lord Berkeley. Brad Verity (personal communication) suggests that Joan was not a Talbot daughter, but the widow of Sir Christopher Talbot.
26. J. Campbell, *At the Cradle of British Monarchy*, Coutances 1959, p. 229.
27. For the early history of the Talbot family in England, see R. Brill, *An English Captain of the Later Hundred Years' War*, unpublished PhD. Thesis, Princeton 1966, and A.J. Pollard, *The Family of Talbot, Lords Talbot and Earls of Shrewsbury in the Fifteenth Century*, unpublished PhD thesis, University of Bristol 1968.
28. Niece and eventual heiress of Aymer de Valence, Earl of Pembroke.
29. N. Pevsner, *The Buildings of England – Herefordshire*, Harmondsworth 1977, pp. 137–139, and plate 15.
30. The Le Strange title was among those which John had inherited.
31. *CPR 1321–1324*, p. 175.
32. VCH *Shropshire*, vol. 4, London 1989, pp. 100, 102. See below, Chapter 5.
33. For basic details of John Talbot's family, see *CP*, vol. 11, part 1, London 1949, pp. 701–705.
34. *TSAS*, Vane, p. 371, cites a Talbot will of 14 April 1425, which refers to *Margaretta domina Talbot*, so John and Margaret must have been married before that date.
35. The exact date of Eleanor's birth is unknown, but it must have taken place at the end of February or the beginning of March 1436 (a leap year).

Chapter 2

1. *EA*, p. 70.
2. *EA*, pp. 70, 85, 126, assumes that John and Margaret both lived mainly in France, but cites no direct evidence.
3. Records of the funeral expenses met by the Steward of Blakemere: Pollard, *Thesis*, p. 33; B. Ross, *Accounts of the Stewards of the Talbot Household at Blakemere 1392–1425*, Keele 2003, p. 156.
4. *EAW*, p. 9.
5. Lady Eleanor Beaufort, *née* Beauchamp, formerly Lady Ros (Roos), was currently the wife of the Earl of Somerset's younger brother, Edmund Beaufort.
6. Future Duke of Somerset.
7. Sixteen was the normal age for the consummation of a marriage in which one (or both) of the contracting partners was a minor: *EAW*, p. 45.
8. The Beauchamp Tower.
9. J. Maclean, ed., J. Smyth, *The Lives of the Berkeleys*, 3 volumes, vol. 2., Gloucester 1883, p. 34.
10. A. Sinclair, *The Beauchamp Pageant*, Donnington 2003, p. 32.
11. Sinclair, *Beauchamp Pageant*, p. 38.
12. Sinclair, *Beauchamp Pageant*, p. 39.
13. Future mother of Isabel, Duchess of Clarence, and of Queen Anne Neville. As Henry Beauchamp's only full-blood sister, Anne was ultimately the Beauchamp heiress.
14. Maclean/ Smyth, *Berkeleys*, vol. 2, p. 28. The original inscription was in Latin.
15. Margaret's only grandson, Thomas Talbot, Viscount Lisle, was killed by the then Lord Berkeley at the battle of Nibley Green.

Chapter 3

1. CPR 1441–1446, p. 79.
2. The earliest surviving mention of Talbot Court dates from 1672: H.A Harben, *A Dictionary of London*, London 1918, p. 567.
3. *EA*, pp. 68, 128, where no source is given. The name can probably be traced back to 1617. Harben, *A Dictionary of London*, p. 567.
4. C.J. Kitching, ed., *London and Middlesex Chantry Certificates, 1548*, London Record Society, vol. 16, 1980, p. 2.
5. 'The Minories'.
6. Leadenhall was held by the Neville family from the early fourteenth century until about 1410, by which time they had acquired 'the Herber' (on the site of the present Canon Street Station): Harben, *Dictionary of London*, pp. 299, 343.
7. According to Talbot, *EA*, pp. 38, 128, the clerks had certainly occupied it entirely by the 1440s. It is listed, however, as one of the possessions of the second Earl of Shrewsbury in his Inquisition *post mortem* in 1460, and was finally granted to the Solicitor General by Francis, Earl of Shrewsbury, in the reign of Edward VI: Harben, *Dictionary of London*, pp. 147–48.
8. *EA*, p. 9, says (citing no authority) that John Talbot 'was reputed to have auburn hair and wide set blue eyes'. However, surviving portraits and manuscript illuminations consistently depict John Talbot with dark, almost black hair, and brown eyes.
9. CPR 1441–1446, p. 79.

10. Her father was created Count of Clermont in 1434, so arguably Eleanor was born a 'lady'.

11. *CPR 144–1446*, p. 106.

12. J. Gairdner, ed., *The Historical Collections of a Citizen of London*, p. 184.

13. *CPR 1441–1446*, p. 448.

14. *CPR 1441–1446*, p. 108.

15. TNA, C 1/43/35. Abstract published in D.M. Gardiner, ed., *A Calendar of Early Chancery Proceedings relating to West Country Shipping, 1388–1493*, Devon and Cornwall Record Society, New Series, vol. 21, 1976, p. 44.

16. *CPR 1436–1441*, p. 408.

17. Pollard, *John Talbot and the War in France*, p.132.

18. Pollard, *John Talbot and the War in France*, p.132.

19. 'You sprinkle me, O Lord, with hyssop, and I shall be clean; you will wash me and I shall be whiter than snow'. The text is from psalm LI, verse 7 (in the enumeration of the *Vulgate*).

Chapter 4

1. Will of Sir Humphrey Talbot: *TV*, vol. 1, London 1826, pp. 409–10 and TNA, PROB 11/10, ff. 156-57.

2. The account given here follows that given in the old *DNB* and assumes that the marriage with Catherine Burnell took place. Pollard, however, is of the opinion that it never progressed further than a betrothal which was subsequently broken. In any event John II married late, as apparently did his sister, Joan (see below). It seems that Lord Talbot took little interest in the marriage plans of his first family.

3. In Joan's case, the only surviving records refer to two subsequent marriages, but she was certainly of an age to have been married by 1443.

4. J. Ward, *Women in Medieval Europe 1200–1500*, London 2002, pp. 16, 19. See also N. Orme, *Education and Society in Medieval and Renaissance England*, London 1989, p. 229.

5. *EAW*, p. 32.

6. N. Orme, *English Schools in the Middle Ages*, London 1973, p. 55, citing the Plumton correspondence.

7. Their father spoke French, which was also a normal accomplishment for aristocratic girls: *EAW*, p. 37.

8. According to Bishop Fisher even a noted bluestocking like Lady Margaret Beaufort was generally unable to read the Latin rubrics in her Book of Hours: *EAW*, p. 37.

9. Ward, *Women in Medieval Europe*, pp. 17, 18.

10. *EAW*, p. 28.

11. Orme, *English Schools*, p. 53.

12. Orme, *English Schools*, p. 55.

13. Orme, *Education and Society*, p. 226.

14. P. Coss, *The Lady in Medieval England 1000–1500*, Stroud, 1998, pp. 152–54, 159.

15. Coss, *Lady*, p. 163.

16. Coss, *Lady*, pp. 156, 157. Orme, *Education and Society*, p. 225.

17. By his first wife, Idoine Hotoft.

18. I am indebted to Brad Verity for information on Elizabeth and Ankaret Barre.

19. J.C. Wedgwood and A.D. Holt, *History of Parliament, 1439–1509*, 2 vols, London 1938, vol. 1, *Biographies*, p. 164, suggest that Jane was Sir William Catesby's first wife, but the

birth dates of the children of his two marriages make this a chronological impossibility. R. Horrox, *ODNB* vol. 10, p. 535, confirms that Jane was Sir William's second wife.

20. Not Henry VII's mother, but her cousin of the same name.

21. Anne (or Agnes) Paston married Sir Gilbert Talbot, younger son of the second Earl of Shrewsbury, and eventual heir of Sir Humphrey Talbot.

22. John, the youngest, used the title 'Duke of Somerset' in exile, but never held it legally in England.

23. When Elizabeth Talbot was in Flanders in 1468, some of her servants called on the exiled Beauforts, provoking the wrath of Edward IV.

24. See Chapter 14.

25. Edmund Beaufort, grandson of John of Gaunt, nephew of the former Chancellor, Cardinal Henry Beaufort, Bishop of Winchester, and younger brother of John, Earl and subsequently first Duke of Somerset, had married Margaret Beauchamp's younger sister, Eleanor, the dowager Lady Roos, in about 1435. In the same year that John Talbot was created Earl of Shrewsbury, Edmund Beaufort was named Earl of Dorset. In 1444, on the death of his elder brother, he became Earl of Somerset, and in 1448, was created Duke of Somerset.

26. *CPR, 1441–1446*, pp. 397–398; p. 220. Perhaps Sir Christopher Talbot's killer was identical with Sir Griffith Vaughan, who was responsible for the capture of Lord Shrewsbury's old friend, the Lollard, Sir John Oldcastle, Lord Cobham. (For details of the latter story see *EA*, p. 43.)

27. *CChR, 1427–1516*, London 1927, p. 50. It is unclear whether, strictly speaking, this barony was an inheritance or a new creation: J.E. Powell and K. Wallis, *The House of Lords in the Middle Ages*, London 1968, p. 476. Later Lord Lisle was raised to the rank of viscount.

28. J. Maclean, ed., J Smyth, *The Berkeley Manuscripts*, 3 volumes, Gloucester 1883–85, vol 2, 1883, pp. 109–110. Thomas reached the age of 21, apparently, in summer 1469, and was 'under the age of 22 years' when he was killed in March 1470. The inquisition *post mortem* of his aunt, Eleanor, Lady Butler, identified him in August 1468 as her nearest heir, and gave his age then as 20, which it defined as being of full age. TNA, C 140/29: '*Thomas Talbot miles, dominus Lisle, est heres eius propinquior, ... et est etatis viginti annos et amplius*'.

Chapter 5

1. Ross, *Thesis*, vol. 1, p. 45; Pollard, *Thesis*, p. 8.

2. Ross, *Thesis*, vol. 1, p. 46.

3. *Et in dono ii hominibus de Salop ludentibus quoddam interludum coram domina die Epiphanie iii s. iiii d.*: Ross, *Thesis*, vol. 2, p. 150, household accounts of Richard Kenleye, 1424-25.

4. S. Landsberg, *The Medieval Garden*, London [n.d], p. 13.

5. Fitzwilliam Museum, Cambridge, MS 41–1950.

6. WRO, L 1/81. See illustrations.

7. J Ashdown-Hill, 'Lady Eleanor Talbot: new evidence; new answers; new questions', *Ric.*16 (2006), pp. 113–32.

8. B. Fogle, *The Encyclopedia of the Dog,* London 1995, p.120.

9. L. Woolley, *Medieval Life and Leisure in the Devonshire Hunting Tapestries*, London 2002, p. 96.

10. They date from *c.*1425–1445, and are believed to have been owned in 1601 by Bess of Hardwick, Countess of Shrewsbury: Woolley, *Devonshire Hunting Tapestries*,

pp.16–23. Their date, and the Talbot connection, together with the fact that the first Earl of Shrewsbury spent much of his time on the Continent, and is known to have commissioned items there, make it plausible that the tapestries belonged to him.

11. Ross, *Thesis*, vol. 1, pp. 1–4.
12. M. Watson and C. Musson, *Shropshire from the Air*, Shrewsbury(?), 1993, p.68.
13. P.A. Baker, *The Medieval Pottery of Shropshire*, Shropshire Archaeological Society, 1970, p. 29; fig. 17.
14. R.W. Griffiths, 'Excavations at Blakemere Castle, Whitchurch', in *Shropshire Newsletter*, vol. 24, Nov. 1963, p. 92.
15. Ross, *Thesis*, pp. 83–88.
16. *EAW*, p. 29.
17. Her own children not excepted.
18. Rous Roll no. 51, quoted in *CP*, vol. 8 (Lisle), p.55, n.f., and Ross, *Thesis*, vol. 1, p.24.
19. John Talbot (like Henry V himself) had been a friend of Sir John Oldcastle (Lord Cobham) in his youth. When Oldcastle was accused of heresy, Talbot (with others) was briefly arrested, but no charge of heresy was ever laid against him. *EA*, Chapter 3 (especially pp. 42–43).
20. It is possible that part of Eleanor's childhood may have been spent in France.
21. *EAW*, p. 27, citing *Privy Purse expenses of the Princess Mary*, xli.
22. Ross, *Thesis*, pp. 43, 44, 121 and *passim.*, *TV*, vol. 1, pp. 409–10, and TNA, PROB 11 / 10, ff. 156–57.
23. Ross, *Thesis*, p. 54, p. 88.
24. A.J. Pollard, *John Talbot and the War in France 1427–1453*, London 1983, p. 98, citing *Calendar of Papal Registers, Papal Letters* 9, p. 239.
25. The volume contains dedicatory verses, a genealogical table showing the descent of Henry VI from St Louis, *la vraye hystoire du bon roy Alixandre*, three *chansons de geste* relating to Charlemagne, the *chanson de geste* of Ogier de Danois, *le livre de Regn[ault] de Montaubain*, the *noble livre du roy de Pontus*, *le livre de Guy de Warrewik*, *lystoire du chevalier au Signe* [*sic: Cygne*], *le livre de larbre de batailes*, *le livre de politique*, *le cronicles de Normandie*, *le breviaire des nobles*, Christine de Pisan's *livre de fais darmes et de chevalerie*, and a French version of the statutes of the Order of the Garter: G.F. Warner and J.P. Gilson, *Catalogue of Western Manuscripts on the old Royal and King's Collections*, 4 vols., London 1921, vol. 2, pp. 177–79.
26. 'Most excellent princess, the Earl of Shrewsbury presents this book to you'.
27. 'My one desire in respect of yourself and the king is to serve you well until I die. That said, one knows all there is to know about my one desire in respect of yourself and the king'.
28. Ward, *Women in Medieval Europe*, p. 34.
29. According to Eleanor's Inquisition *post mortem* Lord Sudeley settled Griff and Great Dorset on her and Thomas in the twenty-eighth year of the reign of Henry VI (1449–50): see below, Appendix 1. Actually Lord Sudeley's deed of gift was dated 1453, but the settlement was probably agreed at the time of the marriage.
30. *CP*, vol. 9, London 1936, pp. 608–609 suggests that John Mowbray and Elizabeth Talbot were married before 27 November 1448, but it seems unlikely, in this case, that Elizabeth would actually have left her parents' home at such an early age.
31. 'John Mowbray, son and heir of John, Duke of Norfolk' was created Earl of Warenne and Surrey on 24 March 1451: *CChR, 1427–1516*, London 1927, p. 114. This date is probably close to that of his marriage.

Chapter 6

1. Both Ralph Butler (his stepson) and Sir John Montgomery (his younger step-daughter's husband) were among those who inherited manors previously held by Sir John Dalyngrygg: *CCR 1441–47*, p. 95, 12 March 1443.
2. The fact that 'Dame Alice Boteler' was appointed Henry VI's governess in 1424 is well known but no one seems previously to have thought about who she might have been. There are two obvious contenders: Ralph Butler's mother and his sister-in-law, both of whom were called Alice. Henry's gifts to his former governess are recorded: *CPR 1436–41*, pp. 46, 127, 367, 434, 534. The fact that the former governess is called 'the King's widow' means that Ralph Butler's sister-in-law is almost certainly the right candidate, as his mother had remarried, and figures in November 1440 as 'Alice Dalyngrrege': *CPR 1441–46*, p. 458. On the other hand Ralph Butler's sister-in-law, Alice, never remarried, as is shown by the fact that in October 1442 she is called 'Alice, late the wife of William Botiller': *CPR 1441–46*, p. 116.
3. Some writers have put his birth as late as 1396.
4. Tudorhistory.org/castles/sudeley/
5. *CP*, vol. 12, part 1, p. 421 (footnote). To crenellate a building (i.e. to put on battlements) created a castle. Since this would affect the king, royal permission was required.
6. D. Verey, *The Buildings of England – Gloucestershire*, vol. 1, *The Cotswolds*, Harmondsworth 1970, pp. 438–41.
7. The following account of the career of Ralph Butler is based largely on that given in *CP*, vol 12, part 1, p. 419 onwards.
8. Portable Antiquities Scheme database, www.finds.org.uk, ESS-CB1310. Lord Sudeley bore the arms of Butler quartering Sudeley, as displayed on his seal (WRO, L1/82). The harness pendant shows only what may possibly be the Sudeley arms.
9. IRO, HA246/B2/508.
10. J. Weever, *Ancient Funeral Monuments of Great Britain*, London 1631, repr. Amsterdam 1979, p. 778.
11. *Guidebook to St Mary, Chilton, Suffolk*, Redundant Churches Fund, London 1985, p. 5.

Chapter 7

1. Alice Deincourt was the grandmother of Francis, Lord Lovel, by her previous marriage.
2. *CP*, vol. 12, part 1, p. 421.
3. C.P. Boyd, *Roll of the Drapers' Company of London*, Croydon 1934, p. 91; S.L. Thrupp, *The Merchant Class of Medieval London 1300-1500*, Chicago 1948, p. 349: see figure 18.
4. B. Burke, *The General Armory of England, Scotland, Ireland and Wales*, London 1984, p. 736.
5. M. Barber, 'John Norbury', *English Historical Review*, vol. 68, 1953, p.66.
6. For Sir John Norbury's career, see Barber, 'John Norbury', pp. 66–76; Burke, *Armory*, p. 736; *CPR 1396–99*, p. 470; *CPR 1399–1401*, p.541; *CPR 1408–13*, pp. 65, 144, 283, 404, 405, 410; *CPR 1413–16*, pp. 161, 162, 419; C.W. Previté-Orton and Z.N. Brooke, eds., *The Cambridge Medieval History*, vol. 8, Cambridge 1964, p. 363, p. 376; E.F. Jacobs, ed., *The Fifteenth Century*, 1399–1485, Oxford 1961, p.1, p.18, p.429; A. Steel, *Richard II*, Cambridge 1962, p.269. For Elizabeth's first marriage see Thrupp, *Merchant Class*, p. 349.

7. Elizabeth Norbury was a relative of the great fifteenth-century abbot of St Albans, who is usually known as John Wheathamstead, but whose family surname was Bostock. It is possible that this relationship was on her mother's side. VCH *Hertfordshire*, vol. 2, p. 375; H.T. Riley, ed., *Registrum Abbatiae Iohannis Whethamstede, Abbatis Monasterii Sancti Albani*, 2 vols., London 1872–73, vol. 1, p. 218 onwards.

8. *CPR 1399–1401*, p. 541; *CPR 1408–13*, p. 404.

9. She was the widow of Thomas Baynarde of Suffolk. Her maiden name is unknown.

10. Henry Norbury is named as Henry IV's godson several times in the patent rolls. See, for example, *CPR 1408–13*, p. 404.

11. *Valens armiger, strenuus ac probus vir.* Barber, 'John Norbury', p. 75. Sir John Norbury was probably in his late fifties at the time of his death, which Barber places in 1414.

12. New York Public Library, Spencer MS. 193.

13. TNA, C 140/7/14.

14. Only the indentures of 1496 survive, so it is not necessarily possible to draw any conclusions as to the date of Eleanor's Corpus Christi endowment from the inclusion of Lady Sudeley in the commemoration. At the time of Eleanor's foundation, the latter could have been still living, and the prayers endowed may have been for her good estate while she lived, and for the repose of her soul after death, which was quite a usual formulation in such cases.

15. The surviving indentures were drawn not by Eleanor but by her sister, Elizabeth (who may not have known the first Lady Sudeley).

Chapter 8

1. *EAW*, pp. 53–55.

2. *CPR 1467–77*, p. 133.

3. WRO, L 1/82.

4. WRO, L 1/79.

5. H.T. Riley, ed., *Registrum Abbatiae Iohannis Whethamstede*, vol. 1, London 1872, p. 227.

6. 22 May 1455.

7. 'Our soveraigne Lorde … cam unto Seint Albanis, with him assembling on his parte … the Lorde Sudeley [and others]. … At the same batelle were hurte: the king our souveraigne Lorde in the nekke with an arow, [and] the duc of Bokingham and the Lorde Sudeley in the visages with an arow': M.L. Kekewich, C. Richmond, A.F. Sutton, L. Visser-Fuchs and J.L. Watts, *The Politics of Fifteenth-Century England: John Vale's Book*, Stroud 1995, pp. 190, 193.

8. *Ac insuper, noveritis nos, praefatus Abbatem et Conventum, quod eum Thomas Bottiler, Miles, Willelmus Beaufitz, et Willelmus Heynes, teneant de nobis, in iure monasterii nostri praedicti, unum messuagium, diversa terras et tenementum, vocata 'Langleys', cum, pertenentiis, in Rykmersworthe praedicta, nuper in tenura Rogeri Lynster, per fidelitatem et redditum decem solidorum annuatim per annum, dedisse, et per preasentes concessisse, praedicto Radulpho Botteller novem solidos et undecim denarios, parcellam dicti redditus decem solidorum*: Riley, *Registrum Abbatiae Iohannis Whethamstede*, vol. 1, p. 227.

9. *CD*, vol. 2, London 1894, p. 308, B 2507, 24 June 21 Henry VI. Thomas Butler's seal on this document unfortunately shows a punning device rather than a coat of arms. It was apparently impressed with a ring, leaving also his fingerprint in the soft sealing wax on the back. The impression is an elongated hexagonal shape 15mm x 10mm, formed by the shape of the top of the ring. The oval bezel depicts three tall bottles with the letters B-OT-[E?]LA-R distributed around them.

10. It is equally possible, therefore, that Thomas Boteler of Meriden was a distant cousin and namesake.
11. *CFR* 1452–61, p. 17.
12. *CD*, vol. 3, London 1900, p. 377, C. 3519, p. 402, C. 3723. The stewardship of Havering-at-Bower subsequently passed into the hands of Sir Thomas Butler's cousin, Sir Thomas Montgomery: W.E. Hampton, 'Sir Thomas Montgomery, K.G.', *Ric.*3, no. 51, p. 10.
13. J. Ashdown-Hill, 'The Inquisition Post Mortem of Eleanor Talbot, Lady Butler', *Ric.*12, no. 159, December 2002, pp. 563–573.
14. WRO, L 1/82.
15. The possibility that the two were identical was canvassed by the present writer in 'Edward IV's uncrowned Queen'.
16. VCH, *Warwickshire*, vol. 4, London 1947, p. 149; N. Pevsner and A. Wedgewood, *The Buildings of England – Warwickshire*, London 1966, p. 354.

Chapter 9

1. Then husband of the younger Butler sister, Elizabeth.
2. Hamon was probably alive on 22 January 1429, when a commission was addressed to him: *CFR, 1422-30*, pp. 258, 236.
3. B. Wolffe, *Henry VI*, London 1981, p. 37.
4. Sir John Montgomery was responsible for the capture of Joan of Arc: *EA*, p. 102.
5. Hampton, 'Sir Thomas Montgomery', p. 9.
6. *CPR 1408–13*, p. 404.
7. I. Nairn & N. Pevsner (revised B. Cherry), *The Buildings of England – Surrey*, London 1962, 1971, pp. 465, 468–469.
8. *CPR 1452–61*, p. 232.
9. The entry in the patent rolls for 1477 is confused and refers to 'John Norbury, knight, son of Henry Norbury, knight and Elizabeth Butler', which could mean either that Henry inherited and his name was accidentally exchanged in the records with that of his father, or alternatively that Henry had died before his uncle and that his son, Sir John Norbury III, inherited from Lord Sudeley, the record having misunderstood John's relationship with Elizabeth Butler, who was not his mother but his grandmother.
10. *CPR 1476–85*, pp. 16, 85, 214, 392, 394, 400, 489, 574.
11. J. Anstis, ed., *The Register of the Most Noble Order of the Garter*, 2 volumes, London 1724, vol. 1, pp. 127, 130, 199.
12. Anstis, *Garter*, vol. 1, pp. 127, 130, 199.
13. *CPR 1452–61*, pp. 87, 481.
14. H. Beaune and J. d'Arbaumont, eds., *Mémoires d'Olivier de la Marche*, 4 vols., vol. 3, Paris 1885, p. 111.
15. *CPR 1476–85*, pp. 542, 430.
16. His inheritance devolved upon the posterity of his sister, Alice. His will is published in H. Nicholas, *TV*, vol. 2, London 1826, p. 396.

Chapter 10

1. See above, p. 58; also *CPR 1467–77*, p.133.
2. Beaune and d'Arbaumont, *Mémoires d'Olivier de la Marche*, vol. 3, p. 107.

3. I am grateful to Dr Anne Sutton for drawing my attention to this portrait, on the subject of which, see L. Campbell, 'Approaches to Petrus Christus', in M.A. Ainsworth, ed., *Petrus Christus in Renaissance Bruges*, New York and Turnhout 1995, pp. 3–5 and figs 1–2.

4. W.J. White, personal communication, January 1997.

5. *EAW*, pp. 32, 192.

6. *In Parochia Omnium Sanctorum ad Fenum*. Riley, *Registrum Abbatiae Iohannis Whethamstede*, p. 233; also pp. 235–36, report of the mayor of London, 4 May 1456.

7. Riley, *Registrum Abbatiae Iohannis Whethamstede*, p. 227.

8. Modern Jenningsbury, near Brickenden, in the rural parish of St John, Hertford. There is still a moated manor house: VCH *Hertfordshire*, vol. 2, p. 120; vol. 3, p. 409.

9. *CCR 1447–54*, p. 317, 5 March 1451.

10. *CCR 1447–54*, p. 228.

11. New York Public Library, Spencer Ms. 193: Winkless, 'Medieval Sudeley', part 2, *Family History* vol. 10, 1977, pp. 21–39.

12. Norfolk's mother, the dowager Duchess Catherine, was the sister of Cecily, Duchess of York.

13. Maclean/Smyth, *Berkeleys*, p. 66.

14. The Catholic Church celebrates a Jubilee or 'Holy Year' at intervals of (usually) twenty-five years – though this has varied from time to time. A 'Holy Year' is regarded as a particularly suitable time for making a pilgrimage to Rome.

15. J. Lees-Milne, *Saint Peters*, London 1967, pp. 124, 125.

16. *EA*, pp. 146; 151,

17. N. Davis, ed., *Paston Letters and Papers of the Fifteenth Century*, 2 volumes, Oxford 1971 and 1976, vol. 2, pp. 74, 76, 77.

18. Maclean / Smyth, *Berkeleys*, p. 62.

19. Maclean / Smyth, *Berkeleys*, p. 67.

20. Maclean / Smyth, *Berkeleys*; Pollard, *Thesis*, pp. 194, 268, 281. Pollard emphasises the close working relationship between Lords Shrewsbury and Somerset.

21. In his will, drawn up in 1452, Lord Shrewsbury instructs his executors to take legal action against Lord Sudeley if necessary to ensure that Eleanor's marriage settlement is honoured. See Appendix 1.

22. WRO, L 1/79. Burton Dassett is referred to in this document as 'Chepingdorset', one of several variants of its name, attested also in 1397 and 1512. See J.E.B. Gover, A. Mawer & F.M. Stenton with F.T.S. Houghton, *The Place Names of Warwickshire*, Cambridge 1936, p. 268.

23. WRO, L 1/80 & L 1/81.

24. The Countess of Shrewsbury's use of the marguerite emblematic of her name is illustrated in her book of hours: Fitzwilliam Museum, Cambridge, MS 41–1950.

25. VCH, *Warwickshire*, vol. 4, London 1947, p. 175, citing *CPR 1467–77*, p. 133.

26. F. Oshaughnessy, *The Story of Burton Dassett Church*, Coventry [n.d.] pp. 4, 7, 8, 11, 12.

27. It could be argued that the Aquitaine was not part of France.

28. Vane, 'Will of John Talbot', *TSAS*, vol. 4, 1904, pp. 371–378.

29. *CPR 1452–1461*, p. 44.

30. W.H. Egerton, 'Talbot's Tomb', *TSAS*, vol. 8, 1885, pp. 413–440.

31. The chapel of Notre Dame de Talbot was destroyed in the French Revolution, but a cross and a column surmounted by a statue of the Virgin Mary, now mark the site.

32. Anatomical report of Dr Groynne *et al.*, quoted in Egerton, 'Talbot's Tomb', p. 425.

33. Wolffe, *Henry VI*, p. 294.

34. J.S. Davies, ed., *An English Chronicle of the Reigns of Richard II, Henry IV, Henry V and Henry VI*, London 1856, p. 72.

35. G. Smith, ed., *The Coronation of Elizabeth Wydeville*, London 1935, reprinted Gloucester 1975, p. 47.

36. See below.

37. TNA, PROB 11/4, f. 205 v: Ashdown-Hill, 'Talbot Wills', *TSAHS* (forthcoming).

38. Davies, ed., *English Chronicle*, p. 72.

39. See Ashdown-Hill, 'Norfolk Requiem'.

40. *CPR 1452–61*, p. 44.

41. M.G.A. Vale, 'The Last Years of English Gascony, 1451–1453', *Transactions of the Royal Historical Society*, fifth series, vol. 19, London 1969, p. 128.

42. *CPR 1452–61*, p. 323.

43. *CCR 1454–61*, p. 269.

44. *Sanis mente licet eger corpore.*

45. *Secundum voluntatem domine Margarete Comitisse de Salop matris mea*: Ashdown-Hill, 'Talbot Wills'.

46. The church floor was repaved in the nineteenth century: A.N. Palmer, *The History of the Parish Church of Wrexham*, Wrexham & Oswestry [n.d.], p. 185. Gresford Church was also 'restored' at that period.

Chapter 11

1. WRO, L1/82.

2. Verey, *Gloucestershire*, vol. 1, p. 437.

3. VCH, *Hertfordshire*, vol. 2, pp. 375–76.

4. Alice Deincourt's exact birth date is unknown, but her parents married in 1400/01 and her father died in 1406, which establishes the possible parameters. Her brother, William, Lord Deincourt, was born *c*.1403.

5. WRO, L1/79.

6. The names of these manors occur in a variety of forms. See W.F. Carter, ed., *The Lay Subsidy Roll for Warwickshire, 6 Edward III (1332)*, London 1926, L. Drucker, ed., *Warwickshire Feet of Fines* vol. 3 (1345-1509), London 1943 and Gover *et al.*, *The Place Names of Warwickshire*.

7. Eleanor's inquisition post mortem, TNA, C 140/29/39.

8. See *EAW*, p. 144.

9. WRO, L 1/82.

10. In her endowment at Cambridge, Eleanor provided for prayers for Lord Sudeley.

11. *EAW*, p. 192.

12. The manor of Fenny Compton was at some stage divided into three. It seems likely that this division postdates Eleanor's death (see below).

13. *EAW*, p. 130. Of the sample considered by Harris, approximately 36 per cent had a jointure of less than £50 *per annum*; 28 per cent had between £50 and £100, 25 per cent had between £100 and £500, and 10 per cent had more than £500.

14. Ashdown-Hill, 'The Inquisition Post Mortem of Eleanor Talbot, Lady Butler', *Ric.*12, p. 572.

15. The total would depend, clearly, on the date at which additional property was acquired. This is unknown.

16. *EAW*, p. 45.

17. The MS has the abbreviation *in dict' com'*, which could imply one county or more than one.

18. *EAW*, p. 43.

19. *EAW*, p. 47.

20. Ashdown-Hill, 'Talbot Wills', *TSAHS* (forthcoming). It was quite usual for siblings not to mention one another in their wills. According to Harris, less than 8 per cent of them did so: *EAW*, p. 185.

21. Eleanor's tenure would, in that case, have been of very limited duration, but she is only known to have held the Wiltshire lands in June 1468. It is not certain when she acquired them.

22. *CFR 1461–1471*, pp. 195-97.

23. Mentioned retrospectively in 1452. *CPR 1446–1452*, p. 108.

24. *CPR 1446–1452*, p. 559; *CPR 1461–1467*, p. 482.

25. J. Ashdown-Hill, 'The elusive mistress: Elizabeth Lucy and her family', *Ric.* 11 (1997–99), pp. 490–505.

26. VCH *Wiltshire*, vol. 10, p. 195.

27. Eleanor *gave (dedisse)* her sister the manor of Fenny Compton, which was not Eleanor's inherited property. On the other hand she granted Elizabeth *the reversion (reversione)* of the Wiltshire properties. This could be construed as implying some right of inheritance. However it could equally imply the repayment of loans from Elizabeth.

28. VCH *Wiltshire*, vol. 10, p. 195.

29. See below and L1/93.

30. Wiltshire and Swindon Record Office: damaged deed and letters of attorney concerning John Cheney, June 1466, ref. 490/1478; marriage settlement referring to John Cheney of Oare, gentleman, 8 June 1678, ref. 9/26/176.

31. Pevsner and Wedgwood, *The Buildings of Britian – Warwickshire*, pp. 222; 293–94, lists an extant seventeenth-century manor house at Burton Dassett, but no manor house at Fenny Compton.

32. *CCR 1447–1454*, p. 228. See also Chapters 6 and 10.

33. Weever, *Ancient Funeral Monuments*, p. 778. See also above, Chapter 6.

34. The present gateway is actually a sixteenth-century rebuilding by the second Howard Duke.

35. Cambridge University Library, Dd. 3. 86. 3c, published in J. Ridgard, ed., *Medieval Framlingham*, Suffolk Record Society, vol. 27, 1985, pp. 129-158.

36. A. Watson and D. Sasitorn, *East Anglia from Above*, London 1998, p. 21.

37. F.J.E. Raby and P.K. Baillie Reynolds, *Framlingham Castle*, English Heritage guidebook, London 1959, revised 1973, p. 17.

38. Details of building construction from Raby and Baillie Reynolds, *Framlingham Castle*.

Chapter 12

1. *CPR 1452–1461*, p.541.

2. C.L. Scofield, *The Life and Reign of Edward the Fourth*, vol. 1, London 1923, p. 120.

3. IRO, HA 246/B2/498.

4. Powell and Wallis, *The House of Lords*, pp. xii–xiii.

5. Beaune and d'Arbaumont, *Mémoires d'Olivier de la Marche*, vol. 3, p. 107.

6. On Edward's hair colour, see A. Sutton and L.Visser-Fuchs, *The Royal Funerals of the House of York at Windsor*, London 2004, pp.113–24. Representations of him from the early 1460s show him with short hair.

7. See Chapter 19.

8. J. Ashdown-Hill, 'The Elusive Mistress', *Ric.*11 (1997-99), pp. 490-505.

9. The *titulus regius* of 1484; Commyne's *Mémoires*; the *Crowland Chronicle*.

10. J. Gairdner, *History of the Life and Reign of Richard the Third*, Cambridge 1898, p. 91.

11. R.A. Griffiths and R.S. Thomas, *The Making of the Tudor Dynasty*, Stroud 1985, p. 30.

12. P. Maddern, 'Honour among the Pastons: gender and integrity in fifteenth-century English provincial society', *Journal of Medieval History*, 14 (1988) p. 358.

13. Maddern, 'Honour among the Pastons', p. 359.

14. This was written with hindsight. In 1460-61 Robert Stillington was not yet a bishop.

15. M. Jones, ed., *Philippe de Commynes: Memoirs*, Harmondsworth 1972, pp. 353-54, 397.

16. Coss, *Lady*, p. 87. Despite this ecclesiastical prohibition, a priest did subsequently officiate at Edward IV's clandestine marriage with Elizabeth Woodville in 1464.

17. For details of Stillington's career, see A.J. Mowat, 'Robert Stillington', *Ric.*4 (June 1976), pp. 23-28, and W.E. Hampton, 'A further Account of Robert Stillington' *Ric.*4 (Sept. 1976), pp. 24-27. Also Emden, *Oxford*, vol. 3, pp. 1777-78 and H.C. Maxwell-Lyte, ed., *The Registers of Robert Stillington, Bishop of Bath and Wells 1466-1491 and Richard Fox, Bishop of Bath and Wells 1492-1494*, Somerset Record Society 1937.

18. *EAW*, p. 10.

19. C.N.L. Brooke, *the Medieval Idea of Marriage*, Oxford 1989, p. 169; Coss, *Lady*, p. 87.

20. Coss, *Lady*, p. 87.

21. J. Gairdner, *History of the Life and Reign of Richard the Third*, Cambridge 1898, p. 91.

22. C.A.J. Armstrong, ed., D. Mancini, *The Usurpation of Richard the Third*, Gloucester 1989, p. 63.

23. Encapsulated in the Act of Parliament of 1484.

24. Jones/Commynes, p. 397.

25. See Chapter 11.

26. A.N. Kincaid, ed., G. Buck, *The History of King Richard the Third*, Stroud 1979, pp. 176, 181.

27. See, for example, *EAW*, p. 137, – the case of Dame Elizabeth Holford, whose disputed marriage was implicity recognised by the courts of Star Chamber and Chancery.

28. *EAW*, p. 15.

29. The secondary Mowbray title 'earl Warren' was used as a courtesy title by the heir to the Dukedom of Norfolk at this period.

Chapter 13

1. *CPR 1461–1467*, p. 72.

2. 30 May 1462. *CPR 1461–1467*, p. 191.

3. The patent rolls record commissions in July 1461, March and October 1462, June, October and December 1464, August 1466, February 1468 and November 1469. There were later appointments in 1470, but these, presumably, were made by the government of the restored Henry VI.

4. *CP*, vol. 12, part 1, p. 421 (footnote).

5. Brooke, *The Medieval Idea of Marriage*, pp. 58, 59. A prohibition extending to the fourth degree of kinship remains the Catholic ruling today: *Catholic Encyclopaedia*, www. newadvent.org/cathen/04261a.htm.

6. Coss, *Lady*, p. 91.

7. Kincaid, ed., Buck, *King Richard the Third*, p. 183.

8. There was nothing exceptional in this. Fifteenth-century aristocratic women in general 'remained devoted to traditional religious practices and were generous about supporting the church': *EAW*, p. 11.

9. Kincaid, ed., Buck, *King Richard the Third*, p. 183, suggests that Eleanor's family knew of the marriage.

10. Dean of St Martin's; archdeacon of Colchester; archdeacon of Taunton; prebend of York; prebend of St David's; prebend of St Stephen's Chapel, Westminster; rector of Ashbury. He was confirmed in these posts early in the reign of Edward IV: H.C. Maxwell-Lyte, ed., *The Registers of Robert Stillington, Bishop of Bath and Wells 1466–1491 and Richard Fox, Bishop of Bath and Wells 1492–1494*, Somerset Record Society 1937, p. x, citing Patent Roll 1 Edward IV part v, m. 9.

11. A.J. Mowat, 'Robert Stillington, *Ric.*4 (June 1976), p. 23.

12. Maxwell-Lyte, *The Registers of Robert Stillington*, p. ix.

13. Powell and Wallis, *The House of Lords*, p. 15.

14. Archbishop William Booth died on or about 12 September 1464.

15. Maxwell-Lyte, ed., *The Registers of Robert Stillington*, p. viii.

16. *CPR 1461–1467*, p. 387.

17. Maxwell-Lyte, ed., *The Registers of Robert Stillington*, p. viii. Pope Paul II (Barbo) had succeeded Pius II (Piccolomini) at the end of August 1464.

18. Maxwell-Lyte, ed., *The Registers of Robert Stillington*, p. viii, citing Patent Roll 4 Edward IV, part 2, m. 2, nos. 37, 38, 51, 52.

19. *Calendar of Papal Registers*, vol. 12, *Papal Letters 1458–1471*, London 1933, p. 519. On Stillington's appointment, see also Mowat, 'Robert Stillington', p. 23, citing *CPR 1461–67*, pp. 149–50, and Emden, *Oxford*, p. 1778.

20. R.H. Helmholz, 'The Sons of Edward IV: A Canonical Assessment of the Claim that they were Illegitimate', in P.W. Hammond, ed., *Richard III: Loyalty Lordship and Law*, London 1986, pp. 95, 96.

21. N. Adams and C. Donahue, eds., *Select Cases from the Ecclesiastical Courts of the Province of Canterbury, c. 1200–1301*, London 1981, p. 337 and *passim*.

22. Adams and Donahue, *Select Cases*, p. 337.

23. Adams and Donahue, *Select Cases*, p. 348.

Chapter 14

1. R. Masters, *The History of the College of Corpus Christi and the Blessed Virgin Mary*, Cambridge 1753, p. 46.

2. Ward, *Women in Medieval Europe*, p. 213.

3. C. Hall, in P.N.R. Zutski, ed., *Medieval Cambridge: Essays on the Pre-Reformation University*, Woodbridge 1993.

4. A.B. Emden, *A Biographical Register of the University of Cambridge to 1500*, Cambridge 1963, p. xviii.

5. Emden, *Cambridge*, p. 81.

6. Parker Library MS. 232, the Markaunt Register. A former master, Thomas Markaunt, left the college his library of seventy-five volumes, for the use of the master and fellows, in 1439. Loans from this collection were recorded in the Markaunt Register and totalled on a yearly basis.

7. Parker Library MS. 232; Emden, *Cambridge*.

8. He paid room rent in 1457–62. Emden, *Cambridge*, p. 230.

9. Masters, *Corpus Christi*, appendix, p. 53.

10. Parker Library, *Liber Albus*, f. 72 (old foliation) or f. 51 (modern pencil foliation). The letter was published in Masters, *Corpus Christi*, appendix, p. 30. See Appendix 1.

11. I am grateful to the ancient archivist at Corpus Christi College, Dr E.S. Leedham-Green, for confirming this point.

12. J. Ashdown-Hill, 'The client network, connections and patronage of Sir John Howard (Lord Howard, first Duke of Norfolk) in north east Essex and south Suffolk', unpublished PhD Thesis, vol. 2, appendices, University of Essex, (2008).

13. *HHB*, part 1, p. 363. There were also Cottons in Cambridgeshire, one of whom was the receiver general of Margaret of Anjou. Eleanor's nephew, Sir Gilbert Talbot, married a Cotton.

14. Masters, *Corpus Christi*, p. 30.

15. Masters, *Corpus Christi*; copy annotated by the author and now in the Parker Library; handwritten note facing p. 53. 'Bichemwell' is presumably Beechamwell, about two miles south west of Swaffham.

16. Emden, *Cambridge*, p. 161.

17. Personal communication of 18 November 1996 from Catherine Hall, former library archivist, Corpus Christi College, citing MS. 232. The sequence of names in the Markaunt Register seems, however, somewhat haphazard.

Chapter 15

1. See illustrations, figure 30, and C.R. Manning, 'Kenninghall', Norfolk and Norwich Archaeological Society, *Original Papers*, vol. 7, part 4, Norwich 1870, pp. 289–299; description pp. 292–94.

2. East Hall remained the property of Elizabeth Talbot until her death in 1507, although she is not known to have lived there in her final years. The new house, Kenninghall Place, was built and habitable by 1526, so the destruction of East Hall must be dated some time within those nineteen years. Parts of the building may have been left standing for the processing of tallow, for the site became known as 'the Candleyards', but by the time of Leland's visit it was, apparently, deserted: L.T. Smith, *The Itinerary of John Leland*, parts 6 and 7, London 1890, p. 120.

3. Elizabeth Fitzalan's first husband had been Sir William de Montagu. After the death of Thomas Mowbray she married two further husbands: Sir Robert Goushill and Sir Gerard Usflete.

4. In 1438. Joan Neville was the sister of Warwick 'the Kingmaker'.

5. M.F. Serpell, *Kenninghall History and St Mary's Church*, Norwich 1982, p. 21.

6. Serpell, *Kenninghall*, pp. 16, 21–27.

7. Serpell, *Kenninghall*, p. 22.

8. Smith, *John Leland*, parts 6 and 7, p. 120.

9. R. Burrows, *Guidelines for Mystical Prayer*, London 1976, p. 65.

10. *EA*, p. 30.

11. CCCC, Parker Library, Ms. XXXI. 121.

12. W.E. Hampton, 'The Ladies of the Minories', *Ric.*4, no. 62, September 1978, pp. 15–22.

13. WRO, L1/81.

14. WRO, L1/85.

15. WRO, L1/86.

16. Ashdown-Hill, 'The Go-between', *Ric.*15 (2005), pp. 119–21.

Notes

17. *HHB*, part 1, pp. 153, 180, 240, 332, 482, part 2, p. 116.
18. *HHB*, part 1, p. 165.
19. See Chapters 12 and 14.
20. *HHB*, part 1, p. 151. 'My Lord' is John Mowbray, fourth Duke of Norfolk.
21. *HHB*, part 1, p. 153.
22. A.B. Emden, *A Biographical Register of the University of Oxford to A.D. 1500*, 3 vols, Oxford 1957–59, vol. 2, pp. 1035–36.
23. CCCC, Parker Library, Ms. XXXI. 121.
24. Ward, *Women in Medieval Europe*, p. 209
25. M.C. Erler, 'Three Fifteenth-Century Vowesses', C.M. Barron and A.F. Sutton, eds., *Medieval London Widows 1300–1500*, London 1994, p. 165.
26. Erler, 'Vowesses', p. 166.
27. NRO, DN/REG 6, book 11, and MF510.
28. H. Kleineke, 'Gerhard von Wesel's Newsletter from England, 17 April 1471', *Ric.*16, 2006, p. 76.
29. Richard Water (or Walter) is named as prior in 1467–70. Probably he succeeded John Keninghale, who died in 1451. By 1470 (and probably earlier) he was *baccalaureus*. About the same period he is named in connection with the Paston family. Prior Water died on 5 March 1485/6, and was buried in a side chapel at the Norwich Carmel. His successor as prior was Thomas Waterpitt (elected August 1486, died December 1505): private communication from Fr Richard Copsey, O. Carm., *Institutum Carmelitanum*, Rome.
30. NRO, DN/REG 6, book 11, f. 130v.
31. The difference between a convent and a monastery is often misunderstood. It has absolutely nothing to do with the gender of the inhabitants. 'Convent' (from Latin *convenire*) is a house where people *come and go*, and is thus to some extent open to the world. 'Monastery' (from Greek μοναχός) is a house more separate from the outside world, where the inmates remain *alone* or apart.
32. Also called in Italy a *mantellata*.
33. J. Smet, *Cloistered Carmel*, Rome 1986. pp. 10–12.
34. J. Smet, *The Carmelites: A History of the Brothers of Our Lady of Mount Carmel*, 3 vols, vol. 1, Darien 1975, trans. A Ruiz Molina, *Los Carmelitos, Historia de la Orden del Carmen*, Madrid 1987, p. 139.
35. Smet, *Cloistered Carmel*, p. 12. The degli Armati were not a unique case. There was a similar married couple in Cologne, *ibid.*, p. 17.
36. Only in recent times have houses of Carmelite nuns been established in England.
37. R.P. Silverio de Santa Teresa, *Saint Teresa of Jesus*, London and Glasgow 1947, p. 21, n. 1.
38. 'Only two per cent of aristocratic women became nuns': *EAW*, p. 11. For Eleanor, as for vowesses, a religious commitment brought certain social and legal advantages, including 'control of temporal resources, free from male intrusion': Erler, 'Vowesses' p. 167.
39. Personal communication from Sister Gillian Leslie OCD, librarian, the Carmelite Monastery, Quiddenham, Norfolk.
40. Personal communication from Sister Gillian Leslie OCD.
41. Ward, *Women in Medieval Europe*, p. 191.
42. C. Wolters, ed., *The Cloud of Unknowing*, Harmondsworth 1961, p. 52.
43. Burrows, *Guidelines*, p. 105.
44. Ward, *Women in Medieval Europe*, pp. 193, 195.

Chapter 16

1. P.M. Kendall, *Richard the Third*, London 1973, p. 52.
2. Jones/Commynes, pp. 354, 397.
3. Kendall, *Richard the Third*, p. 54.
4. Helmholz, 'The Sons of Edward IV', pp. 91–103. Also Brooke, *The Medieval Idea of Marriage*, p. 169.
5. Similarly the marriage between Thomas fitzJames Fitzgerald, Earl of Desmond and Ellis Barry was publicly acknowledged for many years. This did not stop the earl's younger brother, Gerald, from claiming, after Thomas' execution in 1468, that the marriage was invalid, and all the children born of it, bastards. Although Gerald's action failed (because he could not prove his brother's marriage invalid) there is no doubt that had he been able to demonstrate a legal impediment, the children would all have been bastardised, despite having long been held legitimate: *Calendar of Papal Registers*, vol. 11, *Papal Letters 1455–1464*, London 1921, p. 232, and vol. 12, *Papal Letters 1458–1471*, London 1933, p. 672.
6. See Coss, *Lady*, p. 125: 'the courts largely considered cases on the basis of an action brought by an interested party'. Coss is speaking here of suits for nullity or divorce, but the precontract cases cited in Pedersen, *Marriage Disputes in Medieval England*, were all brought to court by one of the disputant 'wives'.
7. See Chapters 11 and 12.
8. Kendall, *Richard the Third*, p. 52.
9. Smith, *The Coronation of Elizabeth Wydeville*.
10. *CCR 1461–1468*, pp. 177, 183, 290; *HHB*, part 1, p. 165.

Chapter 17

1. C.L. Kingsford, ed., *A Survey of London, by John Stow*, 2 vols., Oxford 1908, vol. 1, pp. 336, 337. For the year of the countess's death see TNA, C 140/26 and *Caledarium Inquisitionum Post Mortem*, vol. 4, London 1828, p. 341. A different date was given on her vanished tomb in old St Paul's Cathedral, but this monument was erected twenty-five years after her death, and the year given on it seems to have been an error.
2. The date is given in Eleanor's Inquisition post mortem, TNA, C 140/29/39.
3. Kincaid, ed., Buck, *King Richard the Third*, p. 183.
4. WRO, L 1/85.
5. *Nuper uxor Thome Boteler militis iam defunct'*. It is difficult to see how else Eleanor could have described herself in a legal document at this juncture. If she were not a widow, her freedom to act in the matter would have been in question.
6. *EAW*, p. 9.
7. TNA, C/140/7/14.
8. WRO, L 1/86 and L 1/87.
9. *La duchesse de Norfolck, une moult belle dame d'Angleterre*. Elizabeth's beauty (which Eleanor may have shared) is vouched for by Olivier de la Marche, who met her in Flanders: Beaune and d'Arbaumont, eds., *Mémoires d'Olivier de la Marche*, vol. 3, pp. 106–07.
10. C. Weightman, *Margaret of York, Duchess of Burgundy, 1446-1503*, Gloucester 1989, p. 47.
11. CCCC, Parker Library, Ms. XXXI.121, and J. Ashdown-Hill, 'The Endowments of Lady Eleanor Talbot and Elizabeth Talbot, Duchess of Norfolk, at Corpus Christi College

Cambridge, *Ric.*14 (2004), p. 83. NB my original translation at this point was slightly misleading: *executrix testamenti* refers to a testament, not a will.

12. Personal commmunications from Fr Richard Copsey, O. Carm., *Institutum Carmelitanum*, Rome, citing Bale, Bodleian Library, Oxford, MS 73, f. 51v.

13. 'I bequeath to the Whight Fryers of the said city of Norwich, for I am there a suster, to helpe to pay hir debts xx li.': Will of Agnes Berry (Paston), Davis, *Paston Letters*, vol. 1, p. 49.

14. Davis, *Paston Letters*, vol. 1, p. 625.

15. Eleanor's only surviving brother, Sir Humphrey Talbot, accompanied Elizabeth, Duchess of Norfolk, to the royal wedding in the Low Countries. See Beaune and d'Arbaumont, eds., *Mémoires d'Olivier de la Marche*, vol. 3, p. 111, where he is described as '*son frere, l'ung des filz de monsigneur de Talbot*'.

16. Weightman, *Margaret of York*, pp. 47–59.

17. Smith, *The Itinerary of John Leland*, p. 120.

18. *EAW*, p. 75.

19. Weever, *Ancient Funeral Monuments*, p. 805. The Whitefriars in Norwich was one of the larger Carmelite houses, and was founded in 1256 and dissolved in 1538: D. Knowles and R.N. Hadcock, *Medieval Religious Houses – England and Wales*, London 1953, p. 198.

20. P.G. Lindley, 'The "Arminghall Arch" and contemporary sculpture in Norwich', *Norfolk Archaeology*, vol. 40, part 1, Norwich 1987, pp. 19–43.

21. Erected by the Richard III Society in 1999.

22. W. Dugdale, *Monasticon Anglicanum*, 6 vols, reprinted London 1846, vol. 6, part 3, p. 1574.

23. Tombs of the Lucas family at St Giles' Church in Colchester were desecrated during the Civil War.

Chapter 18

1. *CPR 1467–77*, p. 133.

2. See Chapter 13.

3. *CPR 1461–67; 1467–77*, p. 122.

4. *CPR 1467–1477*, p. 122. The Duke and Duchess of Norfolk had previously been granted such a pardon on 20 March 1468. *CPR 1467–1477*, p. 83. On 28 January 1469 the king also granted a pardon to Sir Humphrey Talbot (*ibid.*).

5. *CPR 1467–77*, p. 133.

6. TNA, Close Roll 8 Edward IV, no. 3 *dorso*, 23 February 1469.

7. Coss, *Lady*, pp. 146–47.

8. Inquisition post mortem of Ralph Butler of Sudeley, TNA, C 140/47/64.

9. The 1492 will of Sir Humphrey Talbot, brother of Eleanor and Elizabeth, ordained prayers for the souls of his faithful servants, John and Elizabeth Wenlock. *TV*, vol. 2, pp. 409–10. An earlier John Wenlock and a William Wenlock had served the Talbots at Blakemere during the period 1401–20: Ross, Thesis, pp. 45, 54, 117, 132, 137, 142-44.

10. Moye, Thesis, p. 438.

11. Moye, Thesis, p. 432.

12. *HHB*, part 1, p. 165; Moye, Thesis, p. 427.

13. He visited his diocese only once in twenty-six years: Ross, *Edward IV*, p. 320. Of the 125 ordinations conducted in Bath and Wells during his episcopate, Stillington was present at none: Maxwell-Lyte, ed., *The Registers of Robert Stillington*, p. xvii.

14. While Stillington held the great seal a number of official documents were dated from his manor of Dogmersfield. See, for example, *CPR 1467–1477*, pp. 11, 17, 31-34. There are many more examples.

15. Maxwell-Lyte, ed., *The Registers of Robert Stillington*, p. xi.

16. A.B. Emden, *Biographical Register of the University of Oxford*, 3 volumes, Oxford 1957–59, vol. 3, p. 1,778.

17. Davis, *Paston Letters*, vol. 1, p. 492; *CPR 1476-1485*, pp. 75, 96; F. Sandford, *Genealogical History of England*, [no place of publication] 1707, [no page numbers].

18. Armstrong/Mancini, pp. 62–63.

19. *CPR 1476–1485*, p. 572.

20. Gairdner, *Richard the Third*, p. 91, n. 1.

21. *CPR 1476–1485*, p. 554.

22. Jones/Commynes, p. 397.

23. *CPR 1476–1485*, p. 102.

24. *RP*, vol. 6, pp. 193-95.

25. When a subject received fealty it was normally offered saving the swearer's duty to the king.

26. Compare, for example Henry VII's long act of attainder against William Stanley, Simon Mountford, William Dawbeney, Robert Ratcliff and Gilbert Debenham; 14 October 1495: *RP*, vol. 6, p. 504.

27. Gairdner, *Richard the Third*, p. 91.

28. Armstong/Mancini pp. 62–63.

29. Ashdown-Hill, 'Norfolk Requiem'.

30. Ashdown-Hill, 'Lady Eleanor Talbot's other husband', and 'Lady Eleanor Talbot: new evidence; new answers; new questions'.

31. Maxwell-Lyte, ed., *The Registers of Robert Stillington*, p. xiii.

32. November 1485: *RP*, vol. 6, p. 270.

33. Compare, for example, *RP*, vol. 6, p. 190; pp. 284–85; pp. 305–6.

34. Arguably the last attempt to replace the Tudors by a sovereign who had a better claim to the English crown was the Spanish Armada of 1588: J. Ashdown-Hill, 'The Lancastrian Claim to the Throne', *Ric.*13, 2003, p. 37.

35. It is interesting to compare the styles of MS. XXXI.121 and MS. XXXI.122. The second indenture, much more laconic in tone, says nothing whatsoever about anybody's family and sticks firmly to the relevant financial arrangements.

36. An anniversary mass was 'save interment ... an exact and annual repetition of the funeral': C. Burgess, 'A service for the dead: the form and function of the anniversary in late medieval Bristol', in S.T. Blake and A. Saville, eds., *Transactions of the Bristol and Gloucestershire Archaeological Society for 1987*, vol. 105, p. 191; Ashdown-Hill, 'Norfolk Requiem', *Ric.*12, no. 152, March 2001, p. 213.

Chapter 19

1. H. Ellis (ed.), *Three Books of Polydore Vergil's English History comprising the reigns of Henry VI, Edward IV and Richard III*, London 1844, pp. 116–17.

2. Ellis/Vergil, p. 183.

3. Ellis/Vergil, p. 184. (Present writer's italics.)

4. A.H. Thomas and I.D. Thornley, eds., *The Great Chronicle of London*, London 1938, pp. 231–32.

5. This is not the place for a detailed analysis of the various texts of More's history and their relationship to one another. That can be found in the introduction to R.S. Sylvester, ed., *The Complete Works of St Thomas More*, vol. 2, *The History of King Richard III*, Yale and London 1963.

6. Sylvester/More, *The History of King Richard III*, p. 62 (abbreviations expanded).

7. Sylvester/More, *The History of King Richard III*, p. 64 (abbreviations expanded).

8. Coss, *Lady*, p.136. Those in minor orders (below the rank of sub-deacon) could marry, but for them, marriage with a widow was classified as 'bigamy'.

9. Sylvester/More, *The History of King Richard III*, p. 64 (abbreviations expanded).

10. Sylvester/More, *The History of King Richard III*, p. 65.

11. Ashdown-Hill, 'The Elusive Mistress', p. 501.

12. E. Halle, *The Union of the two noble families of Lancaster and York (1550)*, Menston 1970, 'Kyng Edward the Fyft', f. 19v.

13. This was first published in 1611, in Speed's *History of Great Britian*. C.M. Markham, *Richard III: his Life and Character*, London 1906, p. 219, n. 1.

14. A.N. Kincaid, ed, *The History of King Richard the Third (1619) by Sir George Buck*, Gloucester 1979, p. 46.

15. Kincaid/Buck, *History of King Richard the Third*, p. 175.

16. In describing Elizabeth Wayte (Lucy): Kincaid / Buck, *History of King Richard the Third*, p. 182.

17. Kincaid/Buck, *History of King Richard the Third*, p. 183.

18. Kincaid/Buck, *History of King Richard the Third*, pp. 176, 183.

19. Kincaid/Buck, *History of King Richard the Third*, p. 176.

20. Kincaid/Buck, *History of King Richard the Third*, pp. 179, 182.

21. Masters, *Corpus Christi*, p. 46. Some of the information published by Masters had previously been incorporated in John Josselin's *Historiola Colegii Corporis Christi*, which dates from the mid-sixteenth century, but this remained unpublished until 1880.

22. Masters, *Corpus Christi*, p. 53.

23. P.W. Hammond, ed., H. Walpole, *Historic Doubts on the Life and Reign of Richard the Third*, Gloucester 1987, pp. 44. (Present writer's italics.)

24. Hammond/Walpole, *Historic Doubts*, p. 45.

25. Hammond/Walpole, *Historic Doubts*, p. 46.

26. Hammond / Walpole, *Historic Doubts*, p. 48.

27. C.A. Halsted, *Richard III, Duke of Gloucester and King of England*, 2 vols., London 1844, vol. 2, p. 91, n. 5.

28. J. Gairdner, *History of the Life and Reign of Richard the Third*, Cambridge 1898, p. 89.

29. Gairdner, *History … of Richard the Third*, p. 90.

30. Gairdner, *History … of Richard the Third*, pp. 90–91.

31. Gairdner, *History … of Richard the Third*, p. 92.

32. Gairdner, *History … of Richard the Third*, p. 92.

33. Markham, *Richard III: his Life and Character*, p. 219 and n. 2.

34. Markham, *Richard III: his Life and Character*, pp. 93–94, p. 218.

35. Markham, *Richard III: his Life and Character*, p. 219.

36. C.L. Scofield, *The Life and Reign of Edward the Fourth*, 2 vols., London 1923, vol. 2, p. 161.

37. Scofield, *The Life and Reign of Edward the Fourth*, vol. 2, p. 213.

38. Scofield, *The Life and Reign of Edward the Fourth*, vol. 2, p. 213 (present writer's italics).

39. P.M. Kendall, *Richard the Third*, London 1955, pp. 216-17, 219.

40. Kendall, *Richard the Third*, pp. 474–75, n. 9.

41. C. Ross, *Edward IV*, London 1974.

42. C. Ross, *Richard III*, London 1981, p. 15.

43. Ross, *Richard III*, p. 89.

44. Ross, *Richard III*, p. 91.

45. The Crowland Chronicle and the *titulus regius* of 1484.

46. A. Hanham, *Richard III and his Early Historians*, Oxford 1975, p. 97.

47. Hanham, *Richard III and his Early Historians*, p. 101.

48. S. Cunningham, *Richard III, a royal enigma*, London 2003, p. 41.

Chapter 20

1. See http://www.bbc.co.uk/legacies/myths_legends/england/leicester/ J. Ashdown-Hill, 'The Fate of Richard III's Body', for an example (and refutation) of such a story.

2. *Jarrolds Magazine*, March 1958 and March 1959, and *Eastern Daily Press*, Wednesday 2 April 1958, p. 6.

3. M. Trotter and G.C. Gleser, 'Estimation of Stature from long-bones of American Whites and Negroes', *American Journal of Physical Anthropology 10* (1952), pp. 463–514, and 'A Re-evaluation of estimation of Stature Taken during Life and After Death', *AJPA* 16 (1958), pp. 79–123.

4. D.R. Brothwell, *Digging Up Bones: the Excavation, Treatment and Study of Human Skeletal Remains*, London 1981.

5. *EA*, pp. 8–9 asserts that the earl's skeleton proves him to have been '5ft 10in in height and strongly built', but this estimate of Lord Shrewsbury's height is incorrect. For a stature of 5ft 10in his femur measurement would have needed to be 19.5in. I am grateful to Mr. W.J. White for his advice on this point.

6. Elkington and Huntsman 'The Talbot Fingers: a study in Symphalangism', *British Medical Journal*, 18 February 1967, p. 409 (quoting Egerton). The calculation of stature is based on Brothwell, *Digging Up Bones*, p. 101.

7. J. Fletcher, *The search for Nefertiti*, London 2004, pp. 368–69.

8. F. Blomefield, *An Essay towards a Topographical History of the County of Norfolk*, 11 vols., London 1805–1810, vol. 4, pp. 421, 422; J. Kirkpatrick, 'The White Friars' in D. Turner, ed., *History of the Religious Orders and Communities and of the Hospital and Castle of Norwich*, Yarmouth 1845, p. 184.

9. J. Gairdner, ed., *Paston Letters*, 3 volumes, vol. 2, London 1874, p. 289. Will of Agnes Paston. This refers to the burial of a number of her relatives at the Carmelite Friary.

10. Blomefield, *Norfolk*, vol. 4, pp. 417, 418.

11. Blomefield, *Norfolk*, vol. 4, p. 417; *International Genealogical Index*: Laura de Vere entry; *CP*.

12. Blomefield, *Norfolk*, vol. 1, pp. 58, 59; vol. 5, p. 291; vol. 10, p. 346.

13. Blomefield, *Norfolk*, vol. 9, p. 191; vol. 11, p. 111.

14. Blomefield, *Norfolk*, vol. 2, pp. 399–401.

15. *CP*, vol. 9, pp. 217, 218; http://en.wikipedia.org/wiki/Baron_Morley.

16. Will of Thomas Pulham the Elder of Stradbrook. IRO, Probate Registry Wills, vol. 2, f. 86.

17. Blomefield, *Norfolk*, vol. 5, pp. 23–26; vol. 8, p. 93.

18. *VN*, p. 28; Gairdner, *Paston Letters*.

19. Blomefield, *Norfolk*, vol. 2, pp. 399–401.

20. *VN*, p. 117.

21. Blomefield, *Norfolk*, vol. 11, p. 65.
22. *VN*, p. 215.
23. *VN*, p 215; *CP*, vol. 6, pp. 156, 157, 358, 359.
24. *VN*, p. 74; M.A. Farrow, *Index to Wills proved in the Consistory Court of Norwich*, London 1945; NRO, wills of William Calthorp (1420) and his second wife, Sybil (1421), widow of Sir John With; N.C.C. wills 75 Hyrnyng and 9l Hyrnyng.
25. Gairdner, *Paston Letters*.
26. Blomefield, *Norfolk*, vol. 11, p. 19.
27. l am grateful to Mr P. Hammond for drawing my attention to 'the Talbot Fingers' and to Mr W.J. White for pointing out the dental anomaly.
28. Elkington and Huntsman, 'The Talbot Fingers', pp 407–11.
29. 'The coffin … had been flattened out on the skeleton'. Report in *The Jarrold Magazine*, March 1959.
30. Medical Report by Dr S. Tayleur Gwynne and Mr John Bromfield, in W.H. Egerton, 'Talbot's Tomb', *TSAS*, vol. 8, 1885, pp. 425–26.
31. Elkington and Huntsman, 'The Talbot Fingers', p. 411.
32. Rushton, 'The Teeth of Anne Mowbray', pp. 335–39.
33. Rushton, 'The Teeth of Anne Mowbray', pp. 355–36.
34. Rushton, 'The Teeth of Anne Mowbray', p. 358.
35. Rushton, 'The Teeth of Anne Mowbray', p. 358.
36. E.g. by Dr Jean Ross; see R. Drewett and M. Redhead, *The Trial of Richard III*, Gloucester 1984, p. 66.
37. From Sixtus IV, St Peter's, Rome, 12 May 1477, 'To Edward King of England. Dispensation at the petition of the king, and also of his son, Richard, Duke of York, of the diocese of Coventry and Lichfield, and Anne de Mowbray of the diocese of Norwich, infants, for the said Richard and Anne, who have completed their fifth and fourth years of age, respectively (*sic*) to contract espousals forthwith, and as soon as they reach the lawful age, to contract marriage, notwithstanding that they are related in the third and fourth degree of kindred': *Calendar of Papal Registers – Papal Letters 1471–1484*, vol. 13, part 1, London 1955, p. 236.
38. Account of Mathieu d 'Escouchy, cited by Elkington and Huntsman, p. 409.

Appendix 1

1. Lambeth Palace Library, Kempe Register, f. 312r.
2. WRO, L1/79.
3. WRO, L1/81.
4. WRO, L1/82.
5. CCCC, Parker Library, *Liber Albus*, f. 72r (old foliation, or f. 51r, new foliation). Published in Masters, *Corpus Christi*, appendix, p. 30.
6. 'Your gentleman, Cotton'. Sir John Howard had one Cotton and his wife in his service in 1466. *HHB*, part 1, p. 363.
7. Let.
8. Buttresses. The reference is to those still standing in the old courtyard of the college.
9. Foundations?
10. Let.
11. WRO, L1/85.
12. WRO, L1/86.

13. WRO, L1/87.

14. TNA, C 140/29/39, f.1.

15. TNA, C 140/29/39, f. 2r.

16. *RP*, vol. 6, pp. 193–95.

17. Perhaps: 'Wherfore therof, although the kynge's Highnesse …'?

18. *RP*, vol. 6, pp. 240–42. In this text both Eleanor Talbot and Elizabeth Woodville are consistently referred to by their married surnames.

19. On the significance of this phrase see above, Introduction.

20. It is evident from this clause that there had never been issue of Edward and Eleanor.

21. Armstrong / Mancini, pp. 62–63; 96–97.

22. *RP*, vol. 6, p. 289.

23. It is noteworthy that this is probably the only instance of an Act of Parliament being repealed both unquoted and unsummarised. The provision for the destruction of all copies is also arguably unique.

24. N. Pronay and J. Cox, eds., *The Crowland Chronicle Continuations: 1459–1486*, London 1986, pp.158–61.

25. Jones / Commynes, pp. 353–54; 397.

26. By modern dating (1495, old style).

27. CCCC, Parker Library Ms. XXXI.121. I am grateful to the master and Fellows of Corpus Christi College, Cambridge, for permission to publish this material.

28. The Latin term *Deo devota* also means 'vowed to God', implying that Eleanor had made a religious commitment. See Chapter 15.

29. This is still the standard formula for prayers for the dead.

30. The feast of St Barnabas is 11 June. 13 June was the vigil of the anniversary of the death of Eleanor's mother, Margaret, Countess of Shrewsbury.

31. 17 July was the anniversary of the deaths of Eleanor's father, the Earl of Shrewsbury and of her eldest brother, Lord Lisle, both killed in France at the battle of Châtillon.

32. I.E. matins of the dead, often known as *Dirige*.

33. CCCC, Parker Library Ms. XXXI.122.

34. Ellis / Vergil, p. 117.

35. Richard Neville, Earl of Warwick, Eleanor's uncle.

36. *L&P*, vol. 6, p. 618.

37. *L&P*, vol. 7, p. 519.

38. L.T. Smith, *The Itinerary of John Leland*, parts 6 and 7, London 1909, p. 120.

Appendix 2

1. The description is from the play's *Dramatis Personæ*. See B.A. Murray, 'Lady Eleanor Butler and John Crowne's *The Misery of Civil War* (1680)', *Ric.*14 (2004), pp. 54–61. Barbara Murray's paper is a welcome and valuable recent addition to the field of Eleanor Talbot studies.

2. Murray '*Civil War*', p. 58.

3. Murray '*Civil War*', pp. 59-60 and n. 17. Murray dismisses the claim that Lucy Walter was married to Charles II, but this claim still has its defendants. Like Eleanor Talbot, Lucy Walter was a descendant of Edward I.

4. J. Tey, *The Daughter of Time*, Harmondsworth 1954, p. 111.

5. It would, perhaps, be more tactful not to name them, but one historian has stated that Eleanor was Edward's mistress in her youth (thus flying in the face of chronology, and

ignoring the fact that Eleanor was actually older than Edward). Another has declared that Eleanor was not the Earl of Shrewsbury's daughter, and that her parentage was unknown.

6. R.H. Jarman, *The King's Grey Mare*, London 1975, pp. 158–59.
7. Lumby / More, *History of King Richard III*, pp. 61–64.
8. E. Lytton, *The Last of the Barons*, London 1843, pp. 151–55.
9. Lytton, *Last*, p. 273.
10. Lytton, *Last*, pp. 114; 306; 335.
11. Tey, *Daughter*, p. 111.
12. S. Penman, *The Sunne in Splendour*, London 1982, pp. 558–59.
13. See Chapter 19.
14. S. Wilson, *Wife to the Kingmaker*, London 1974, p. 121.
15. Wilson, *Wife*, p. 90.
16. Wilson, *Wife*, pp. 90–91.
17. R.H. Jarman, *We Speak no Treason*, London 1971, p. 367.
18. Jarman, *Grey Mare*, pp. 159; 316.
19. Tey, *Daughter*, pp.115, 128.
20. Penman, *Sunne*, pp. 559–60.
21. M. Bowen, *Dickon*, London 1971; Rhoda Edwards, *Some Touch of Pity*, London 1976; Jean Plaidy, *The Goldsmith's Wife*, London 1950.
22. Bowen, *Dickon*, p. 74. The intended date can be deduced from Bowen's reference to the marriage of Margaret of York as having taken place in the previous year.
23. Bowen, *Dickon*, p. 195.
24. Bowen, *Dickon*, p. 69.
25. Bowen, *Dickon*, p. 78.
26. Jarman, *Treason*, p. 253.
27. Penman, *Sunne*, p. 562.
28. Penman, *Sunne*, pp. 556–57.
29. Edwards, *Some Touch of Pity*, p. 78.
30. Edwards, *Touch of Pity*, p. 79.
31. Plaidy, *Goldsmith's Wife*, p. 176.
32. Wilson, *Wife*, pp. 98–99.
33. Lytton, *Last*, pp. 292–93; 300–1; 343; 354.
34. Penman, *Sunne*, pp. 671–73.
35. Penman, *Sunne*, p. 556.
36. Plaidy, *Goldsmith's Wife*, p. 175.

Appendix 3

1. In the fifteenth century it seems to have been applied also to women of a certain personal status such as the wives of mayors of London: A.F. Sutton and L. Visser Fuchs 'The Cult of Angels in Late Fifteenth-Century England' in J.H.M. Taylor and L. Smith, *Women and the Book*, London 1997, p. 245.

List of Abbreviations

CCCC   Corpus Christi College, Cambridge
CD   *Catalogue of Ancient Deeds in the Public Record Office* (6 vols)
CP   *The Complete Peerage*
CChR   *Calendar of Charter Rolls*
CCR   *Calendar of Close Rolls*
CPR   *Calendar of Patent Rolls*
DNB   *Dictionary of National Biography*
HHB   A. Crawford, ed., *The Household Books of John Howard, Duke of Norfolk, 1462–1471, 1481–1483*
EA   H. Talbot, *The English Achilles*
EAW   B.J. Harris, *English Aristocratic Women, 1450–1550*
IRO   Suffolk Record Office (Ipswich Branch)
L&P   *Letters and Papers, Foreign and Domestic: Henry VIII*
NRO   Norfolk Record Office
ODNB *Oxford Dictionary of National Biography*
Ric.11   *The Ricardian*, vol. 11 (&c)
RP   *Rotuli Parliamentorum*
TNA   The National Archives
TSAS   *Transactions of the Shropshire Archaeological Society*
TSAHS *Transactions of the Shropshire Archaeological and Historical Society*
TV   N.H. Nicolas, *Testamenta Vetusta*
VCH   *Victoria County History*
VN   W. Rye, ed., *Visitations of Norfolk: 1563, 1589 and 1613*
WRO   Warwickshire County Record Office

Acknowledgements

I should like to offer my most sincere thanks to all the many people who have helped me in various ways in preparing this book. These include (in chronological order of Eleanor's life and career) the staff at the Warwickshire County Record Office; Jean Bray, archivist at Sudeley Castle; the staff of the Parker Library, Corpus Christi College, Cambridge – and most particularly Catherine Hall, formerly library archivist, Gill Cannell, assistant librarian, and Dr Elizabeth Leedham-Green, ancient archivist; modern members of the Carmelite Order, including the community of the Carmelite Monastery at Quidenham in Norfolk – and most especially Sister Shelagh OCD and Sister Gillian Leslie OCD – Fr Richard Copsey, O. Carm., of the *Institutum Carmelitanum* in Rome, and the librarian at Aylesford Priory, Kent; the staff of Norwich Museums Service – and especially Bill Milligan, Sue Margeson, keeper of archeology, and John Renton, assistant keeper of Social History; Peter Salt, former archivist at Jarrolds; Bill White, curator of the Centre for Human Bioarchaeology, Museum of London, and Christine Meadway BDS (who carried out examinations of the human remains in Norwich which may be those of Eleanor Talbot). Last, but not least, I should like to thank all those who helped me in various ways with aspects of my text: Dr Anne Sutton, Dr Lesley Boatwright, Dr Livia Visser Fuchs, Annette Carson, and Dave Perry. Any errors which remain are, of course, my responsibility.

Bibliography

UNPUBLISHED PRIMARY SOURCES

IRO, HA246/B2/498
IRO, HA246/B2/508
NRO, DN/REG 6, book 11, and MF510
TNA, C140/7/14 (*ipm* of Elizabeth Norbury, Lady Sudeley)
TNA, C140/47/64 (*ipm* of Ralph Butler, Lord Sudeley)

BOOKS

Adams, N. and Donahue C., eds., *Select Cases from the Ecclesiastical Courts of the Province of Canterbury, c. 1200–1301*, London, 1981
Ainsworth, M.A., *Petrus Christus, Renaissance Master of Bruges*, New York, 1994
Anstis, J., ed., *The Register of the Most Noble Order of the Garter*, 2 volumes, London, 1724
Armstrong, C.A.J., ed., Mancini D., *The Usurpation of Richard the Third*, Gloucester, 1989
Baker, P.A., *The Medieval Pottery of Shropshire*, Shropshire Arcaeological Society, 1970
Beaune, H. and d'Arbaumont, J., eds., *Mémoires d'Olivier de la Marche*, 4 vols., Paris, 1883-88
Blomefield, F., *An Essay towards a Topographical History of the County of Norfolk*, 11 vols., London, 1805–1810
Boyd, C.P., *Roll of the Drapers' Company of London*, Croydon, 1934
Brooke, C.N.L., *The Medieval Idea of Marriage*, Oxford, 1989
Brothwell, D.R., *Digging Up Bones: the Excavation, Treatment and Study of Human Skeletal Remains*, London, 1981
Brunschvicg, L., ed., Blaise Pascal, *Pensées*, fifth edition, 1909
Buck, G., see Kincaid A.N.
Burke, B., *The General Armory of England, Scotland, Ireland and Wales*, London, 1984
Burrows, R., *Guidelines for Mystical Prayer*, London, 1976
Calendar of Charter Rolls, 1427–1516, London, 1927
Calendar of Papal Registers, vol. 11, Papal Letters, 1455–1464, London, 1921

Calendar of Papal Registers, vol. 12, Papal Letters, 1458–1471, London, 1933

Calendar of Papal Registers, vol. 13, Papal Letters, 1471–1484, London, 1955

Caledarium Inquisitionum Post Mortem, vol. 4, London, 1828

Campbell, J., *At the Cradle of British Monarchy*, Coutances, 1959

Carter, W.F., ed., *The Lay Subsidy Roll for Warwickshire*, 6 Edward III (1332), London, 1926

Calendar of Close Rolls 1441–1447; 1447–1454

Calendar of Fine Rolls, 1422–1430; 1461–1471

Clark, J.W., ed., *John Josselin's Historiola Colegii Corporis Christi*, Cambridge, 1880

Clive, M., *This Sun of York, A Biography of Edward IV*, London, 1973

Commynes, P. de, see Jones M.

Coss, P., *The Lady in Medieval England 1000–1500*, Stroud, 1998

Crawford, A., ed., *The Household Books of John Howard, Duke of Norfolk, 1462–1471, 1481–1483*, Stroud, 1992

Calendar of Patent Rolls, 1321–1324; 1396–99; 1399–1401; 1408–13; 1413–16; 1441–1446; 1446–1452; 1452–1461; 1461–1467; 1467–1477; 1476–85

Cunningham, S., *Richard III, a royal enigma*, London, 2003

Davies, J.S., ed., *An English Chronicle of the Reigns of Richard II, Henry IV, Henry V and Henry VI*, London, 1856

Davis, N., ed., *Paston Letters and Papers of the Fifteenth Century*, 2 volumes, Oxford, 1971, 1976

Descriptive Catalogue of Ancient Deeds in the Public Record Office, 6 vols., vol. 2, London, 1894; vol. 3, London, 1900

Dictionary of National Biography

Drewett, R. and Redhead, M., *The Trial of Richard III*, Gloucester, 1984

Drucker, L., ed., *Warwickshire Feet of Fines* vol. 3 (1345–1509), London, 1943

Duffy, E., The Stripping of the Altars, London, 1992

Dugdale, W., *Monasticon Anglicanum*, 6 vols, reprinted London, 1846, vol. 6, part 3

Ellis, H., ed., *Three Books of Polydore Vergil's English History comprising the reigns of Henry VI, Edward IV and Richard III*, London, 1844

Emden, A.B., *A Biographical Register of the University of Oxford*, 3 volumes, Oxford 1957–59

——, *A Biographical Register of the University of Cambridge to 1500*, Cambridge, 1963

Erler, M.C., 'Three Fifteenth-Century Vowesses', Barron C M and Sutton A F, eds., *Medieval London Widows 1300–1500*, London, 1994, pp. 165–183

Fabyan's Chronicle – see Thomas

Farrow, M.A., *Index to Wills proved in the Consistory Court of Norwich*, London, 1945

Fogle, B., *The Encyclopedia of the Dog*, London, 1995

Gairdner, J., ed., *Paston Letters*, 3 volumes, vol. 2, London, 1874

——, ed., *The Historical Collections of a Citizen of London*, London, 1876

——, *History of the Life and Reign of Richard the Third*, Cambridge, 1898

Gardiner, D.M., ed., *A Calendar of Early Chancery Proceedings relating to West Country Shipping, 1388–1493*, Devon and Cornwall Record Society, New Series, vol. 21, 1976

Gover, J.E.B., Mawer, A. and Stenton, F.M. with Houghton, F.T.S., *The Place Names of Warwickshire*, Cambridge, 1936

Griffiths, R.A. and Thomas, R.S., *The Making of the Tudor Dynasty*, Stroud, 1985

Halle, E., *The Union of the two nobles families of Lancaster and York (1550)*, Menston, 1970

Hallam, E., ed., *The Plantagenet Encyclopedia*, London, 1990

Halsted, C.A., *Richard III, Duke of Gloucester and King of England*, 2 vols., London 1844, (and reprinted Gloucester, 1977)

Hammond, P.W., ed., Walpole H, *Historic Doubts on the Life and Reign of Richard the Third*, Gloucester, 1987

Hanham, A., *Richard III and his Early Historians*, Oxford, 1975

Harben, H.A., *A Dictionary of London*, London, 1918

Harris, B.J., *English Aristocratic Women, 1450–1550*, Oxford, 2002

Hicks, M., *False, Fleeting, Perjur'd Clarence*, Gloucester, 1980

Jacobs, E.F., ed., *The Fifteenth Century*, 1399–1485, Oxford, 1961

Jones, M., ed., Commynes P de, *Memoires*, Harmondsworth, 1972

Josselin – see Clark

Kekewich, M.L., Richmond, C., Sutton, A.F., Visser-Fuchs, L. and Watts, J.L., *The Politics of Fifteenth-Century England: John Vale's Book*, Stroud, 1995

Kendall, P.M., *Richard the Third*, London, 1973

Kincaid, A.N., ed., Buck, G., *The History of King Richard the Third*, Stroud, 1979

Kingsford, C.L., ed., *A Survey of London, by John Stow*, 2 vols., Oxford, 1908

Kitching, C.J., *London and Middlesex Chantry Certificates 1548*, London Record Society, vol. 16, 1980

Knowles, D. and Hadcock, R.N., *Medieval Religious Houses – England and Wales*, London, 1953

Landsberg, S., *The Medieval Garden*, London, [n.d]

Lees-Milne, J., *Saint Peters*, London, 1967

Letters and Papers, Foreign and Domestic: Henry VIII, vol. 6

Lumby, J.R., ed., Sir Thomas More, *History of King Richard III*, Cambridge, 1924

Maclean, J., ed., Smyth, J., *The Lives of the Berkeleys*, 3 volumes, vol. 2., Gloucester, 1883

Mancini D – see Armstrong

Marche, O de la – see Beaune

Markham, C.M., *Richard III: his Life and Character*, London, 1906

Masters, R., *History of the College of Corpus Christi*, Cambridge, 1753

Maxwell-Lyte, H.C., ed., *The Registers of Robert Stillington, Bishop of Bath and Wells 1466-1491 and Richard Fox, Bishop of Bath and Wells 1492–1494*, Somerset Record Society, 1937

More, T. – see Lumby; Sylvester

Nairn, I. and Pevsner, N. (revised Cherry B), *The Buildings of England – Surrey*, London, 1962, 1971

Nicolas, N.H., *Testamenta Vetusta* 2 vols., London, 1826

Orme, N., *English Schools in the Middle Ages*, London, 1973

———, *Education and Society in Medieval and Renaissance England*, London, 1989

Pascal, B., – see Brunschvicg

Pevsner, N., *The Buildings of England – Herefordshire*, Harmondsworth, 1977

Pevsner, N. and Wedgewood, A., *The Buildings of England – Warwickshire*, London, 1966

Pollard, A.J., *John Talbot and the War in France, 1427–1453*, London, 1983

Powell, J.E. and Wallis, K., *The House of Lords in the Middle Ages*, London, 1968

Previté-Orton, C.W., and Brooke, Z.N., eds., *The Cambridge Medieval History*, vol. 8, Cambridge, 1964

Pronay, N. and Cox, J., eds., *The Crowland Chronicle Continuations*, London, 1986

Ridgard, J., ed., *Medieval Framlingham*, Suffolk Record Society, vol. 27, 1985

Riley, H.T., ed., *Registrum Abbatiae Iohannis Whethamstede, Abbatis Monasterii Sancti Albani*, 2 vols., London, 1872–73

Ross, B., *Accounts of the Stewards of the Talbot Household at Blakemere 1392–1425*, Keele, 2003

Bibliography

Ross, C., *Edward IV*, London, 1974

———, *Richard III*, London, 1981

Rot. Parl., vol. 6

Rye, W., ed., *The Visitations of Norfolk, 1563, 1589 and 1613*, London, 1891

Sandford, F., *Genealogical History of England*, [no place of publication] 1707

Scofield, C.L., *The Life and Reign of Edward the Fourth*, 2 vols., London, 1923

Serpell, M.F., *Kenninghall History and St Mary's Church*, Norwich, 1982

Sinclair, A., *The Beauchamp Pageant*, Donnington, 2003

Silverio de Santa Teresa, R.P., *Saint Teresa of Jesus*, London and Glasgow, 1947

Smet, J., Cloistered Carmel, *A Brief History of the Carmelite Nuns*, Rome, 1986

———, *The Carmelites: a history of the brothers of Our Lady of Mount Carmel*, 3 vols, vol. 1,
   Darien, 1975, trans. A. Ruiz Molina, Los Carmelitas, Historia de la Orden del Carmen,
   Madrid, 1987

Smith, G., ed., *The Coronation of Elizabeth Wydeville, a Contemporary account from a 15th
   century Ms.*, London 1935, reprinted Gloucester, 1975

Smith, L.T., *The Itinerary of John Leland*, parts 6 and 7, London, 1907–10

Smyth, J. – see Maclean

Steel, A., *Richard II*, Cambridge, 1962

Stowe, J., – see Kingsford

Sutton, A.F. and Visser Fuchs, L., 'The Cult of Angels in Late Fifteenth-Century England'
   – see Taylor and Smith

———, *The Royal Funerals of the House of York at Windsor*, London, 2004

Sylvester, R.S., ed., *The Complete Works of St Thomas More, vol. 2, The History of King
   Richard III*, Yale and London, 1963

Talbot, H., *The English Achilles: the life and campaigns of John Talbot, 1st Earl of Shrewsbury*,
   London, 1981

Taylor, J.H.M. and Smith, L., *Women and the Book*, London, 1997

Thomas, A.H. and Thornley, I.D., eds., *The Great Chronicle of London*, London, 1938

Thrupp, S.L., *The Merchant Class of Medieval London 1300–1500*, Chicago, 1948

V.C.H. *Hertfordshire*, vols. 2 and 3; *Shropshire*, vol. 4; *Warwickshire*, vol. 4, *Wiltshire*, vol. 10

Verey, D., *The Buildings of England – Gloucestershire,* vol. 1 *The Cotswolds* Harmondsworth, 1970

Vergil, P. – see Elllis

Walpole, H. – see Hammond

Ward, J., *Women in Medieval Europe 1200–1500*, London, 2002

Warner, G.F. and Gilson, J.P., *Catalogue of Western Manuscripts on the old Royal and King's
   Collections*, 4 vols., London, 1921

Watson, A. and Sasitorn, D., *East Anglia from Above*, London, 1998

Watson, M., and Musson, C., *Shropshire from the Air*, Shrewsbury(?), 1993

Wedgwood, J.C. and Holt, A.D., *History of Parliament, 1439–1509*, 2 vols., London, 1938,
   vol. 1, *Biographies*

Weever, J., *Ancient Funeral Monuments of Great Britain*, London, 1631, repr. Amsterdam, 1979

Weightman, C., *Margaret of York, Duchess of Burgundy, 1446–1503*, Gloucester, 1989

Welch, J., *The Carmelite Way*, Leominster, 1996

White, G.H., ed., *Complete Peerage*

Wolffe, B., *Henry VI*, London, 1981

Woolley, L., *Medieval Life and Leisure in the Devonshire Hunting Tapestries*, London, 2002

Wolters, C., ed., *The Cloud of Unknowing*, Harmondsworth, 1961

Zutski, P.N.R., ed., *Medieval Cambridge: Essays on the Pre-Reformation University*, Woodbridge, 1993

PUBLISHED ARTICLES, PAPERS OR PAMPHLETS

Ashdown-Hill, J., 'Edward IV's Uncrowned Queen; The Lady Eleanor Talbot, Lady Butler', *The Ricardian*, vol. 11, no. 139, Dec. 1997, pp. 166–90

——, 'Seeking the genes of Lady Eleanor Talbot' *Genealogists' Magazine*, vol. 26, no. 3, September 1998

——, 'Further Reflections on Lady Eleanor Talbot', *The Ricardian*, vol. 11, no. 144, March 1999

——, 'The elusive mistress: Elizabeth Lucy and her family', *The Ricardian*, vol. 11, no. 145, June 1999, pp. 490–505

——, 'Norfolk Requiem: the Passing of the House of Mowbray', *The Ricardian*, vol. 12, no. 152, March 2001

——, 'The Inquisition Post Mortem of Eleanor Talbot, Lady Butler', *The Ricardian*, vol. 12, no. 159, December 2002, pp. 563–573

——, 'The Lancastrian Claim to the Throne, *The Ricardian*, vol. 13, 2003, pp. 27–38

——, 'Lady Eleanor Talbot's other husband', *The Ricardian*, vol. 14, 2004, pp. 62–81

——, 'The Endowments of Lady Eleanor Talbot and of Elizabeth Talbot, Duchess of Norfolk, at Corpus Christi College, Cambridge' *The Ricardian*, vol. 14, 2004, pp. 82–94

Ashdown-Hill, J. and Carson, A., 'The Execution of the Earl of Desmond', *The Ricardian*, vol. 15, 2005, pp. 70–93

Ashdown-Hill, J., 'The Wills of John Talbot, first Earl of Shrewsbury, and of his sons, Lord Lisle and Sir Louis Talbot', *Transactions of the Shropshire Archaeological and Historical Society* (forthcoming)

——, 'Lady Eleanor Talbot: new evidence; new answers; new questions', *The Ricardian*, vol. 16, 2006, pp. 113–132

Barber, M., 'John Norbury', *English Historical Review*, vol. 68, 1953, pp. 66–76

Burgess, C., 'A service for the dead: the form and function of the anniversary in late medieval Bristol', in S.T. Blake and A. Saville, eds., *Transactions of the Bristol and Gloucestershire Archaeological Society for 1987*, vol. 105

Campbell, L., 'Approaches to Petrus Christus', in M.A. Ainsworth, ed., *Petrus Christus in Renaissance Bruges*, New York and Turnhout 1995, pp. 3–5

Eastern Daily Press, Wednesday 2 April 1958

Egerton, W.H., 'Talbot's Tomb', *Transactions of the Shropshire Archaeological Society*, vol. 8, 1885, pp. 413-40

Elkington, S.G. and Huntsman, R.G., 'The Talbot Fingers: a study in Symphalangism', *British Medical Journal*, 18 February 1967, pp. 407–11

Griffiths, R.W., 'Excavations at Blakemere Castle, Whitchurch', in *Shropshire Newsletter*, vol. 24, Nov. 1963

Guidebook to St Mary, Chilton, Suffolk, Redundant Churches Fund, London, 1985

Hampton, W.E., 'Sir Thomas Montgomery, K.G.', *The Ricardian*, vol. 3, no. 51, December 1975, pp. 9-14

——, 'A further Account of Robert Stillington' *The Ricardian*, vol. 4, no. 54, September 1976, pp. 24-27

——, 'The Ladies of the Minories', *The Ricardian* vol. 4, no. 62, September 1978, pp. 15–22.

Helmholz, R.H., 'The Sons of Edward IV: A Canonical Assessment of the Claim that they were Illegitimate', in Hammond, P.W., ed., *Richard III: Loyalty Lordship and Law*, London, 1986, pp. 91–103

Jarrold Magazine, March 1958 and March 1959

Johnson, V., The Message of St Thérèse of Lisieux, CTS, London, 1997

Kirkpatrick, J., 'The White Friars' in Turner D, ed., *History of the Religious Orders and Communities and of the Hospital and Castle of Norwich*, Yarmouth, 1845

Kleineke, H., 'Gerhard von Wesel's Newsletter from England, 17 April 1471', *The Ricardian*, vol. 16, 2006, pp. 66–83

Lindley, P.G., 'The "Arminghall Arch" and contemporary sculpture in Norwich', *Norfolk Archaeology*, vol. 40, part 1, Norwich 1987, pp. 19–43

Maddern, P., 'Honour among the Pastons: gender and integrity in fifteenth-century English provincial society', *Journal of Medieval History*, 14 (1988) pp. 357–371

Manning, C.R., 'Kenninghall', Norfolk and Norwich Archaeological Society, *Original Papers*, vol. 7, part 4, Norwich 1870, pp. 289-299

Mowat, A.J., 'Robert Stillington', *The Ricardian*, vol. 4, no. 53, June 1976, pp. 23–27

Murray, B.A., 'Lady Eleanor Butler and John Crowne's *The Misery of Civil War* (1680)', *The Ricardian*, vol. 14, 2004, pp. 54–61

Oshaughnessy, F., *The Story of Burton Dassett Church*, Coventry [n.d.]

Palmer, A.N., *The History of the Parish Church of Wrexham*, Wrexham & Oswestry, [n.d.]

Raby, F.J.E. and Baillie Reynolds, P.K., *Framlingham Castle*, English Heritage guidebook, London, 1959, revised 1973

Richmond, C., '1485 and all that', in Hammond, P.W., ed., *Richard III: Loyalty Lordship and Law*, London, 1986

Rushton, M.A., 'The Teeth of Anne Mowbray'. *British Dental Journal*, no. 119. 1965, pp. 335–39

Serpell, M.F., 'Kenninghall History and St Mary's Church', Norwich, 1982

Vale, M.G.A., 'The Last Years of English Gascony, 1451–1453', *Transactions of the Royal Historical Society*, fifth series, vol. 19, London, 1969, pp. 119–38

Vane, G.H.F., 'The Will of John Talbot, First Earl of Shrewsbury', *Transactions of the Shropshire Archaeological Society*, third series, vol. 4, 1904, pp. 371–378

Watson, G.W., 'William Heroun, Knight, Lord Say', *Miscellanea Genealogica et Heraldica*, 5th series, part 9

Winkless, D., 'Medieval Sudeley, part 2: the Fifteenth Century Roll Chronicle of the Kings of England with the Sudeley and Boteler Pedigree', *Family History* vol. 10, 1977, pp. 21–39

UNPUBLISHED SECONDARY MATERIAL

Ashdown-Hill, L.J.F., *The client network and connections of Sir John Howard (Lord Howard, first Duke of Norfolk) in north east Essex and south Suffolk*, unpublished PhD Thesis, University of Essex (2008)

Brill, R., *An English Captain of the Later Hundred Years' War*, unpublished PhD. Thesis, Princeton, 1966

Moye, L.E., *The Estates and Finances of the Mowbray Family, Earls Marshal and Dukes of Norfolk, 1401–1476*, unpublished PhD thesis, Duke University, 1985

Pollard, A.J., *The Family of Talbot, Lords Talbot and Earls of Shrewsbury in the Fifteenth Century*, unpublished PhD thesis, University of Bristol, 1968

Ross, B., *An account of the Talbot Household at Blakemere in the County of Shropshire, 1394-1425*, unpublished M.A. thesis, 2 vols., University of Canberra, 1970

White, W.J., *Report on a Skeleton (Inhumation II) from the Excavation of the Carmelite Friary, Norwich* (1958), unpublished report, 1996 (Castle Museum Norwich and Richard III Society Library)

WEBSITES

www.newadvent.org/cathen/04264a.htm *Catholic Encyclopaedia*

Church of Jesus Christ of the Latter Day Saints: *International Genealogical Index*

www.finds.org.uk Portable Antiquities Scheme database

Tudorhistory.org/castles/sudeley/

J. Ashdown-Hill, 'The Fate of Richard III's Body', http://www.bbc.co.uk/legacies/myths_legends/england/leicester/

NOVELS

Bowen, M., *Dickon*, London, 1971

Edwards, R., *Some Touch of Pity*, London, 1976

Jarman, R.H. *We Speak no Treason*, London, 1971

——, *The King's Grey Mare*, London, 1975

Lytton, E., *The Last of the Barons*, London, 1843

Penman, S., *The Sunne in Splendour*, London, 1982

Plaidy, J., *The Goldsmith's Wife* London, 1950

Tey, J., *The Daughter of Time*, Harmondsworth, 1954

Index

For kings and popes see first name. For all other individuals see surname. Women are listed under maiden surname if known, but all entries are cross-referenced.